D1457519

The Prehistory of Cognitive Science

Also by Andrew Brook

Books

A UNIFIED THEORY OF CONSCIOUSNESS (*with Paul Raymont*)

KNOWLEDGE AND MIND (*with Robert J. Stainton*)

KANT AND THE MIND

Edited Collections

PHILOSOPHY AND NEUROSCIENCE: A Maturing Movement (*co-editor with Kathleen Akins*)

DANIEL DENNETT (*co-editor with Don Ross*)

SELF-REFERENCE AND SELF-AWARENESS (*co-editor with R.C. DeVidi*)

DENNETT: A Comprehensive Assessment (*co-editor with D. Ross and D. Thompson*)

The Prehistory Of Cognitive Science

Edited by

Andrew Brook

First published 2007 by
PALGRAVE MACMILLAN
Houndmills, Basingstoke, Hampshire RG21 6XS and
175 Fifth Avenue, New York, N.Y. 10010
Companies and representatives throughout the world

PALGRAVE MACMILLAN is the global academic imprint of the Palgrave
Macmillan division of St. Martin's Press, LLC and of Palgrave Macmillan Ltd.
Macmillan® is a registered trademark in the United States, United Kingdom
and other countries. Palgrave is a registered trademark in the European
Union and other countries.

ISBN-13: 978–0–230–01339–1   hardback
ISBN-10: 0–230–01339–2   hardback

This book is printed on paper suitable for recycling and made from fully
managed and sustained forest sources.

A catalogue record for this book is available from the British Library.

Library of Congress Cataloging-in-Publication Data

The prehistory of cognitive science/Andrew Brook, ed.
    p. cm.
    Includes bibliographical references and index.
    ISBN-13: 978-0-230-01339-1 (cloth)
    ISBN-10: 0-230-01339-2 (cloth)
      1. Cognition–History. 2. Cognitive science–History. I. Brook, Andrew.

BF311.P739 2007
153.09–dc22

                                                                2006050337

10   9   8   7   6   5   4   3   2   1
16   15   14   13   12   11   10   09   08   07

Transferred to digital printing 2007

Contents

List of Table

List of Contributors

Arthur L. Blumenthal, History of Psychology, Graduate Faculty, New School for Social Research, New York, NY, USA.

Andrew Brook, Chancellor's Professor of Philosophy and Director, Institute of Cognitive Science, Carleton University, Ottawa, ON, Canada.

Noam Chomsky, Institute Professor, Massachusetts Institute of Technology, Cambridge, MA, USA.

Marcelo Dascal, Professor of Philosophy, Tel Aviv University, Tel Aviv, Israel, Editor, *Pragmatics and Cognition* and recipient of the Humboldt Prize.

Tracy B. Henley, Professor and Head, Department of Psychology and Special Education, Texas A & M University-Commerce, Commerce, TX, USA.

Anne Jaap Jacobson, Professor of Philosophy and Electrical and Computer Engineering, Associate Director of the UH Center for Neuro-Engineering and Cognitive Science, University of Houston, Houston, TX, USA.

Patricia Kitcher, Professor of Philosophy and Chair, Dept of Philosophy, Columbia University, New York, NY, USA.

Stellan Ohlsson, Professor of Psychology, University of Illinois, Chicago, IL, USA.

Don Ross, Professor of Philosophy, Professor of Economics, University of Alabama–Birmingham, Birmingham, AB, USA and University of Cape Town, Cape Town, South Africa.

Peter Simons, FBA, Professor and Fellow of the British Academy, Leeds University, Leeds, UK.

Preface

As we define it, the prehistory of cognitive science is the period up to about 1900. There then followed an interregnum during which cognition was not much studied, then the period of cognitive science proper. We call the first period the 'prehistory' because while philosophers and psychologists certainly studied the mind in this period, few envisaged a *science* of the mind. A partial exception was David Hume (Jacobson[1]). Even he was only a partial exception because, while he hoped to build a scientific *model* of the mind, he did not do a scientific *investigation* of the mind. The prehistory comes to an end with a group of otherwise diverse theorists who began to do just that: Wundt, James, and Freud (Blumenthal, Henley, Kitcher). With the exception of Aristotle (Ohlsson), all the figures we study worked in the 'early modern' period, which is usually dated from about 1600.

The interregnum was the period in which behaviorism reigned supreme in psychology and logical empiricism in philosophy. Then begins the period of the cognitive revolution (the *second* cognitive revolution according to Chomsky, Descartes and colleagues having launched the first). The first glimmerings of the revolution can be variously dated: from the development of programmable computers in the Bletchley code-breaking establishment of which Alan Turing was a member in England during the World War II (Turing wrote the seminal papers on computational theory that underpin the computational model of the mind before, during, and shortly after this period),[2] the famous Hixon Fund Conference, *Cerebral Mechanisms in Behavior*, at Caltech in 1948, the publication of Chomsky's *Aspects of Syntax* in 1956 (a work that revolutionized the way not only language but the whole of

---

[1] We will refer to chapters in this collection using simply the author's name.
[2] For many years, Americans in particular claimed ENIAC (Electronic Numerical Integrator And Computer), built at the University of Pennsylvania in 1946, as the first programmable computer. We now know that it was not. The group at Bletchley had created Colossus and other computers a few years earlier in the course of developing tools to break Enigma and Ultimate, Germany's ultra-high-secret military codes. Some versions of Colossus were programmable. Being under a thirty- to fifty-year gag order, the Bletchley group could do nothing about this misinformation until recently. Indeed, very few people knew much if anything about Colossus until recently (Donald Michie, personal communication).

human cognition was conceived), and perhaps other dates. The year 1956 was also the year in which the idea of a unified, multidisciplinary research programme into human and artificial cognition was first officially articulated, at the now-famous *Symposium on Information Processing* at MIT, September 10–12, 1956. Whatever, by the mid-1970s, cognitive science was well established. The name was being used, the Cognitive Science Society had been formed (1977) and *Cognitive Science*, the Journal of the Cognitive Science Society, had been started (1979).

This volume is concerned with the first period, the prehistory, when research into human cognition had not yet even become separated off as a distinct intellectual enterprise.

The chapters of this volume are not intended to be a history of the period. Every contributor does research in some cutting-edge area of contemporary cognitive research, not historical research, and the task we set ourselves was to see how the work on cognition of the figure of interest to us connects to contemporary cognitive science. And the results are invariably revealing and informative in many different ways. All the figures studied in this volume have, of course, had a major influence on contemporary thought about cognition but, and this is very interesting, some of their contributions have not had much influence at all. They have not only not been superseded by contemporary cognitive science, they have not even been assimilated into it. Dascal, Chomsky, Brook, Jacobson, Ross, and Simons all argue that this is true in one way or another of the figure we studied.

Another way in which this volume is not a history is that we have by no means covered everyone with a claim to appear in a volume such as this. Among possible further figures, one thinks, for example, of Antoine Arnauld, logician extraordinaire and Descartes's great interlocutor, John Locke, the source of what came to be called 'British empiricism', Thomas Reid, Scottish contemporary of Kant's and advocate of common sense as a source of genuine knowledge, John Stuart Mill and Jeremy Bentham, worthy successors to Hume, Hermann von Helmholtz, successor to both Hume and Kant and teacher of Freud's teachers, or John Babbage, inventor of the first mechanical calculating machine. Nor would we claim to have treated all the new ideas about cognition that appeared in our period. But we do think that we have treated the figures and ideas that were most influential.

Like many other scientists, cognitive scientists tend to know relatively little about the history of their own subject. Such lack of knowledge would be a pity anywhere but it is perhaps particularly unfortunate in a discipline such as cognitive science, where the history is so long and where so much in the conception of the mind of at least classical cognitive science was handed down to us from long-past predecessors and still governs our thinking without much critical assessment.

All the contributors to this volume are active cognitive scientists and approach the history of cognitive research from this perspective. As befits a volume such as this, they have a wide range of backgrounds and teach a wide range of subjects. Three of the contributors are trained in and teach philosophy. Three are psychologists. One is a linguist. Two teach cognitive science. And one teaches economics.

So far as we know, no one else has attempted to do what we are doing in this volume. The closest previous work is J.-C. Smith's *Historical Foundations of Cognitive Science* (1990). Smith's work should certainly be acknowledged as a trailblazer in this kind of study but the book has been out of print for many years and even major research libraries often do not have a copy.

A number of people have played a role in bringing this volume to completion. John Logan played an important role in the early stages. Rob Stainton made helpful suggestions on a number of chapters. Marcelo Dascal, Noam Chomsky, Don Ross, and anonymous referees made useful comments on the Introduction. Alex Taylor and Alain El Hofi, research assistants, played a vital and sometimes thankless role. The volume was put together with the assistance of funding from Carleton University and the Social Sciences and Humanities Research Council of Canada. Finally, Daniel Bunyard of Palgrave Press has been a delight to work with and one of the project's keenest supporters. To all, our thanks.

Andrew Brook
Ottawa
June 2006

A version of Noam Chomsky's paper has been published previously. We thank the following publishers who hold copyright in the earlier version for their permission:

Allen & Unwin Book Publishers, 83 Alexander Street, Crows Nest, NSW 2065 (Australia and New Zealand)
South End Press, 7 Brookline Street #1, Cambridge, MA (USA)
Pluto Publishing Ltd, 345 Archway Road, London N6 5AA (Europe)
Between the Lines, 404–720 Bathurst Street, Toronto, Ontario (Canada)

Introduction

1. The collection

In this collection, we aim to identify and explore the most important, enduring work on cognition done in the European tradition up to about 1900, focusing on the period from 1600 on.

If the history of research into cognition can be roughly divided into three periods, pre-1900, then to somewhere between 1956 and 1977, and from between those dates to the present, then the year 1879 is often taken as the watershed in the transition from the first to the second period. Wundt is credited with creating the first-ever psychology laboratory in the Department of Philosophy of the University of Leipzig in that year. In fact, he had been doing psychological experiments for almost twenty years by 1879 (Henley), but 1879 has stuck as the year in which experimental psychology began.

Likewise, in 1879 Frege published *Begriffsschrift* [Concept-Notation], the seminal work that presaged his epoch-making *Foundations of Arithmetic* (1884). His work launched the formal apparatus of logic and semantics in the contemporary era, apparatus that continues to constitute the formal foundations of cognitive science, and also of logic and analytical philosophy of language, to this day (Simons). Prior to Frege, logic had hardly made any progress since the time of Aristotle and was most often done as a sideline when it was done at all. Kant is a good example (Brook); he simply took Aristotelian logic over lock, stock, and barrel, and proceeded from there. To be sure, there were exceptions. Medieval writers such as St. Anselm, William of Occam, and Nicholas à Cusa did important work, though broadly within the Aristotelian tradition. As Chomsky shows, Descartes, Arnauld, and the Port Royal logicians did work of enduring value at the intersection of logic and language; it was lost again

1

soon after. As Dascal makes clear, Leibniz formulated a grand research program for logic, one, indeed, that Frege sometimes saw himself as carrying out (Simons). One might also mention Boole (of Boolean algebra fame), though he worked only a couple of decades before Frege. Nevertheless, in general it is true to say that there were few major developments in logic from Aristotle to Frege.

The last decades of the nineteenth century were a period of considerable ferment in cognitive research. In these years, psychology, linguistics, and logic and semantic theory developed into distinct intellectual enterprises. Prior to then, such work as had been done in these areas had been done mainly by researchers who identified themselves as philosophers or philosopher/psychologists. Even the separation of psychology from philosophy occurred only in the nineteenth century; Wundt, for example, was a member of a Department of Philosophy, not Psychology. Prior to this time, cognitive theorists of all stripes called themselves philosophers. (Of course, so did a lot of other researchers. Sir Isaac Newton's Chair at Cambridge, for example, was called the Chair in Natural Philosophy and many physics chairs in the UK and Australia bear that title to this day.) By shortly after 1900, psychology had decisively separated from philosophy, linguistics had come into its own as a separate discipline (though with few exceptions – Whorf's work in Harvard's famous five-cultures study of the 1950s comes to mind[1] – work on language did not have much influence on general cognitive research until Chomsky and the 1950s), and the logical/semantic tradition that Frege's work made possible had established itself as a dominant influence within English-speaking philosophy.

In this collection, we explore thinking on cognition from the very beginning of the modern era (and even before [Ohlsson]) to the brink of these twentieth-century developments. Our aim is not to produce an introductory history (Gardner 1984 has done that). Rather, our aim is to identify contributions to cognitive research prior to 1900 that have had an enduring influence. The authors were asked to identify what was of permanent value in the figure(s) or movement on which they chose to write and focus on that. (It is interesting, as we said in the Preface, that a number of them urge that some of their target's contributions should have had more influence than they have had: Dascal, Chomsky, Brook,

---

[1] In what is widely considered to be the first major empirical project in anthropology, a group of Harvard anthropologists and linguistics studied five linguistic/cultural groups in the four-corners area where Arizona, Utah, New Mexico, and Colorado meet. The groups were Hopi, Apache, Navaho, English-speaking ranchers, and Hispanics.

Jacobson, Ross, and Simons.) The result is a volume much closer in both topics and style to contemporary cognitive science than one usually finds in histories. Likewise, the chapters integrate the past with the present and one discipline with another better than standard histories do. The contributors are all active cognitive scientists and all but one of the chapters (Chomsky's) were prepared for this collection and are previously unpublished. Given this uniformity of origin, it is interesting to see how much the essays themselves vary one from another. We think that this variation is significant; it reflects something deep about the state of cognitive science as a whole right now. If cognitive science is unified as a conception, it is much less unified as an activity and the chapters of this volume reflect the latter state of affairs. A great many voices and a great many topics contend with one another, voices ranging from hard empirical and computational modeling at one end to broad speculations about situated cognition and chaotic systems at the other, topics ranging from 'classical' ones such as syntax, lexical processing, perception, and reasoning systems to such things as connectionism, dynamic systems, and cognitive neuroscience.[2] In the way the authors write, what they chose to emphasize, the balance of empirical and conceptual considerations, the extent of their interest in biography, and in other ways, they display aspects of this range and diversity. Indeed, there is even great diversity in the scope of the chapters. Some authors start from one figure to write on broad movements and themes (Ohlsson, Chomsky, Dascal, Ross), others stick closely to a single figure (Jacobson, Brook, Simons, Henley) and the rest fall in between (Blumenthal, Kitcher). Instead of trying to iron these differences out, we view them as a valuable part of the collection and have left them as they are.

2. The prehistory of cognitive science

The story of serious, systematic thinking about cognition goes back as far as Aristotle, indeed perhaps even to Plato (see Table 0.1 for their dates). Aristotle articulated a distinction between practical and theoretical reason that is still accepted and continues to be influential (Ohlsson). Theoretical reasoning is reasoning about what to believe, what is the case, etc., while practical reasoning is reasoning about what do, what ought to be the case, etc. Aristotle saw so far into the distinction that he

---

[2] Sometimes one finds both ends in one person. William Clancey is a good example. Compare his book *Situated Cognition* (1996) with his earlier AI work developing expert systems such as MYCIN.

Table 0.1.   Main figures in the prehistory of cognitive research

	Plato (438BC–347BC)	
	Aristotle (384BC–322BC)	
	Descartes (1596–1650)	
	Hobbes (1588–1679)	
Empiricism		Rationalism
Locke (1632–1704)		Spinoza (1632–1677)
Hume (1711–1776)		Leibniz (1646–1716)
	Kant (1724–1804)	
	Darwin (1809–1882)	
	Wundt (1832–1920)	
	Frege (1848–1925)	
	James (1842–1910)	
	Freud (1856–1939)	

even connected it to the distinction between teleological and mechanistic explanations. Practical reasoning concerns what he called final causes, that is to say, goals and purposes. Theoretical reasoning, though concerned with final causes, also concerns itself with what he called efficient causes or what we now would call causes, period. Aristotle articulated a system of sentential logic that survived unscathed until the time of Frege. And his account of what we would now call human cognition in *De Anima* is the first attempt ever to give something like a systematic description of human cognition.

Nevertheless, in important respects the story of cognitive *science* begins later. Aristotle described something recognizable as cognitive functions, indeed saw them as functions of the body and arguably as biological functions, but he had no conception of representation as we now understand it, nor of consciousness, nor of memory, nor of perception as the processing of information in the brain, nor ... nor ... nor .... That he did not have a concept of a mental representation, a concept, that is to say, of something that functions by standing for or referring to something else, is arguably the thing that most centrally separates his work from all work on cognition in the modern era, which begins about 1600.[3] Aristotle held that perception, for example, consists roughly in

---

[3] There is an interesting and complicated story to be told about the history of the notion of a representation. While there is not much evidence of any clear notion of a *mental* representation prior to the time of Descartes and Hobbes, something like our current notion of a *linguistic* representation, a sign, goes all the way back to the Stoics (Dascal and Dutz 1997). Why one notion of something presenting or standing for something else should have developed so much sooner than the other is an interesting question.

taking the essential structure of the perceived object into the mind. Thus perception is 'built out of' aspects of the thing perceived (Jacobson), not out of states and processes that *represent or stand for* the thing perceived. Aristotle's view of perception was the view adopted (or assumed) by most theorists, both Platonists and Aristotelians, till the modern era. St. Thomas Aquinas is a good example.

Though there are anticipations of our current conception of a representation in some late medieval thinkers (Pasnau 1997), it achieved its current form at about the time of Descartes and Hobbes (see Table 0.1 for dates). It is with this conception that the study of cognition as we now understand it really begins (though the idea of a *science* of cognition was still centuries away even at that point). We are not saying that nothing happened in the roughly two thousand years between Aristotle and Descartes. In fact, a great deal happened, more than is usually realized. In late Roman times, for example, St. Augustine had already articulated the inference for which Descartes is famous, the inference *cogito, ergo sum* (I think, therefore I am). But Augustine had no precise conception of *what* the 'I' is, indeed probably did not get much further than Aristotle on that score. (We are painting with a very broad brush here.) Descartes did (Chomsky), and so did Hobbes (Dascal).

Descartes held that the mind is 'a thing that thinks'. What he meant by 'thinks' was something very different from what Aristotle would have had in mind. Descartes conceived of the materials of thinking as representations in the contemporary sense. And Hobbes was the first to clearly articulate the idea that thinking is operations performed on representations. Here we have two of the dominating ideas underlying all subsequent cognitive thought: the mind contains and is a system for manipulating representations.

Descartes's contribution to our conception of human cognition was massive. The central aspects of it endured with no serious competitors until about fifty years ago. These aspects include:

- the notion of a representation, i.e., something cognitive that stands for something else,
- the idea that representations are 'in the head', and,
- the idea of the mind as a unified system of representations, a unified being to whom representations represent.

Dennett (1991) calls the last notion, the idea of the mind as a being to whom representations represent in a kind of quasi-spatial arena

inside the head, the Cartesian Theater. All these ideas endure to this
day. They all figure, for example, in Fodor's Representational Theory
of Mind. Many of the most persistent problems about cognition also
stem from them, e.g., the problem of knowledge of the external world
and of other minds (Jacobson). Many recent developments in cognitive
thinking are direct reactions to them, e.g., Gibson's ecological cognition (Gibson 1979) and externalism about the content of representations (the claim that 'meanings just ain't in the head' in Putnam's
memorable 1975 phrase). In addition to Gibson, other serious alternatives to the Cartesian picture as a whole since World War II have
included behaviorism (Skinner 1974; Ryle 1949), Dennett's multiple-
drafts alternative to the Cartesian Theater (1991, for commentary, see
Brook and Ross 2002), and connectionism and neurophilosophy (P.M.
Churchland, 1984, 1994; P. S. Churchland 1986) but the Cartesian
picture remains overwhelmingly the dominant picture in cognitive
science.

In addition to articulating a representational model of the mind,
Descartes was also the first to pay serious attention to the balance
between the role played by the mind and the role played by sensible
experience in the acquisition of knowledge. In the form of the battle
between empiricism and rationalism, this problem achieved its first
resolution only with Kant (Brook) and continues to be a live issue
today, in the controversies over innatism and over the mind's 'top-
down' contribution to extracting patterns from sensible stimulations,
for example.

The chapters that discuss Descartes (Chomsky and Dascal) do not
devote much attention to his general model of the mind. With Ryle's
(1949) critique of the 'ghost in the machine' and Dennett's (1991)
critique of the Cartesian Theater, the topic has been extensively canvassed in recent decades. Descartes's notion of a representation is now
part of everyone's cognitive coinage, so we do not spent much time on
it, either. Instead, the chapters that discuss Descartes focus on aspects of
the Cartesian, rationalist tradition that are not so well known. Though
these latter ideas go back to the seventeenth century, they are extremely
interesting, so interesting that Chomsky takes them to amount to a first
cognitive revolution (the one going on now being, in his view, the second).

Nor was Descartes's revolutionary originality limited to the mind. With
Galileo and others, he was also one of the originators of the mechanistic
conception of the universe, for example, and he did extensive experimental neurophysiology. Indeed, he laid down a neurophysiological

conception of vision and of cognition more generally.[4] Descartes made language a central indicator of the presence of a mind (though, as Dascal shows, he also *separated* language from cognitive activity more radically than most would now). He had a major influence on the work on logic and language of his contemporaries at Port Royal. (Many of the best ideas of this group rapidly were lost again, or so Chomsky argues.) Finally and against the empiricist-sounding dictum of Aristotle that 'nothing is in the mind that is not first in the senses', Descartes argued that what the mind achieves by *reflection* on things is far closer to knowledge of their nature than what it *observes* about them.[5] All of these ideas are of enduring value, lost again though many of them were.

To be sure, not everything that Descartes believed about the mind has lived on. For modern tastes, he placed the balance between the contribution of the mind and the world too far on the mind side, being the good rationalist that he was. Rationalism as exemplified by theorists such as Spinoza and Leibniz is the view that the representations to be trusted are the ones arrived at entirely inside the head by processes of reasoning alone. (The crucial kind of reasoning here is the exploring of the semantic implications of one's concepts and propositions.) When cast less austerely and therefore more plausibly, a modest form of rationalism lives on in Chomsky's conception of universal, innate grammar and in Fodor's language of thought hypothesis (the latter is the view that the materials out of which our concepts are constructed are also universal and innate). However, few theorists now would push the idea as far as Descartes seems to have done.

More importantly, strongly impressed by the complexity of language and the free creativity that it made possible, Descartes held that minds able to use language are things entirely 'separate and apart' from the body, nonspatial, nonmaterial entities made up of who knows what and, together with this, that nonhuman animals do not have minds. (He held, for example, that nonhuman animals cannot feel pain and can be

---

[4] In connection with this, Descartes and his tradition achieved the first clear articulation of the problem of unifying knowledge formulated at different levels and in different vocabularies, goal-directed language vs. mechanistic language, for example. Aristotle had anticipated some aspects of the issue (Ohlsson) but Descartes confronted it head-on. It is a major issue today.

[5] Aristotle's dictum might appear to be ultra-empiricist but we should be cautious about this. His picture of perception was utterly different from ours; he thought that essential features of the structure of objects literally move from the objects into us. His picture being so different, nothing but confusion is likely to result from giving the two conceptions of the source of knowledge the same name.

dissected without anaesthetic.) Few contemporary cognitive scientists follow him in any of this. His explanatory dualism persists. Many cognitive scientists think that we are permanently stuck with a duality of explanations – explanations of neurological processes in the language of the neurosciences and explanations of cognitive function in the language of folk psychology or some other teleological language. (This is one way in which Aristotle's distinction between theoretical and practical reasoning lives on.) Some cognitive scientists even think that we must retain a dualism of properties, e.g., between neurological composition and cognitive functioning, or between cognitive functioning and qualitative feel, 'qualia' in philosophers' jargon (Chalmers 1996). But few now accept Descartes's ontological dualism, however obvious it seemed to him; few now think of a person as a 'union' of two utterly different kinds of thing. Indeed, the reverse seems obvious to most people.

In this Hobbes has had the more enduring influence. Hobbes was a near-contemporary of Descartes's, indeed wrote the best known of the six series of objections to Descartes's *Meditations* of 1645. On the fundamental nature of the mind, Hobbes and Descartes utterly disagreed. Hobbes urged that the mind simply is the brain or certain aspects of it. This is connected to his single greatest contribution to our conception of cognition, the idea, as he put it, that 'all reasoning is but reckoning' (1651, I, 5, pp. 1–2) – all thinking is computation (Dascal). Put Hobbes's mechanistic materialism together with Descartes's notion of representation and you have the fundamentals of the contemporary picture of cognition: cognition consists of computations over representations.

Dascal shows, however (and this is one of the most interesting aspects of his chapter), that if Hobbes was a materialist, there is a good deal more to his view of knowledge than simple empiricism. (In a different way, Chomsky shows much the same about the parallel picture of Descartes as the father of dualism and rationalism.) As Dascal shows, Hobbes's claims about the tight relationship between language and thought are closer to the spirit of rationalism, to Spinoza and Leibniz, than to empiricists such as Locke and Hume. Indeed, Hobbes inspired a research program on thinking that was at the center of both rationalism and empiricism in the seventeenth and eighteenth centuries, a program that continued at least as far as Stewart in the nineteenth century. On the other hand, though Descartes is supposed to be the father of rationalism, his separation of language and thought was much more in the spirit of empiricism than of rationalism. Indeed, both Hobbes and Descartes but particularly Hobbes cut across the time-worn division of early modern cognitive thinking into empiricism and rationalism.

Rationalism of one kind or another was one of the great stances on knowledge acquisition and validation of the early modern period. The other was empiricism, as in the Aristotelean dictum that 'nothing is in the mind that is not first in the senses' interpreted as we would now interpret it (see note 5). The British philosopher John Locke is generally viewed as the originating figure of what came to be called British empiricism. However, there is at least some ambiguity about the extent of Locke's empiricism. By contract, the Scottish philosopher David Hume was unambiguously and radically an empiricist. He carried out the empiricist program more comprehensively and rigorously than anyone before him (and maybe since). Hume held that there is no source of knowledge except sense experience. As Jacobson shows, he also held that an empiricism rigorously followed out will end up denying that sensible experience has anything like the structure of a language – sensible representations are like pictures, not propositional structures, and associations govern their relationships, not propositional relations. (This is enough by itself to make Hume the grandfather of behaviorism and of connectionism.) Hume also saw a set of skeptical problems as lying at the heart of empiricism. According to him, we can never justify our beliefs about: the world external to us; the future; or even the past! Jacobson shows that how one views this skeptical streak in Hume's work depends very much on how one views his project as a whole. If one views him as holding to a picture of representations as like objects of some kind, then one must see him as mired in deep skeptical problems indeed. If one sees him as holding, in the spirit of later thinkers, that representations are cognitive acts of some kind, the issue about skepticism may take on a quite different appearance.

Hume not only took empiricism about the contents of knowledge more seriously than anyone before him and maybe since, he also insisted that theories of mind stay within empiricist bounds. In particular, he insisted on what we would now called a naturalized epistemology. Not just the mechanisms by which we acquire knowledge but also the *standards by which we assess knowledge claims* have to be derived entirely from what nature provides. Likewise, by insisting even more rigidly than Descartes that everything about the content of representation is 'in the head', he formulated a picture of the content of representations that is still orthodoxy.

Now often called *internalism*, it remains the view of most cognitive theorists even in the face of a recent challenge, *externalism*. Externalism is the view that the content of representations, what representations are about, consists of a relationship of some kind between what is going on in the head and what is found in the world (Putnam 1975). Externalism is largely confined to some philosophers of mind. It has never had much influence in the rest of the cognitive community. (Some philosophers view J.J. Gibson and the more recent situated cognition movement as varieties of externalism but this view is disputable [Brook 2005].)

Kant brought empiricism and rationalism together. Gaps, as Kant saw it, in Hume's empiricism and the skeptical problems about the nature of the self and the knowledge that it seemed to him to entail aroused him from what he called his 'dogmatic slumbers' – an uncritical submersion in the rationalism of his time. Spurred by the example of the trouble that radical empiricism had caused Hume, Kant argued that the element in knowledge advocated by rationalism and the element advocated by empiricism are both necessary – to acquire knowledge, we need both sensible input and activities of the mind. As he put it in a famous aphorism, 'thoughts without content are empty, intuitions without concepts are blind' (1781, p. A 51=B 75). That is to say, we cannot confirm or disconfirm conceptualizations without experiential evidence, no matter how carefully we think about the conceptualizations – but we cannot organize experience without applying concepts to it. The first cuts against full-blown rationalism, the second cuts against extreme forms of empiricism. Kant's resolution of the empiricist/rationalist tension is now widely accepted in cognitive science, some connectionists being among the few exceptions. As Brook shows, some of Kant's other views about the mind have also been incorporated into cognitive science, Kant's view about the mind as a system of functions and his views about the right method to study the mind in particular. For these reasons, Kant can even be viewed as the grandfather of cognitive science.

If some of Kant's central ideas about the mind live on, it is interesting that a number of the ideas that he held most dear have played hardly any role in contemporary cognitive science at all. This is true of Kant's claims about the mind's synthesizing powers, about its various mental unities (in particular, the unity of consciousness), and about consciousness of self. As Brook argues, not only have these views not been superseded by cognitive science, they have never even been assimilated by it – and they deserve to be.

If Wundt, Frege, and 1879 are the divide between the prehistory of cognitive science and the next period, Kant and the *Critique of Pure Reason* of 1781 are the divide between the eighteenth and nineteenth centuries and therefore the two parts of this book. Empiricism as Hume had laid it out in the *Treatise of Human Nature* (1739) continued to influence thought about cognition in the nineteenth century but the dominant influence, certainly in the German-speaking world, was Kant. Except for a few stubborn empiricists, work in German on cognition in the nineteenth century and even a lot of work in English consisted of spelling out and beginning to test ideas that Kant had articulated. Indeed, that is true of a lot of work on cognition up to the present. (The influential Cartesian ideas that we listed earlier live on in Kant's picture, so Kant's picture continuing to have influence is also Descartes's picture continuing to have influence.) There have been movements that rejected the Kantian picture of cognition, of course. We have already mentioned connectionism and could add behaviorism (a form of extreme empiricism), though the latter has never been part of cognitive science. But classical cognitive science and the great majority of cognitive researchers up to the present hold to a model of the mind that is Kantian in many essentials. Though, as we said, contemporary theorists have neglected some topics dear to Kant's heart, they conceive of the mind largely as Kant conceived of it.

The nineteenth century saw a blossoming of theorizing about cognition. A great deal of it did not add much that was really original to the two models that we were left with at the end of the eighteenth century, radical empiricism and the Kantianism synthesis. J.S. Mill, Herbart, and Helmholtz might be considered as examples. Among nineteenth century figures who did add major new ideas, one thinks immediately of Darwin.

Anticipations of Darwin's theory of evolution can be found earlier but as a well-articulated theory based on imposing and powerful evidence, Darwin's work had no antecedents. As Ross shows, evolutionary theory is coming to play a central role in cognitive science, and that for a variety of reasons. First, evolutionary theory is an excellent way to approach the important task of reuniting cognitive theory and neuroscience. Cognitive theorizing and biology were deeply interanimated in Darwin's time but by the time of the great cognitive revolution of the 1970s, the two had come apart. Entranced by the computer metaphor, cognitive scientists of the classical period urged that, like computer system designers, we can understand the functioning, the 'software', of the mind/brain without needing to know much about how those functions are implemented in the brain. (Indeed, it was common to refer to the brain as the 'wetware'.)

Second, evolutionary theory is an excellent way to approach the task (and also, some think, the limitations) of building a purely naturalistic epistemology – an account of knowledge acquisition within the limits of what nature has provided (including acquisition of knowledge about the mind itself). Ross may be overplaying his hand a bit when he says that Darwin was the greatest cognitive scientist. For one thing, it took a very long time for evolutionary theory to come to play any important role in cognitive science. But it would surely be right to say that cognitive scientists who ignore Darwin do so at their peril.

Wundt introduced a second element that was largely new: the idea that claims about cognition should be submitted to empirical test. Of course, the experimental method did not originate with Wundt. What he found was a way to apply it to claims about cognition. Few would disagree with Wundt about the importance of experimental verification today.

For Wundt, the experimental method was not an end in itself. As Blumenthal shows, Wundt thought that it revealed deep aspects of the mind that other methods do not reveal. Interestingly enough, for Wundt, the mind thus revealed fits Kant's picture better than the empiricist picture. However, Wundt's picture was not Kantian in every respect. His rejection of the idea of discrete, persisting representations resonates more with anti-representational views such as situated cognition than it does with Kant, for example.

A third new development in the nineteenth century from an entirely different direction was Frege's invention late in the century of the concepts and tools of modern symbolic logic and semantic theory. As Simons shows, most of the formal foundations of contemporary cognitive science were articulated by Frege. His work is the basis not just of logic and semantic theory but also of computational theory, which was the basis in turn of the computer revolution and artificial intelligence. Given that Frege himself fought to separate logic and semantic theory from psychology with everything at his disposal, there is, as Simons notes, a certain irony in the fact that his work laid the foundations for the whole formal side of cognitive science.

James's place in this volume is a bit different from Darwin's, Wundt's, or Frege's. With James there are no stunning new ideas that changed the shape of cognitive research forever. His body of work as a whole had a major influence but because of its accessibility and the breadth of issues that James took on, not because of major innovations. His best-known contributions are to a topic that slid from view not long after his time and surfaced again only about a decade ago – consciousness. Probably the single best-known concept in James is the stream of consciousness. As Henley shows, James also made significant contributions to our understanding of association, memory, imagery, imagination, and reasoning. Perhaps his most important contribution was his distinction between explanation by reference to biological foundations and explanation by reference to social/behavioral factors – the explanatory dualism that, as we showed earlier, goes all the way back to Aristotle. Finally, and reason enough by itself for including James as a central figure of the prehistory of cognitive science, his articulation of the idea of the mind as a system of functions is fuller than any prior to about thirty years ago. James did not originate the functionalist conception of the mind, of course. The basic idea goes back to Plato and Aristotle and we find a full statement of what a mental function is and how the mind as system of functions works in Kant (Meerbote 1990; Brook 1994). James merely carried an already-existing idea further. However, he carried it a long way further. (There is a nice irony to James unwittingly following Kant in this way: James ridiculed Kant as few others have ever done – Brook gives an example.)

Freud fits into the prehistory of cognitive science in yet another different way. He was a great innovator, of course: his theories of the unconscious mind and his method of free association for studying the mind changed the way we conceive of the mind. But Freud's ideas have not directly influenced cognitive science in the way that Darwin's, Frege's, and Wundt's have. Indeed, far from being influenced by psychoanalytic theory, many cognitive scientists harbor deep suspicions about it. His importance, as Kitcher argues, lies in a different direction.

What makes Freud important to cognitive science is that he was the first to attempt to built a comprehensive interdisciplinary model of the mind. Where he succeeded and especially where he failed still have a great deal to teach us. Freud's fullest statement of his model (1895) was not published in his lifetime but, as Kitcher shows, the ideas in it shaped Freud's thinking for the rest of his life. Among the many striking things that Kitcher says about such interdisciplinary models, perhaps the most striking is her suggestion that such models are utterly hostage to the state of knowledge at the time. Freud attempted to draw together in a single model everything significant that was known (or believed) about the mind by the relevant disciplines, neurobiology, psychology, and anthropology/archaeology, in his time. Unfortunately, it is entailed by this effort that if any of them were wrong about anything important, his model was going to be wrong, too. There is no way to avoid this problem – and the same is true of the interdisciplinary models of cognitive science today. In addition, as Kitcher shows, Freud made further mistakes, mistakes he did not have to make, mistakes that led him even further astray – and important cognitive scientists today are making precisely the same mistakes. These are arresting, sobering claims.

We will close where we began. No single collection of essays could begin to do justice to the huge range of ideas about cognition that was articulated prior to 1900. Nor was that our aim. Rather, ten active contemporary cognitive researchers examine ideas from that time that continue to shape how we conceive human cognition, and examine them from their point of view as contemporary cognitive researchers. To conduct this investigation, we look at ten major figures and a number of others who were the original sources of these ideas.

References

Brook, A. (1994). *Kant and the Mind*. New York and Cambridge: Cambridge University Press.
Brook, A. (2005). My blackberry and me: Forever one or just friends? In Nyiri, K. (ed.), *Mobile Understanding: The Epistemology of Ubiquitous Communication*. Vienna: Passagen Verlag, pp. 55–66.
Brook, A. and Ross, D. (2002). *Daniel Dennett* (in the series, Contemporary Philosophy in Focus). New York: Cambridge University Press.
Chalmers, D. (1996). *The Conscious Mind*. Oxford: Oxford University Press.
Churchland, P.M. (1984). *Matter and Consciousness*. Cambridge, MA: MIT Press, 1984 (2nd edn, 1988).
Churchland, P.M. (1994). *The Engine of Reason, the Seat of the Soul*. Cambridge, MA: MIT Press.
Churchland, P.S. (1986). *Neurophilosophy*. Cambridge, MA: MIT Press.
Clancey, W. (1996). *Situated Cognition*. New York: Cambridge University Press.
Dascal, M. and Dutz, K. (1997). Beginnings of scientific semiotics. In R. Posner, K. Robering, and T.A. Sebeok (eds). *Semiotics – A Handbook on the Sign-Theoretic Foundations of Nature and Culture*, Vol. 1. Berlin: W. De Gruyter, pp. 746–762.
Dennett, D.C. (1991). *Consciousness Explained*. Boston: Little, Brown, 1991.
Freud, S. (1895). *Project for a Scientific Psychology*. In J. Strachey (trans. and ed.). *The Complete Psychological Works of Sigmund Freud* Vol. 1. London: Hogarth Press and the Institute of Psychoanalysis, 1966.
Gardner, H. (1984). *The Mind's New Science*. New York: Basic Books.
Gibson, J. (1979). *The Ecological Approach to Visual Perception*. Boston: Houghton-Mifflin.
Hobbes, T. (1651). *Leviathan or the Matter, Forme and Power of a Commonwealth Ecclesiastical and Civil*. E. Curley (ed.) Indianapolis, IN: Hackett [1994].
Hume, D. (1739). *Treatise of Human Nature*. L.A. Selby-Bigge (ed.) Oxford: University Press, 1962.
Kant, I. (1781). *Critique of Pure Reason* (2nd edn, 1787). (Trans.) N. K. Smith as: *Immanuel Kant's Critique of Pure Reason*. London: Macmillan, 1963.
Meerbote, R. (1990). Kant's functionalism. In J-C. Smith (ed.), 1990, pp. 161–187.
Pasnau, R. (1997). *Theories of Cognition in the Later Middle Ages*. Cambridge and New York: Cambridge University Press.
Putnam, H. (1975). The meaning of 'meaning'. In his *Mind, Language and Reality* Philosophical Papers Vol. 2. New York: Cambridge University Press, pp. 215–271, at p. 227.
Ryle, G. (1949). *The Concept of Mind*. New York: Barnes and Noble.
Skinner, B.F. (1974). *About Behaviorism*. New York: Random House.
Smith, J-C. (ed.) 1990. *Historical Foundations of Cognitive Science*. Dordrecht: Reidel Publishers.

Part I The Roots of Cognitive Science in the Early Modern Era

1

The Separation of Thought and Action in Western Tradition

Stellan Ohlsson

Thought and action are abstract categories, but concrete instances easily come to mind. As examples of thinking, the proverbial person in the street might mention among other events, deciding what house to buy, making a bid in bridge or figuring out a murder mystery before the last chapter. Action covers most of everyday life, from cooking and driving to playing softball at the company picnic.

How are thought and action related? Intuition offers several partial and mutually inconsistent answers. The West has a long-standing tradition of regarding thought and action as separate. According to standard stereotypes, the theoretician wanders around with his or her head in the clouds, while the man or woman of practical affairs has little use for contemplation.

Other intuitions suggest bridges between thought and action. We would like to believe that our actions derive from our thoughts, or at least that our most rational actions are so grounded. Intuition also suggests that the bridge is two-way: our thinking is based on information gathered by acting on the world and observing the subsequent outcomes. The prehistory of cognitive science – as well as the history of cognitive science proper – is, in part, a series of attempts to make sense of these intuitions and replace them with more precise theoretical formulations.

The purpose of this chapter is to review three qualitatively different formulations of the distinction between thought and action, two of which antedate cognitive science by millennia. I trace each conceptual lineage forward from its origins and demonstrate how each projects into cognitive science proper. Along the way, I note the surprising extent to which these conceptual lineages have evolved in isolation from each other.

1. Theory versus practice

The pursuit of theoretical knowledge for practical purposes belongs to the modern era. To the ancients, knowledge and action did not seem so intertwined. The classical Greek philosophers sharply distinguished between *'episteme'* and *'techne'*. Their term *'episteme'* is approximately translatable as (the pursuit of) clear and certain knowledge; our terms 'science' and 'theory' (as the latter term is used on the European continent) can serve as contemporary equivalents. The classical term *'techne'* shares semantic features with each of our terms 'art', 'craft' and 'technology'; perhaps 'practice' is the closest English translation.[1]

If we consider the material practices available to philosophical reflection in ancient Greece, we can understand why the distinction between *'episteme'* and *'techne'* seemed sharp to Aristotle and his contemporaries. Architecture, agriculture, glass making, leather making, metal working, pottery and weaving lacked any basis in what we today would call theory and existed only in the uncodified skills of practitioners. Examples of deep and certain knowledge, on the other hand, were found primarily in arithmetic and geometry, domains in which truths could be discovered without engaging in significant physical action.

A millennium later, the split between theory and practice had acquired a religious connotation. In the transformation from the Greek *'episteme'* to the Latin *'scientia'*, clear and certain knowledge came to be associated with the sacred. In the scholastic theory of the world, God was the ultimate axiom and the only source of certainty. The exalted truths the scholastics deduced from this axiom stood in stark contrast to the grubby activities of the craftsmen who out of leather, iron and wood fashioned the creaky contraptions that constituted the leading-edge technology of medieval Europe. Scholastic philosophy strengthened rather than attenuated the ancient distinction between science and craft, theory and practice.

As Europe moved through the scientific and industrial revolutions, two forces worked to overcome this opposition: technology and professionalization. A machine functions in accordance with the laws of nature, yet serves a practical purpose. Its design must be responsive to both theory and practice and thus brings the two closer together.

---

[1] See Rothenberg (1995) for a discussion of *'techne'* versus *'episteme'* in the context of technology, specifically.

The gradual growth of systematic knowledge not only within engineering, but also in architecture, medicine, law and other fields led in the nineteenth century to *professionalization*, the creation of social organizations and institutions to authorize and regulate these knowledge-based practices (Abbot 1988; Bledstein 1978). Professional organizations nurture a self-understanding based on the Baconian idea that professionals can offer unique services because they possess esoteric but applicable knowledge (Faulkner 1993).

However, the gap between theory and practice has persisted into the modern era. Many professionals claim that what they do is not, in fact, applied science. In *What Engineers Know and How They Know It*, Walter G. Vincenti, a veteran aeronautical engineer, argues that although the activities of airplane designers have a 'scientific look' – very quantitative, sometimes experimental and typically concerned with the forces of nature – engineering cannot be equated with applied physics, because engineers are concerned with the human purpose of the devices they design, the operating principles and configurations of those devices and the practicalities of implementation, concepts which have no natural place in the theories of physicists (Vincenti 1990). Although technology and professionalization narrowed the gap between theory and practice, science and craft, they did not close it.

The gap is clearly visible in the organization of Western institutions of higher learning. University departments teach science – sometimes further specified as *basic* science – while schools of medicine, business and engineering train students to deal with practical affairs. The degree of separation between departments and professional schools on university campuses is an index of the strength of the intuition that theory and practice are separate realms.

The separation is also prevalent in popular culture. In everyday life, it is commonplace for a proposal to be countered with the objection, 'that might be correct in theory but it doesn't work in practice'. One consequence of this attitude is a tendency to sort individuals into thinkers and doers. The brilliant dreamer or theoretician who bumbles through simple, everyday tasks while issuing visionary but impractical schemes is a recurring stereotype in fiction, as is the achiever who relentlessly pursues this or that career goal without reflecting on its meaning.

The separation of theory and practice made its way into cognitive science too. Artificial Intelligence (AI) work on expert systems aims to design and implement computer programs that perform professional tasks such as design and diagnosis. Such programs must include an explicit representation of the expert's knowledge. Researchers in this field insist that the relevant knowledge is not a theory for the target performance. They contrast the concise, mathematical theories of natural science with the vast, loosely organized, irregular and only partially conscious knowledge that underpins practice. F. Hayes-Roth, D. Waterman and D. Lenat wrote:

... most of the difficult and interesting problems [addressed by experts] do not have tractable algorithmic solutions since many important tasks originate in complex social or physical contexts, which generally resist precise description and rigorous analysis. Planning, legal reasoning, medical diagnosis, geological exploration, and military situation analysis exemplify these problems.

(Hayes-Roth, Waterman & Lenat, 1983, p. 4)

Empirical studies of expertise concur. For example, Vimla L. Patel, David A. Evans and Guy J. Groen conducted experimental investigations to clarify the relative role of biomedical (i.e., theoretical) knowledge and clinical (i.e., practical) knowledge in medical diagnosis. 'Our goal is to illuminate the interaction of basic-scientific knowledge and clinical knowledge in medical problem solving' (Patel, Evans & Groen 1989, p. 57). After comparing expert practitioners and novices under a variety of conditions, they concluded; 'The most striking observation is that mature, clinical problem solving shows a preponderance of forward reasoning with little or no reliance on principles from basic science' (Patel, Evans & Groen 1989, p. 108). Biomedical theory is one thing; clinical practice another.

In summary, the distinction between theory and practice has been present in Western tradition since the beginning of systematic reflection. The unifying forces of technology and professionalization notwithstanding, it still forms one of the implicit axioms of our educational organizations as well as popular culture. The two branches of cognitive science that concern themselves with practice – implementation of AI expert systems and empirical studies of experts – agree that the competence that underpins expert practice is not theory-like.

In this conceptual lineage, the distinction between theory and practice is explicated as a distinction between two different types of *activities*. To theorize is one activity, to pursue goals is another. This way of drawing the distinction invites the objection that successful practice – whether in engineering, medicine or elsewhere – requires thinking as well. If so, perhaps the distinction can be reformulated in terms of two different kinds of thinking.

2. Theoretical versus practical inference

People disagree – and hence reason – about what to believe (i.e., about what reality is like) but also about what to do (i.e., about which action is most useful in a given situation). This observation suggests that rather than distinguishing theorizing from goal attainment we ought to distinguish between types of thought. Theoretical thinking, whether in science or in craft, strives to attain knowledge through valid, truth-preserving inferences. Practical thinking, in whatever field, aims for goal attainment through right decisions.

Aristotle implicitly made such a distinction by discussing the logic of syllogisms – a class of theoretical arguments – in his *Prior Analytics* and *Posterior Analytics* while saving his analysis of practical reasoning for the *Nichomachean Ethics*. This separation was so influential that the logic of truth and the logic of action moved along independent trajectories for two millennia.

Theoretical logic

Theoretical logic developed slowly from Aristotle's syllogisms to medieval logic, picked up speed in the nineteenth century with the works of Augustus De Morgan, George Boole and Gottlob Frege and matured when Bertrand Russell and Alfred North Whitehead in *Principia Mathematica* laid the foundation for the formal, first-order predicate logic that has since been reformulated in textbook after logic textbook.

Throughout the history of theoretical logic, thought has been viewed as a process of passing from (assumed true) premises to true conclusions by the application of truth-preserving inference rules. For example, if we have established the truth of the implication, *if global warming is happening, then the temperature is rising*, as well as the proposition, *the temperature is not rising*, then the Modus Tollens inference rule,

$$\{P \rightarrow Q, \text{ not } Q\} \Rightarrow \text{ not } P,$$

generates (or warrants) the conclusion, *global warming is not happening*. This is a valid inference regardless of the factual veridicality of the conclusion.

Logical systems differ in several respects: the notation for premises and rules, the set of inference rules and the definition of truth. Nevertheless, they share the idea that to reason is to apply inference rules to already accepted propositions in order to generate (or determine the truth value of) other propositions. Indeed, this feature can be taken to define the terms 'logical system' and 'logical reasoning'. Thinking, so defined, moves from truth to truth; it cannot address questions about what to do. There is no exit from the system of propositions into the spatio-temporal realm of action, no symbolic machinery for representing goals and intentions and no way to resolve conflicts between multiple attractive but mutually exclusive courses of action.

Theoretical logic projects into cognitive science along many paths. Formal logic was one of the background disciplines that led to abstract automata theory, the principled basis for symbolic computer programming and hence computer simulation.[2] The notation developed in formal logic is also the origin of the propositional knowledge representations often used in computational models of long-term memory and text comprehension (see, e.g., Kintsch 1974). Finally, the so-called resolution proof method that lies at the heart of logic programming languages (e.g., Prolog) is based on formal results from theoretical logic.[3]

More important for present purposes, theoretical logic has served as a model for cognitive theories of human reasoning. The relation between theoretical logic and the psychology of reasoning is somewhat paradoxical. On the one hand, theoretical logic made its greatest advances after it rid itself of the notion that the laws of logic are the laws of mind and pursued its goals independently of psychology. On the other hand, once formalized, logic became a tool for theorizing about human reasoning. In the 1960s, pioneers like Peter Wason – a transitional figure, schooled in the pre-cognitive tradition of British experimental psychology but with a strong impact on cognitive research – asked whether the logician's description of valid reasoning is also a theory of human reasoning, and if not, why not.

The enterprise of building a logic-based model of human reasoning is well defined: the experimental tasks usually taken to be relevant for a theory of reasoning are to draw and evaluate assertions, assuming

---

[2] See Arbib (1969) for a classic treatment of abstract automata. For an outline of the rationale for computer simulation of human cognition that highlights its basis in abstract automata theory, see Ohlsson (1988).

[3] For a formal, yet readable introduction to resolution theorem proving and logic programming, see Nilsson (1980), Chapters 4–5. See also Jackson, Reichgelt and van Harmelen (1989).

the truth of certain other assertions. The face validity of these tasks is obviously a reflection of the idea that an inference is a passage from some premises to a conclusion. To build a theory to account for data from such tasks, define a propositional notation for the premises and formulate inference rules such that those rules, when applied to the relevant premises, generate precisely those conclusions that people generate (or judge as valid) and no others; if people make errors, the rules should generate those same errors; if people take longer to draw or evaluate one conclusion than another, then the rules should imply that a greater number of inferential steps are involved. The explanation by I.M.L. Hunter of how people reason about so-called linear syllogisms was perhaps the first systematic attempt at carrying out this explanatory program (Hunter 1957), but other efforts soon followed.[4]

Cognitive science models of this sort go further than pre-cognitive models in that they also specify the control structure, i.e., the machinery by which the individual inference rules are selected and applied in the course of reasoning. This enables such theories to account for processing data, e.g., variations in the time it takes people to draw or judge particular conclusions. Works by Daniel N. Osherson, Martin D.S. Braine, Lance J. Rips and others exemplify this approach (Osherson 1974, 1975; Braine & O'Brien 1998; Rips 1994). Although Rips's theory differs from formal logic in its concern with real-time processing, its relation to theoretical logic is so clear that Aristotle would have been able to pick up his *The Psychology of Proof* and immediately understand the purpose of the work.

For present purposes, the central observation is that logic-based reasoning theories do not bring thought into contact with action. Such theories describe how people decide whether some proposition follows from certain other propositions. There is no mechanism for deciding what to do. According to theories of this sort, thought is locked into a universe of propositions that has neither perceptual entrance nor motor exit, the defining feature of theoretical as opposed to practical reasoning.

Practical logic

In addition to the celebrated theoretical syllogism, which was the starting point for theoretical logic and still supplies the raw material for countless psychological experiments, Aristotle recognized a second class of arguments that philosophers and logicians call *practical syllogisms*.

[4] Two other pioneers were Peter Wason (1969) and Mary Henle (1962).

The key feature of a practical syllogism is that it ends not with an assertion but with an action.

In *On the Motion of Animals*, Aristotle sets out to 'inquire how the soul moves the body' and asks 'how is it that thought (viz. sense, imagination, and thought proper) is sometimes followed by action, sometimes not; sometimes by movement, sometimes not?' (*De Motu Animalium*, 701a). In his answer, Aristotle implicitly introduces a class of arguments that parallel theoretical arguments in structure, but differ in outcome: 'What happens seems parallel to the case of thinking and inferring about the immovable objects of science. There the end is the truth seen (for, when one conceives the two premises, one at once conceives and comprehends the conclusion), but here [i.e., in the case of practical reasoning] the two premises result in a conclusion which is an action ...'.

The examples given by Aristotle are peculiar: if one thinks of the principle that every person ought to walk (the major premise), and of the fact that oneself is a person (the minor premise), then 'straightway one walks'. Alternatively, if one thinks that nobody should walk, 'straightway one remains at rest'. The formulation suggests that practical reasoning exerts causal force on the thinking person's own body.

The same view is advanced in the *Nichomachean Ethics*: '... when a single opinion [i.e., conclusion] results from the two [premises], the soul must in one type of case affirm the conclusion, while in the case of opinions concerned with production it must immediately act' (*Ethica Nicomachea*, 1147a). Once again, the example given is peculiar: '... if "everything sweet ought to be tasted", and "this is sweet", in the sense of being one of the particular sweet things, the man who can act and is not prevented must at the same time actually act accordingly', i.e., actually taste it.

What are we to make of these passages? It is easy to agree with George von Wright's assessment that 'Aristotle's own treatment of the topic is very unsystematic and his examples are often confusing' (von Wright 1971, pp. 26–27). Von Wright summarizes his own interpretation of Aristotle's view as follows:

> The starting point or major premise of the [practical] syllogism mentions some wanted thing or end of action; the minor premise relates

[5] The question of how to decide what to do was seriously considered in economics, ultimately leading to the theory of decision-making. The distinctive character of this intellectual lineage is the effort to quantify the problem and to find mathematically well-defined solutions. Reviewing this development would take us outside the boundary of the current investigation.

some action to this thing, *roughly* as a means to the end; the conclusion finally, consists in use of this means to secure that end. Thus, as in a theoretical inference the affirmation of the premises leads of necessity to the affirmation of the conclusion, in a practical inference assent to the premises entails action in accordance with them.

(von Wright 1971, p. 27)

Aristotle only mentions the practical syllogism in works on ethics and empirical science, not in his *Organon*. Thus split off from epistemology and logic, and hence isolated from what was to become the mainstream of Western philosophy, the question of how human beings decide what to do hibernated in the relatively obscure and neglected corner of philosophical ethics.[5] Medieval works of logic such as the highly influential *Port-Royal Logic* (Arnauld & Nicole 1683/1996) did not discuss practical syllogisms, and neither did nineteenth-century works such as George Boole's *Laws of Thought* (1854/1958).

This situation did not change until the publication of G.E.M. Anscombe's *Intention* in 1957. Anscombe pointed out that the practical syllogism was one of Aristotle's more interesting discoveries in logic. Once philosophers focused on practical reasoning, they discovered knotty problems therein. In two influential articles, George von Wright set up the following practical reasoning schema:

X intends to make it true that E.
Unless he does A, he will not achieve this.
Therefore X will do A.

and asked whether arguments of this form are logically valid (von Wright 1963 a,b, 1972). A closely related question is whether practical logic can be reduced to theoretical logic or requires unique logical constructs; as one might expect, philosophers are divided on the issue (Aune 1977). Other philosophers have focused on the first premise in the schema and asked what it means to have an intention and whether intentions have unique logical characteristics, and yet others wonder whether the premises in a practical argument are causally or logically related to the subsequent action. These strands of analysis come together into a type of inquiry into human action that is distinctly philosophical rather than psychological (see, e.g., Aune 1977; Schick 1991 and Velleman 1989).

Unlike its theoretical cousin, practical logic and the philosophy of action have had minimal impact on cognitive science. One reason is that cognitive science has a logic of action of its own, usually referred to as general methods for problem solving or planning. Consider means-ends analysis: to reach goal X, determine the difference between X and your current situation; then think of some action that might reduce that difference; identify the constraints on applying that action; call the conjunction of those constraints Y; pose attaining Y as your next goal; continue this process until you reach an action that you can perform in your current situation; execute that action; repeat until done (Newell & Simon 1972).

To see the close conceptual relations between general problem-solving methods and practical logic, compare the specification of means-ends analysis in the previous paragraph with Aristotle's discussion of deliberation in the *Nichomachean Ethics*:

> We deliberate not about ends but about means. [Practitioners] assume the end and consider how and by what means it is to be attained; and if it seems to be produced by several means they consider by which it is most easily and best produced, while if it is achieved by one only they consider how it will be achieved by this and by what means *this* will be achieved, till they come to the first cause, which in the order of discovery is the last. ... And if we come on an impossibility, we give up the search, e.g., if we need money and this cannot be got; but if a thing appears possible we try to do it.
>
> (*Ethica Nicomachea* 1112b)

The conceptual similarity between practical logics and general methods for problem solving and planning has been obscured by differences in style, notation and terminology. These differences originate in the cognitive scientist's concern with process. Executable specifications of means-ends analysis (or any other general method) must specify not only the underlying logic of the method but also the details of how a physically realizable agent – brain or machine – can execute that logic in real time. Because the computational details are complicated and extensive while the underlying logic is simple and concise, the details tend to obscure the logic.

To highlight the conceptual relations, we can shave off the machinery for execution and restate means-ends analysis as two practical inference rules: The first rule is, [if your goal is G and action A helps you reach G, then perform A] and the second rule is, [if you need to perform A, and B is a prerequisite to performing A, set yourself the goal of attaining B].

The first of these rules is virtually identical to the practical reasoning schema proposed by von Wright (1963 a,b, 1972) and dissected by Aune (1977) and other philosophers. In short, general methods for problem solving and planning occupy the practical reasoning niche in the intellectual ecology of cognitive science. These methods are expressed in a powerful formal notation (symbolic programming languages) and supported by a special technology (computers). The existence of such formidable defenders at home has ensured that practical logic as formulated by philosophers has made little headway into cognitive territory.

One exception is an overlooked paper, 'On reasoning about actions', by Herbert A. Simon in which this giant of cognitive science sketches a formal calculus of action that allows the derivation of conclusions like 'Can attain state X', given certain premises about what the agent can and cannot do (Simon 1972).

In Simon's calculus, the symbol CAN(c) is defined to mean that the agent can attain situation c (from some given starting situation). Simon sets up the two axioms:

$$CAN(c_1,c_2), CAN(c_2,c_3) \rightarrow CAN(c_1,c_3)$$

which says that if the agent knows how to attain c_2 from c_1 and how to attain c_3 from c_2, then he or she knows how to attain c_3 from c_1, and

$$CAN(c_1), CAN(c_1.c_2,c_3) \rightarrow CAN(c_2,c_3)$$

which says that if the agent knows how to get to c_1 and also how to achieve c_3 from a state that combines c_1 and c_2, then he or she also knows how to get to c_3 from c_2.

From these axioms, Simon derives several formal results, including the principle that

$$CAN(c_1), CAN(c_2) \rightarrow CAN(c_1.c_2),$$

i.e., the statement that if the agent knows how to achieve c_1 and how to achieve c_2, then he or she knows how to achieve a state that combines c_1 and c_2. This calculus is applied in the analysis of a variety of action problems, including the famous monkey and banana problem (Simon 1972, p. 418).

Conceptually, the main difference between Simon's action calculus and the practical logics formulated by philosophers is that the former deals with the question of how to prove that some end result is attainable, while the latter typically address the question how one decides that some particular end result is desirable. Simon's attempt at formulating a practical logic from within cognitive science is an isolated effort. It did not grow out of prior work in practical logic, and, to the best of my knowledge, it has had no successors.

In spite of the close conceptual relations between practical reasoning, on the one hand, and problem solving and planning, on the other, there is no historical evidence for a dialogue between the two intellectual lineages. Newell and Simon did not reference any prior work on practical logic when they introduced the notion of general problem-solving methods, nor do works in practical logic reference cognitive science works on problem solving, planning and other relevant topics. Parallel, non-interacting development has been the rule.

Discussion

Contemporary theoretical and practical logics share certain notational conventions and analytical techniques, but their very existence as separate disciplines is an implicit claim that thinking about what to believe and thinking about what to do are distinct processes. To many, this is not an historical accident. Scholars tend to believe that it is, in principle, impossible to derive 'ought' from 'is' or vice versa. Attempts to reduce one to the other are made from time to time, but so far without convincing success. The intellectual enterprise of logic thus continues to depict thought as split down the middle, the pursuit of truth and the pursuit of goals rolling along on parallel, non-intersecting tracks.

Cognitive science has followed suit. Psychological research on what is commonly called reasoning, as summarized in textbook chapters, falls squarely into the tradition of theoretical logic. The common experimental tasks of deriving and judging the validity of conclusions with respect to given premises reflect the conception of thinking as a passage from premises to conclusions via inference rules, and at least some theories proposed to account for data from such experiments mimic the form of formal logic. Such theories lack any mechanism for interfacing thought with action.

Research on what is commonly called either problem solving or planning, on the other hand, focuses on tasks that require a sequence of

---

[6] This practice is quite prevalent and shows no sign of abating. See, for example, Reisberg (1997), Goldstein (2005), and Willingham (2007).

actions, and the goal is to explain how the problem solver decides which action to take at any moment in time, the very question posed by practical logics. General methods for problem solving and planning proposed to account for data from action tasks can be conceptualized as executable implementations of practical inference rules. Those theories have no mechanism for deciding what to believe or for judging whether an assertion follows from a given set of premises.

Hence, in the contrast between reasoning and problem solving, current cognitive psychology reproduces the distinction between theoretical and practical logic and thus implicitly agrees with the claim that there are two types of thought, one concerned with deciding what is true and one concerned with what to do. This distinction is so established that contemporary textbooks in cognitive psychology typically treat deductive reasoning and problem solving in separate chapters.[6]

Once proposed, the idea that there are two distinct types of thought is puzzling. Why is human thinking divided in this way? A third way of formulating the intuitive distinction between thought and action contains a possible explanation.

3. Knowing that versus knowing how

In *Concept of Mind*, published in 1949, Gilbert Ryle expressed his concern that attempts to understand mind overemphasized thought at the expense of action:

> Theorists have been so preoccupied with the task of investigating the nature, the source, and the credentials of the theories that we adopt that they have for the most part ignored the question what it is for someone to know how to perform tasks. In ordinary life, on the contrary, as well as in the special business of teaching, we are much more concerned with people's competences than with their cognitive repertoires, with the operations than with the truths that they learn.
>
> (Ryle 1949/1963, p. 28)

To remedy this imbalance, Ryle introduced a distinction between knowing *that* and knowing *how*. Ryle does not explicitly define these two concepts, but he provides many examples. To know *that* is to possess some fact about the world (e.g., that Sussex is a county in England), while to know *how* is to possess a skill, to be able to carry out some action successfully (e.g., to play chess). Ryle insists that the two are irreducibly distinct: '"Intelligent" cannot be defined in terms of "intellectual" or "knowing how" in terms of "knowing that"' (p. 32).

One reason for so insisting is that the two types of knowledge are acquired in different ways:

> Learning *how* or improving in ability is not like learning *that* or acquiring information. Truths can be imparted, procedures can only be inculcated, and while inculcation is a gradual process, imparting is relatively sudden. It makes sense to ask at what moment someone became apprised of a truth, but not to ask at what moment someone acquired a skill.
>
> (Ryle 1949/1963, p. 58)

The novel element in Ryle's formulation is that he distinguishes between two types of *knowledge*, as opposed to two types of activities or two types of arguments. Facts constitute a qualitatively different type of knowledge than skills.

Ryle's distinction resonates with practitioners in many fields. Although opposed to Ryle's epistemology, Michael Polanyi agrees that there are two types of knowledge, which in his terminology are called 'pure' and 'applicable': 'The conceptual framework of applicable knowledge is different from that of pure knowledge. It is determined primarily in terms of the successful performances to which such knowledge is relevant' (Polanyi 1958/1973, p. 175). Applicable knowledge is characteristic of crafts and the professions: 'The medical diagnostician's skill is as much an art of doing as it is an art of knowing' (p. 54).

Vincenti makes a similar distinction between what he calls *descriptive* and *prescriptive* knowledge in the context of aeronautics: 'Descriptive knowledge is knowledge of how things are. Descriptive data needed by designers include physical constants (acceleration of gravity, for example) as well as properties of substances (failing strength of materials, coefficient of viscosity of fluids, etc.) and of processes (rate of chemical reactions and so forth). ... Prescriptive knowledge is knowledge of how things should be to attain a desired end – it says, in effect, 'in order to accomplish this, arrange things in this way' (Vincenti 1993, pp. 216–17).

Jerome Bruner, in discussing the relation between psychology and education, makes the same distinction:

> One might ask why a theory of instruction is needed, since psychology already contains theories of learning and of development. But theories of learning and of development are descriptive rather than

prescriptive. ... A theory of instruction, on the other hand, ... is concerned with how what one wishes to teach can best be learned, with improving rather than describing learning.

And again:

A theory of instruction is *prescriptive* in the sense that it sets forth rules concerning the most effective way of achieving knowledge or skill.

(Bruner 1966, p. 40)

In short, practitioners in many fields recognize a distinction between the two types of knowledge distinguished by Ryle. One kind is knowledge about what the world is like; the other kind is knowledge of how to accomplish particular results.

In 1975, Terry Winograd introduced this distinction into cognitive science in a paper entitled, 'Frame representations and the declarative/ procedural controversy' (Winograd 1975). Writing in the context of an ongoing debate within AI research, Winograd used the terms 'declarative' and 'procedural', but the distinction is the same as Ryle's. Cognitive science augments Ryle's distinction with the notion of formal representation, applied to both types of knowledge. Declarative knowledge is typically represented in propositions, while procedural knowledge can be represented by sets of rules or other programming constructs. In a computer program, the fact [San Francisco is north of Los Angeles] is most naturally encoded as a proposition, while the prescription [if you are in Los Angeles and you want to go to San Francisco, you must travel north] is most naturally encoded as a procedure.

Although Terry Winograd's 1975 paper is the first publication in which the terminology of declarative and procedural knowledge appears in print, it was not written to introduce the distinction. On the contrary, Winograd treats it as well known. Indeed, his purpose was to suggest directions for how to go beyond it. This attitude characterized subsequent work within AI. Two decades later, the only trace of the so-called declarative-procedural controversy within AI is the continuing debate over the supposed advantages of logic programming, a methodology that emphasizes declarative over procedural representations.

The distinction fared better in cognitive psychology. In 1976, John R. Anderson placed it at the center of his ACT theory of human cognition.[7]

---

[7] See Anderson (1983), Anderson (1993) and Anderson & Lebiere (1998) for successive versions of this highly influential theory.

The ACT model makes a fundamental distinction between procedural knowledge and declarative knowledge – between knowing how and knowing that. Procedural knowledge is represented in terms of productions whereas declarative knowledge is represented in terms of a propositional network.

(Anderson 1976, p. 116)

Although many other constructs have come and gone in the successive versions of the ACT model, this distinction has remained stable.[7] As neuroscientific evidence for the two types of knowledge accumulates, the distinction is likely to remain central to cognitive psychology (see, e.g., Squire 1987).

How was the distinction between knowing *that* and knowing *how* projected into cognitive science? Winograd mentions the 'old philosophical distinction between "knowing that" and "knowing how"' (Winograd 1975, p. 186). He does not give a reference, but the terminology indicates familiarity with Gilbert Ryle's *Concept of Mind*. However, this clue is slender. According to Professor Winograd's recollections, the distinction was part of the culture of the AI community at that time, with no specific publication serving as starting point (personal communication, spring 1998). If we follow his references backwards in time, the trail disappears into unpublished technical reports that deal primarily with other topics.

It is therefore possible that the distinction was made *de novo* in the development of AI programming practices. The distinction might have asserted itself, as it were, in attempts to supply AI systems with knowledge: How do you encode it? Where do you put it? What form of access is needed? The struggle to find workable solutions to these problems might have forced the distinction on the system builders. The connection backwards to Ryle and the philosophical tradition might have been made later. What we know is that sometime between 1958 (the recognized date for the birth of AI; for the history of the cognitive revolution, see Gardner 1985) and 1975 (the date of Winograd's paper), the distinction between the two types of knowledge appeared within cognitive science.

Conclusion

The intuition that the mind is split down the middle goes deep in the Western tradition. There is contemplation and there is activity; there are thinkers and there are achievers; there is insight into the nature of things and there is the ability to get things done; there are truths and there are skills; and there are descriptions and there are prescriptions.

The conceptual lineages surveyed in this chapter formulate the distinction in three ways, differentiated by the type of entities being distinguished. The theory-versus-practice (or science-versus-craft) formulation distinguishes between *activities*. Theory (in the sense in which this term is used on the European continent) is a reflective enterprise directed towards the creation of true descriptions. This activity might require action, e.g., traveling to distant places for the purpose of observation, constructing instruments, conducting experiments, and so on. However, those actions do not aim to accomplish material results. They serve reflection, and their only relevant outcomes are intellectual (measurements, observations, descriptions and explanations). Practice, on the other hand, consists of acting towards a material result or state of affairs that is desirable in itself, not merely for the information it provides.

This way of drawing the distinction fails to deal with the fact that practitioners think. It is true that the expert practitioner can carry out many activities within his or her field in a routine manner, but the novice is not so quick and even the master can encounter problems that stretch his or her skills and force reflection. Our admiration for the achievements of the expert practitioner makes us overlook the intellectual work that guides his or her performance. Locating thought exclusively within the domain of theory is contrary to the experience of any craftsman or practitioner.

The logic tradition avoids this mistake by formulating the distinction differently. Logicians differentiate between types of *arguments*, not activities or enterprises. On the one hand, there are arguments (and hence thought processes) that go from true premises to true conclusions via truth-preserving inference rules. The conclusion is a new assertion about the world, a new piece of knowledge. On the other hand, there are arguments that start from a goal and end in an action or exhortation, using other types of inference rules than those employed in theoretical logics.

With this distinction in hand, we can re-conceptualize the difference between theory and practice as follows: both activities involve thought and action, both theoretical and practical reasoning, but they differ as to which type of reasoning dominates. A scientist engages in practical reasoning while conducting an investigation, but most of his or her mental energy is devoted to developing predictions from theories, drawing conclusions from data and other forms of theoretical reasoning. On the other side of the coin, the practitioner must engage in theoretical reasoning to understand the situation he or she is trying to change, but the bulk of his or her reasoning effort is devoted to deciding what to do next. In short, the logical distinction between types of arguments suggests that the distinction between theory and practice is a matter of balance between theoretical and practical inferences.

Why are there two distinct types of inferences? A possible answer emerges if we reformulate the distinction as a distinction between two types of *knowledge* (or two ways of representing knowledge). Propositions describe reality in a task-neutral way. They carry truth-values but must be interpreted vis-à-vis the task at hand. Rules, on the other hand, are neither true nor false, but more or less appropriate or useful. They specify what to do with respect to the task at hand, at the cost of task-specificity.

Both representations can be supplied with inference engines that enable them to compute new results. A general inference engine running over a propositional database carries out a process that in logical terminology would be called theoretical reasoning; a Prolog interpreter is such an engine (Jackson, Reichgelt & van Harmelen 1989 is an introduction). A rule interpreter running over a set of condition-action rules carries out a process that closely resembles the arguments discussed within practical logic, especially if the condition parts of the rules contain goal expressions; a production system architecture is such an interpreter.[8] In short, the distinction between two types of knowledge, in conjunction with the computational concept of process, explains why there are two distinct types of reasoning: each type arises as the natural way to process a distinct type of knowledge representation.

The three ways of drawing the distinction between thought and action reappear within cognitive science. AI efforts to build expert systems and empirical research on expertise distinguish expert competence from

[8] Klahr, Langley & Neches (1987) contains a systematic overview of production system architectures, as well as several examples of how they are used in cognitive modeling.

[9] The preparation of this chapter was completed while I was Senior Scientist at the Learning Research and Development Center, and I thank James Voss for his input. Andrew Brook was generous in offering this intriguing opportunity to try my hand at intellectual history, an unfamiliar art to me. His insightful editorial comments helped me to overcome structural problems in the first version of the chapter. Gershon B. Berkson and James G. Kelly, two colleagues at the University of Illinois at Chicago (UIC) with extensive knowledge of the history of psychology, also provided useful comments. My wife, Elaine Ohlsson, kept my motivation high with her steadfast encouragement.

theory. Within cognitive psychology, the gap between research on reasoning and research on problem solving reproduces the distinction between theoretical and practical reasoning as it appears within logic. Finally, the distinction between declarative and procedural knowledge is a reformulation of a distinction common to multiple fields of scholarship: knowing *that* versus knowing *how*, pure versus applied, descriptive versus prescriptive and so on. The three ways of drawing the distinction between thought and action antedate, but are present in, cognitive science.

Works in one of these lineages rarely reference those in either of the others. The advantage of explicating the distinction between theory and practice in terms of the relative balance between theoretical and practical reasoning has not been pursued. The possibility of mapping types of arguments onto types of knowledge has largely gone unnoticed. The implications of the declarative-procedural distinction for the contrast between theory and practice remain to be worked out. One lesson from the prehistory of this topic is that cognitive science might benefit from a synthesizing approach that integrates long-standing conceptual lineages.[9]

References

Abbot, A. (1988). *The System of Professions*. Chicago: The University of Chicago Press.

Anderson, J.R. (1976). *Language, Memory, and Thought*. Hillsdale, NJ: Erlbaum.

Anderson, J.R. (1983). *The Architecture of Cognition*. Cambridge, MA: Harvard University Press.

Anderson, J.R. (1993). *Rules of the Mind*. Hillsdale, NJ: Erlbaum.

Anderson, J.R., & Lebiere, C. (1998). *The Atomic Components of Thought*. Mahwah, NJ: Erlbaum.

Anscombe, G.E.M. (1957). *Intention*. Oxford, UK: Basil Blackwell.

Arbib, M.A. (1969). *Theories of Abstract Automata*. Englewood Cliffs, NJ: Prentice-Hall.

Aristotle, *The Works of Aristotle* (1952). (Vols 1 and 2). Chicago, IL: Encyclopedia Britannica, Inc.

Arnauld, A., & Nicole, P. (1683/1996). *La Logique ou l'art de penser*, 5th edn, orig. publ. 1683. English translation under the title *Logic or the Art of Thinking* (transl. by J.V. Buroker). Cambridge, UK: Cambridge University Press, 1996.

Aune, B. (1977). *Reason and Action*. Dordrecht, Holland: D. Reidel.

Bledstein, B.J. (1978). *The Culture of Professionalism*. New York: Norton.

Boole, G. (1854/1958). *An Investigation of the Laws of Thought on which are Founded the Mathematical Theories of Logic and Probabilities*, orig. publ. by Macmillan in 1854. Paperback edition by Dover Publications, New York, 1958.

Braine, M.D.S., & O'Brien, D.P. (1998). *Mental Logic*. Mahwah, NJ: Erlbaum.

Bruner, J.S. (1966). *Toward a Theory of Instruction*. Cambridge, MA: Belknapp Press.

Faulkner, R.K. (1993). *Francis Bacon and the Project of Progress*. Lanham, MD: Rowman & Littlefield.

Gardner, H. (1985). *The Mind's New Science*. New York: Basic Books.

Goldstein, E.B. (2005). *Cognitive Psychology: Connecting Mind, Research, and Everyday Experience*. Belmont, CA: Thomson Wadsworth.

Hayes-Roth, F., Waterman, D.A., & Lenat, D.B. (1983). An overview of expert systems. In F. Hayes-Roth, D.A. Waterman, & D.B. Lenat (eds), *Building Expert Systems* (pp. 3–29). London: Addison-Wesley.

Henle, M. (1962). On the relation between logic and thinking. *Psychological Review*, 69, 366–378.

Hunter, I.M.L. (1957). The solving of three-term series problems. *The British Journal of Psychology*, 48, 286–298.

Jackson, P., Reichgelt, H., & van Harmelen, F. (eds) (1989). *Logic-Based Knowledge Representation*. Cambridge, MA: MIT Press.

Kintsch, W. (1974). *The Representation of Meaning in Memory*. Hillsdale, NJ: Erlbaum.

Klahr, D., Langley, P. & E Neches, R. (eds) (1987). *Production system Models of Learning and Development*. Cambridge, MA: MIT Press.

Newell, A., & Simon, H.A. (1972). *Human Problem Solving*. Englewood Cliffs, NJ: Prentice-Hall.

Nilsson, N.J. (1980). *Principles of Artificial Intelligence*. Los Altos, CA: Kaufmann.

Ohlsson, S. (1988) Computer simulation and its impact on educational research and practice. *International Journal of Education*, 12, 5–34.

Osherson, S. (1974). *Logical Inference: Underlying Operations* (Logical abilities in children, Vol. 2). Potomac, MD: Erlbaum.

Osherson, S. (1975). *Reasoning in Adolescence: Deductive Inference* (Logical abilities in children, Vol. 3). Hillsdale, NJ: Erlbaum.

Patel, V.L., Evans, D.A., & Groen, G. (1989). Biomedical knowledge and clinical reasoning. In D.A. Evans, & V.L. Patel (eds), *Cognitive Science in Medicine* (pp. 53–112). Cambridge, MA: MIT Press.

Polanyi, M. (1958/1973). *Personal Knowledge*. London, UK: Routledge & Kegan Paul.

Reisberg, D. (1996). *Cognition: Exploring the Science of the Mind*. New York: Norton.

Rips, L.J. (1994). *The Psychology of Proof*. Cambridge, MA: MIT Press.

Ryle, G. (1949/1963). *The Concept of Mind*. London, UK: Penguin Books.

Schick, F. (1991). *Understanding Action*. Cambridge, UK: Cambridge University Press.

Simon, H.A. (1972). On reasoning about actions. In H.A. Simon and L. Siklossy (eds), *Representation and Meaning* (pp. 414–430). Englewood Cliffs, NJ: Prentice-Hall.

Squire, L.R. (1987). *Memory and Brain*. New York: Oxford University Press.

Velleman, J.D. (1989). *Practical Reflection*. Princeton, NJ: Princeton University Press.

Vincenti, W.G. (1990). *What Engineers Know and How They Know It*. Baltimore, MD: John Hopkins University Press.

Wason, P.C. (1968). Reasoning about a rule. *The Quarterly Journal of Experimental Psychology*, 20, 273–281.

Willingham, D.T. (2007). *Cognition: The Thinking Animal* (3rd edn). Upper Saddle River, NJ: Prentice-Hall.

Winograd, T. (1975). Frame representations and the declarative/procedural controversy. In D. G. Bobrow & A. Collins (eds), *Representation and Understanding* (pp. 185–210). New York: Academic Press.

Wright, von, G.H. (1963a). Practical inference. *Philosophical Review*, 72, 159–179.
Wright, von, G.H. (1963b). *Norm and Action*. London, UK: Routledge & Kegan Paul.
Wright, von, G.H. (1971). *Explanation and Understanding*. London, UK: Routledge & Kegan Paul.
Wright, von, G.H. (1972). On so-called practical inference. *Acta Sociologica*, 15, 39–53.

2
Language and Thought: Descartes and Some Reflections on Venerable Themes

Noam Chomsky

The study of language and mind goes back to classical antiquity – to classical Greece and India in the pre-Christian era. It has often been assumed over these millennia that the two inquiries have some intimate relation. Language has sometimes been described as a 'mirror of mind', so that the study of language should then give unique insight into human thought. That convergence, which has been repeated over the centuries, took place again about forty years ago, at the origins of what is sometimes called the 'Cognitive Revolution'. I will use the term intending you to hear quotes around the phrase 'cognitive revolution', expressing some skepticism; it was not all that much of a revolution in my opinion.

In any event, however one assesses it, an important change of perspective took place: from the study of behavior and its products (texts, and so on) to the internal processes that underlie what people are doing, and, their origin in the human biological endowment. The approach to the study of language that I want to consider here has developed in that context, and was a significant factor in its emergence and subsequent progress.

The first cognitive revolution

Much the same convergence had taken place in the seventeenth century, in what we might call 'the first cognitive revolution', perhaps the only real one. This was part of the general scientific revolution of the period – the 'Galilean revolution', as it is sometimes called. There are interesting features in common between the contemporary cognitive revolution and its predecessor. The resemblance was not appreciated at the outset (and still is hardly well known) because the history had been largely forgotten. Such scholarly work as existed was misleading or worse, and even basic texts were not available or considered of any interest. The topic merits attention, in my opinion, not just for anti-quarian reasons. My own view is that we have much to learn from the earlier history, and that there has even been some regression in the modern period. I will come back to that.

One element of similarity is the stimulus to the scientific imagination provided by complex machines. Today that means computers. In the seventeenth and eighteenth centuries it meant the automata that were being constructed by skilled artisans, a marvel to everyone. Both then and now the apparent achievements of these artifacts raise a rather obvious question: are humans simply more complex machines? That is a topic of lively debate today, and the same was true in the earlier peri-od. It was at the core of Cartesian philosophy – but it is worth remembering that the distinction between science and philosophy did not exist at the time: a large part of philosophy was what we call 'science'. Cartesian science arose in part from puzzlement over the difference – if any – between humans and machines. The questions went well beyond curiosity about human nature and the physical world, reaching to the immortality of the soul, the unchallengeable truths of established religion, and so on – not trivial matters.

In the background was 'the mechanical philosophy', the idea that the world is a complex machine, which could in principle be constructed by a master craftsman. The basic principle was drawn from simple common sense: to interact, two objects must be in direct contact. To carry through the program of 'mechanization of the world-view', it was necessary to rid science of neoscholastic sympathies and antipathies and substantial forms, and other mystical baggage, and to show that contact mechanics suffices. This endeavor was considerably advanced by Descartes's physics and physiology, which he regarded as the heart of his achievement. In a letter to Mersenne, his confidant and most influential supporter in the respectable intellectual world of the day, Descartes wrote that his *Meditations on First Philosophy*, today commonly considered his fundamental contribution, was a work of propaganda designed to lead readers step-by-step to accept his physics without realizing it, so that by the end, being entirely convinced, they would renounce the dominant Aristotelian picture of the world and accept the mechanical worldview. Within this context, the question of limits of automata could not fail to be a prominent one.

The Cartesians argued that the mechanical worldview extended to all of the inorganic and organic world apart from humans, even to a substantial part of human physiology and psychology. But humans nevertheless transcend the boundaries of any possible machine, hence are fundamentally different from animals which are indeed mere automata, differing from clocks only in complexity. But however intricate a mechanical device might be, the Cartesians argued, crucial aspects of what humans think and do would lie beyond its scope, in particular, voluntary action. Set the machine in a certain state in a particular external situation, and it will be 'compelled' to act in a certain way (random elements aside). But under comparable circumstances, a human is only 'incited and inclined' to do so. People may tend to do what they are incited and inclined to do; their behavior may be predictable, and a practical account of motivation may be possible. But theories of behavior will always miss the crucial point: the person could have chosen to act otherwise.

In this analysis, the properties of language played a central role. For Descartes and his followers, notably Géraud de Cordemoy, the ability to use language in the normal way is a criterion for possession of mind – for being beyond the limits of any possible mechanism. Experimental procedures were devised that could be used to determine whether some object that looks like us is actually a complicated machine or really has a mind like ours. The tests typically had to do with what I have called elsewhere the 'creative aspect of language use', a normal feature of everyday usage: the fact that it is typically innovative, guided but not determined by internal state and external conditions, appropriate to circumstances but uncaused, eliciting thoughts that the hearer might have expressed the same way. If an object passes all the tests we can devise to determine whether it manifests these properties, it would only be reasonable to attribute to it a mind like ours, the Cartesians argued.

Notice that this is normal science. The available evidence suggests that some aspects of the world, notably the normal use of language, do not fall within the mechanical philosophy – hence cannot be duplicated by a machine. We therefore postulate some further principle, a kind of 'creative principle', that lies beyond mechanism. The logic was not unlike Newton's, to which I will return. In the framework of the substance metaphysics of the day, the natural move was to postulate a second substance, mind, a 'thinking substance' alongside of body. Next comes the problem of unification: how do we relate these two components of the world? This was a major problem of the period.

These intellectual moves were not only normal science, but also pretty reasonable. The arguments that were given are not without force. We would frame the issues and possible answers differently today, but the fundamental questions remain unanswered, and puzzling.

Fascination with the (possible) limits of automata is one respect in which the first cognitive revolution has been in part relived in recent years, though the usual preoccupation today is the nature of consciousness, not the properties of normal human action that concerned the Cartesians; crucially, the apparent fact that it is coherent and appropriate, but uncaused. Another similarity has to do with what are nowadays called 'computational theories of mind'. In a different form, these were also a salient feature of the first cognitive revolution. Perhaps Descartes's most lasting scientific contribution lies right here: his outline of a theory of perception with a computational flair (though our notions of computation were unavailable), along with proposals about its realization in bodily mechanisms.

To establish the mechanical philosophy, Descartes sought to eliminate the 'occult properties' invoked by the science of the day to account for what happens in the world. The study of perception was an important case. How, for example, can we see a cube rotating in space when the surface of the body – the retina, in this case – records only a sequence of two-dimensional displays? What is happening in the outside world and in the brain to bring about this result?

Prevailing orthodoxy held that somehow, the form of the cube rotating in space passes into your brain. So there is a cube in your brain, rotating presumably, when you see a cube rotating. Descartes ridiculed these fanciful and mysterious notions, suggesting a mechanical alternative. He asked us to consider the analogy of a blind man with a stick. Suppose there is an object before him, say a chair, and he taps on it with the end of his stick, receiving a sequence of tactile sensations in his hand. This sequence engages the internal resources of his mind, which compute in some manner, producing the image of a chair by means of their inner resources. In this way, the blind man perceives a chair, Descartes reasoned. He proposed that vision is much the same. According to the mechanical worldview, there can be no empty space: motion is caused by direct contact. When Jones sees a chair, a physical rod extends from his retina to the chair. If Jones's eye is scanning the surface of the chair, his retina is receiving a series of sensations from the rod that extends to it, just as the fingers of the blind man are stimulated when he taps on the chair with a stick. And the mind, using its intrinsic computational resources, constructs the image of a chair – or a cube rotating in space, or whatever it may be. In this way, the problem of perception might be solved without mysterious forms flitting through space in some immaterial mode and mystical fashion.

That was an important step towards eliminating occult ideas and establishing the mechanical worldview. It also opened the way to modern neurophysiology and theory of perception. Of course, Descartes's efforts to work all of this out have a quaint tone: tubes with animal spirits flowing through them and so on. But it is not very hard to translate them into contemporary accounts in terms of neural systems transmitting signals which somehow do the same thing – still just stories in a certain measure, in that not a great deal is understood. The logic is rather similar whether it is instantiated by tubes with animal spirits or neural nets with chemical transmitters. A good deal of the modern theory of vision and other sensorimotor activities can be seen as a development of these ideas, obviously a huge improvement, but based on similar thinking. The mechanisms are no longer mechanical; rather, electrical and chemical. But the pictures are similar. And at a more abstract level, explicit computational theories of the operations of the internal mechanisms have now been devised, providing much insight into these matters: for example, Shimon Ullman's demonstration that remarkably sparse stimulation can lead to rich perception when intrinsic design interprets it in terms of rigid objects in motion – his 'rigidity principle'.

These two achievements – the establishment of the mechanical worldview and of the basis for modern neurophysiology and theory of perception – fared very differently. The latter was developed in the medical sciences and physiology in the years that followed, and has in a certain sense been revived today. But the mechanical philosophy collapsed within a generation. Newton demonstrated that the world is not a machine. Rather, it has occult forces after all. Contact mechanics simply does not work for terrestrial and planetary motion. Some mystical concept of 'action at a distance' is required. That was the great scandal of Newtonian physics. Newton was harshly criticized by leading scientists of the day for retreating to mysticism and undermining the achievements of the mechanical philosophy. He seems to have agreed, regarding the idea of action at a distance as an 'absurdity', though one must come to terms somehow with the refutation of the mechanical philosophy.

Notice that Newton's invocation of immaterial forces to account for ordinary events is similar in its basic logic to the invocation of a second substance by the Cartesians to overcome the limits of mechanism. There were, of course, fundamental differences. Newton *demonstrated* that the mechanical philosophy could not account for the phenomena of nature; the Cartesians only argued – not implausibly, but not conclusively – that aspects of the world fell beyond these limits. Most important, Newton provided a powerful theoretical account of the operation of his occult force and its effects, whereas the Cartesians had little to say about the nature of mind – at least, in what records we have (some were destroyed). The problems that Newton sought to overcome remained very troubling for centuries, and many physicists feel that they still are. But it was soon understood that the world is not a machine that could in principle be constructed by a skilled craftsman: the mechanical philosophy is untenable. Later discoveries demolished the picture even more fully as science moved on.

We are left with no concept of body, or physical, or material, and no coherent mind-body problem. The world is what it is, with its various aspects: mechanical, chemical, electrical, optical, mental and so on. We may study them and seek to relate them, but there is no more a mind-body problem than an electricity-body problem or a valence-body problem. One can doubtless devise artificial distinctions that allow such problems to be formulated, but the exercise seems to make little sense, and indeed is never undertaken apart from the mental aspects of the world. Why it has been commonly felt that these must somehow be treated differently from others is an interesting question, but I am aware of no justification for the belief, nor even much recognition that it is problematic.

So the most important thesis – the mechanical philosophy – did not last; it was gone in a generation, much to the consternation of leading scientists. On the other hand, Cartesian physiology had a lasting impact, and ideas of a somewhat similar cast about neurophysiology and perception have reemerged in modern theories in the cognitive and brain sciences.

An interest in language provides a third point of contact between the first and second cognitive revolutions. The study of language was greatly stimulated by Cartesian thought, leading to a good deal of productive work which, in a rational world, would have provided much of the foundations of modern linguistics, had it not been forgotten. This work had two components: particular grammar and rational grammar, also called 'universal grammar' or sometimes 'philosophical grammar', a phrase that translates as 'scientific grammar' in modern terminology (these notions did not mean quite the same thing, but we can abstract from the differences). Rational grammar was the study of the basic principles of human language, to which each particular language must conform. Particular grammar was the study of individual cases: French, German, etc. By the mid-seventeenth century, studies of the vernacular were being undertaken, and interesting discoveries were made about

French, notably 'the rule of Vaugelas', which was the focus of inquiry for many years. The first explanation for it was given by the linguists and logicians of Port Royal in the 1660s, in terms of concepts of meaning, reference, and indexicals in pretty much their contemporary sense. Much influenced by Cartesian thought along with earlier traditions that remained alive, these same investigators also formulated the first clear notions of phrase structure, along with something similar to grammatical transformations in the modern sense. They also developed a partial theory of relations and inference involving relations, among other achievements. In the case of language, these early modern contributions were scarcely known, even to scholarship, until they were rediscovered during the second cognitive revolution, after somewhat similar ideas had been independently developed.

The last prominent inheritor of this tradition before it was swept aside by behaviorist and structuralist currents was the Danish linguist Otto Jespersen, who argued seventy-five years ago that the fundamental goal of linguistics is to discover the 'notion of structure' of sentences that every speaker has internalized, enabling the speaker to produce and understand 'free expressions' that are typically new to speaker and hearer or even the history of the language, a regular occurrence of everyday life. A specific 'notion of structure' is the topic of particular grammar, in the sense of the tradition.

This 'notion of structure' in the mind of the speaker finds its way there without instruction. There would be no way to teach it to anyone, even if we knew what it is; parents certainly do not, and linguists have only limited understanding of what is a very hard problem, only recently studied beyond the surface of phenomena. The 'notion of structure' somehow grows in the mind, providing the means for infinite use, for the ability to form and comprehend free expressions.

This observation brings us to a much deeper problem of the study of language: to discover the basis in the human mind for this remarkable achievement. Interest in this problem leads to the study of universal grammar. A theory of universal grammar can be envisaged for syntax, Jespersen believed, but not for morphology, which varies among languages in accidental ways.

These ideas seem basically correct, but they made little sense within the prevailing behaviorist or structuralist assumptions of Jespersen's day. They were forgotten – or worse, rejected with much scorn and little comprehension – until new understanding made it possible to rediscover something similar, and still later, to discover that they entered into a rich tradition.

It makes sense, I think, to view what happened in the 1950s as a confluence between ideas that have a traditional flavor but that had been long forgotten, and new understanding that made it possible to approach at least some of the traditional questions in a more serious way than heretofore. Previously, fundamental problems could be posed, though obscurely, but it was impossible to do very much with them. The core idea about language, to borrow Wilhelm von Humboldt's formulation in the early eighteenth century, is that language involves 'the infinite use of finite means', something that seemed paradoxical. The means must be finite, because the brain is finite. But the use of these means is infinite, without bounds; one can always say something new, and the array of expressions from which normal usage is drawn is astronomical in scale – far beyond any possibility of storage, and unbounded in principle, so that storage is impossible. These are trivially obvious aspects of ordinary language and its use, though it was not clear how to come to grips with them.

The new understanding had to do with computational processes, sometimes called 'generative' processes. These ideas had been clarified enormously in the formal sciences. By mid-twentieth century, the concept of 'infinite use of finite means' was very well understood, at least in one of its aspects. It is a core part of the foundations of mathematics and led to startling discoveries about decidability, completeness, and mathematical truth; and it underlies the theory of computers. The ideas were implicit as far back as Euclidean geometry and classical logic, but it was not until the late nineteenth and early twentieth century that they became really clarified and enriched. By the 1950s, certainly, they could readily be applied to traditional problems of language that had seemed paradoxical before, and that could only be vaguely formulated, not really addressed. That made it possible to return to some of the traditional insights – or more accurately, to reinvent them, since everything had unfortunately been forgotten; and to take up the work that constitutes much of the contemporary study of language.

In these terms, the 'notion of structure' in the mind is a generative procedure, a finite object that characterizes an infinite array of 'free expressions', each a mental structure with a certain form and meaning. In this sense, the generative procedure provides for 'infinite use of finite means'. Particular grammar becomes the study of these generative procedures for English, Hungarian, Warlpiri, Swahili or whatever. Rational or universal grammar is the study of the innate basis for the growth of these systems in the mind when presented with the scattered, limited, and ambiguous data of experience. Such data fall far short of determining one or another language without rigid and narrow initial restrictions.

While the newly available ideas opened the way to very productive study of traditional problems, it is important to recognize that they only partially capture traditional concerns. Take the concepts 'infinite use of finite means' and production of 'free expressions'. A generative procedure incorporated in the mind/brain may provide the *means* for such 'infinite use', but that still leaves us far from what traditional investigators sought to understand: ultimately, the creative aspect of language use in something like the Cartesian sense. To put it differently, the insights of the formal sciences allow us to identify and to investigate only one of two very different ideas that are conflated in traditional formulations: the infinite scope of finite means (now a topic of inquiry), and whatever enters into the normal use of the objects that fall within this infinite scope (still a mystery). The distinction is crucial. It is basically the difference between a cognitive system that stores an infinite array of information in a finite mind/brain and systems that access that information to carry out the various actions of our lives. It is the distinction between knowledge and action – between competence and performance, in standard technical usage.

The problem is general, not restricted to the study of language. The cognitive and biological sciences have discovered a lot about vision and motor control, but these discoveries are limited to mechanisms. No one even thinks of asking why a person looks at a sunset or reaches for a banana, and how such decisions are made. The same is true of language. A modern generative grammar seeks to determine the mechanisms that underlie the fact that the sentence I am now producing has the form and meaning it does, but has nothing to say about how I chose to form it, or why.

Yet another respect in which the contemporary cognitive revolution is similar to its predecessor is in the importance assigned to innate structure. Here the ideas are of much more ancient vintage, traceable back to Plato, who famously argued that what people know cannot possibly be the result of experience. They must have far-reaching prior knowledge.

Terminology aside, the point is hardly controversial, and has only been considered so in recent years – one of those examples of regression that I mentioned earlier (I put aside here the traditional doctrine that 'nothing is in the mind that is not first in the senses', to be understood, I think, in terms of rich metaphysical assumptions that are properly to be reframed in epistemological terms). Hume is considered the arch-empiricist, but his inquiry into 'the science of human nature' recognized

that we must discover those 'parts of [our] knowledge' that are derived
'by the original hand of nature' (Hume 1748, Stn 9, Para. 85) – innate
knowledge, in other terms. To question this is about as sensible as to suppose that the growth of an embryo to a chicken rather than a giraffe is
determined by nutritional inputs.

Plato went on to offer an explanation of the fact that experience
scarcely accounts for the fringes of knowledge attained: the reminis-
cence theory, which holds that knowledge is remembered from an earlier existence. Today many are inclined to ridicule that proposal, but
mistakenly. It is correct, in essence, though we would put it differently.
Through the centuries, it has been understood that there must be something right about the idea. Leibniz, for example, argued that Plato's
conception of innate knowledge is basically correct, though it must be
'purged of the error of pre-existence' (Leibniz 1686, Section XXVI) –
how, he could not really say. Modern biology offers a way to do so: the
genetic endowment constitutes what Plato mistakenly thought we
'remember from an earlier existence'. Like the neurophysiological
rephrasing of Cartesian tubes with animal spirits, this too is a kind of a
story, because so little is known about the matter, even in far simpler
domains than language. Nevertheless, the story does provide a plausible
indication of where to look for an answer to the question of how we
remember things from an earlier existence, bringing it from the domain
of mysteries to that of possible scientific inquiry.

As in the theory of vision, and the cognitive sciences generally (in
fact, much of science), we can study these questions at various levels. At
one level, we can seek to identify the cellular structures involved in
these operations. Or we can study the properties of these objects more
abstractly – in this case, in terms of computational theories of mind and
the symbolic representations they make available. Such investigations
have something of the character of the study of structural formulas of
chemistry or the periodic table. In the case of language, we can be reasonably confident that the computational structure is largely innate;
otherwise, no language could be acquired. A reasonable conjecture is
that, at root, there is only one fixed computational procedure that
underlies all languages, and enough is understood for us to be able to
spell out some of its likely properties. These have been major topics of
inquiry during the past forty years. From the 1950s, and particularly in
the past fifteen years as new theoretical ideas became available,
languages of a very broad typological range have come under intensive
scrutiny, and surprising properties have been discovered, sometimes
with fairly plausible explanations for them. Vastly more is known about

languages as a result of this work, and some of the leading questions on the research agenda today could not have been formulated or even imagined not many years ago.

The second cognitive revolution

In such ways as these, the second cognitive revolution has rediscovered, reformulated, and to some extent addressed some of the most venerable themes of our cultural tradition, back to its early origins.

As I mentioned, the second cognitive revolution involved a shift of perspective from the behaviorist, structuralist approaches that constituted the orthodoxy of the day: a shift from the study of behavior and its products to the study of states and properties of the mind that enter into thought and action. Reconsidered in these terms, the study of language is not the study of texts or their elements, or of procedures for identifying such elements and their arrangement, the primary concerns of European and American structuralism. Still less so is it the study of 'dispositions to respond' or other constructs of behaviorist doctrine that cannot even be coherently formulated, in my opinion, though they have been taken seriously in philosophy of mind – to its detriment, I believe.

What had been the topic of inquiry – behavior, texts, etc. – is now just data, with no privileged status, standing alongside any other data that might prove relevant for the investigation of the mind. Behavior and texts are of no more intrinsic interest than, say, observations of electrical activity of the brain, which has become quite suggestive in recent years. We cannot know in advance what data will advance the study of the 'notion of structure' that enters into the normal use of language, and its origins in initial endowment.

The perceptual judgments called 'linguistic intuitions' are also just data, to be evaluated alongside other kinds: they do not constitute *the* database for the study of language, any more than observed behavior and its products do. The contrary is widely argued, but mistakenly, I think. These data may have a special status, however, in a different sense. A theory that departs too radically from linguistic intuitions will not be an account of language, but of something else. Furthermore, we cannot exclude the possibility that a future science of mind may simply dispense with the concept of language in our sense, or those of other cultures that relate to the same obscure and complex domain. That has already happened in contemporary linguistics. It is also the norm, as understanding progresses.

The shift of perspective was, in essence, a shift from something like natural history to at least potential natural science. It should also not be controversial, in my opinion. Contrary to what is often maintained, sometimes with great passion, it in no way conflicts with pursuit of other interests. If anything, it may facilitate them, insofar as it progresses.

Also pointless, in my opinion, is the controversy that has arisen over the abstract (in this case, computational) approach to the study of mind. Efforts to allay uneasiness about the approach commonly introduce computer metaphors: the hardware–software distinction, for example. A computer has hardware and we write software for it; the brain is the hardware and the mind the software. The metaphors are harmless if not taken too seriously, but it should be borne in mind that the proposed analogues are much more obscure than the original they are supposed to clarify. The hardware–software distinction raises all sorts of problems that do not arise in the study of an organic object. What is hardware and what is software is largely a matter of decision and convenience. But the brain is a real natural object, just as a molecule is, whether we study its abstract properties (say, structural formulas) or its postulated components. The problems that plague the hardware–software distinction, which are probably unanswerable, do not arise in the study of the mind/brain. So the metaphor should not be pressed beyond the point where it may be helpful.

The second cognitive revolution has led to real advances in certain areas, among them language and vision, which also figured prominently in the first cognitive revolution. It is less clear that there have been advances in second-order reflection about these matters. I will come back to that, but first a few comments about the study of language.

The language faculty

It seems now reasonably well established that there is a special component of the human brain (call it 'the language faculty') that is specifically dedicated to language. That sub-system of the brain (or the mind, from the abstract perspective) has an initial state which is genetically determined, like all other components of the body: the kidney, the circulatory system, and so on. The study of that initial state is a contemporary version of traditional universal (rational, philosophical) grammar. This aspect of biological endowment appears to be close to uniform across the species, apart from pathology. It also seems to be unique in essentials. That is, its essential properties do not seem to be found in other organisms, perhaps even elsewhere in the organic world.

The language faculty changes from its initial state during early life, as do other biological systems. It 'grows' from the initial state through childhood, reaching a relatively steady state at some stage of maturation. This is the process of language acquisition, sometimes misleadingly called 'language learning'; the process seems to bear little resemblance to what is called 'learning'. It seems that growth levels off before puberty, perhaps as early as six to eight, some investigators believe. After the system stabilizes, changes still take place, but they seem to be at the margins: acquisition of new words, social conventions of usage, and so on. Other organs develop in rather similar ways.

The steady state incorporates a computational (generative) procedure that characterizes an infinity of possible expressions, each of which has properties that determine its sound, its meaning, its structural organization, and so on. We could reasonably call the computational procedure itself the 'language', thinking of a language more or less as 'a way of speaking', one traditional notion.

Adopting this terminology, we take a language to be – to first approximation – a particular state of the language faculty. For Jones to have (know) a language is simply for the language faculty of Jones's mind to be in a particular state. If the state of your language faculty is similar enough to the state of mine, you may understand what I say. Spelling it out a bit further, when my mind produces something that induces my articulatory apparatus to produce noises, and those signals hit your ear, they stimulate your mind to construct some sort of an 'image' (a symbolic structure of some sort), your counterpart to what I was trying to express. If our systems are similar enough you may understand me, more or less, comprehension being a 'more or less' affair.

How does perception of language work? A common assumption is that one component of the mind is a 'parser', which takes a signal and turns it into a symbolic representation. Clearly the parser accesses the language. When you interpret what I say, you are using your knowledge of English, not Japanese (if you happen to know Japanese). What the parser yields is of course enhanced and enriched by other systems; you interpret what I say on the basis of beliefs, expectations, and so on, which reach far beyond language.

This approach embodies a number of assumptions that are less than obvious. One is that a parser exists at all – that there is a faculty of the mind that interprets signals independently of other features of the environment. That may well be true, but it need not be. It is commonly assumed that we can be fairly confident of the existence of the parser, while the status of the generative procedure is more problematic. But that is incorrect; the opposite is true. The existence of the generative procedure is far better established from a scientific point of view, and embedded in a much richer theoretical matrix.

A second assumption is that parsers do not grow. Unlike languages and organs of the body generally, they are fixed. The parser for Japanese is the same as for English. The reason for this rather implausible assumption is that we do not know that it is wrong. In a situation of ignorance, one begins with the simplest assumption, expecting it to be disproven as more is learned.

On these assumptions, the changes that take place during language acquisition are in the cognitive state alone; in the 'storage of information', the language, the generative procedure that distinguishes English from Japanese.

A third assumption is that the parser works very efficiently: parsing is 'easy and quick', according to a slogan that has motivated a good deal of research seeking to show that language design yields this result. But the belief is incorrect. Parsing is often difficult, and often fails, in the sense that the symbolic representation produced by the perceptual mechanism is not the one determined by the language, and may well be incoherent even for expressions with a determinate and sensible meaning. Many cases are known, including quite simple ones. Thus all sorts of problems arise in interpretation of expressions involving some kind of negative meaning, with such words as 'unless', or 'doubt', or 'miss'. If I had hoped to see you last summer, but did not, do I say 'I missed seeing you'? 'I missed not seeing you'? Neither? Confusion is so compelling that it has even been established in idiomatic usage. If two airplanes pass too close for comfort, they nearly hit; they do not nearly miss. But the event is called a 'near miss', not a 'near hit'.

For many categories of expressions, parsing fails completely or is extremely difficult. Such 'parsing failures' have been a major topic of inquiry in recent years, because they provide a good deal of evidence into the nature of language processing.

Why then does parsing seem so easy and quick, giving rise to the conventional false belief? The reason is that when I say something, you ordinarily understand it instantaneously, without effort. That much is generally true. In practice, the perceptual process is close to instantaneous and effortless. But from that fact we cannot conclude that language is designed for quick and easy parsing. It shows only that there is a part of language that we parse easily, and that is the part we tend to use. As a speaker, I draw from the same scattered part that you are able to deal with as a hearer, giving rise to the illusion that the system is somehow 'designed for efficient use'. In fact, the system is 'inefficient', in the sense that large parts of the language – even short and simple expressions – are unusable, though they have quite definite sound and meaning, determined by the generative procedure of the language faculty. The language is simply not well adapted to parsing.

In the background there is a familiar fairy tale sometimes called 'Darwinism' that probably would have shocked Darwin: that the systems of the body are well adapted to their functions, perhaps superbly so. What that is supposed to mean is unclear. It is no principle of biology. On some interpretations, the statement just seems false. Nothing follows about the theory of evolution, which in no way suggests that the systems that have developed should be well adapted to conditions of life. They may be the best that nature could do under the constraints within which organisms evolve, but the outcome may be far from ideal. For all sorts of reasons, specific organs might turn out to be more poorly designed than is possible even within these constraints; perhaps because such design failures contribute to modifications elsewhere in the highly integrated system that improve reproductive capacity. Organs do not evolve independently, of course, and a viable organism has to hang together in complicated ways; breeders know how to breed bigger horses, but it would not help if size increases without highly intricate corresponding changes in the brain, the circulatory system, and much more. In general, little can be said without an understanding of the physical and chemical properties of complex organisms, and if we had that understanding, it would hardly be a surprise to discover significant 'design errors' in organisms that are a 'biological success' (meaning, plenty of them are around).

A familiar example is the human skeleton. Few people escape back problems, because the system is poorly designed from an engineering standpoint. That may be true for large vertebrates generally (though cows do not know how to complain about back pains). The system works well enough for reproductive success, and perhaps it is the 'best solution' under the conditions of vertebrate evolution. But that is as far as the theory of evolution reaches. In the case of language, there would be no reason to expect the system to be 'well adapted to its functions', and it seems not to be (at least, if we try to give some natural meaning to these obscure notions). The fact that large parts of language are unusable does not bother us; we use the parts that are usable, hardly an interesting fact.

There are similar assumptions in the theory of learnability. It is often assumed that languages must be learnable. Natural languages are sometimes defined as those learnable under normal conditions. But that need not be true. We could have all sorts of possible languages in our heads, which we cannot access. There would be no way to acquire them, though they are possible states of our language faculty. There is recent work suggesting that languages may indeed be learnable, but if so, that is an empirical discovery. It is not a conceptual necessity.

I have said nothing so far about the production of language. The reason is that there is little to say of any interest. Apart from peripheral aspects, it remains largely a mystery. As I have already discussed, that is no small gap in our understanding: it has to do with the very criterion of mind, from the Cartesian perspective – not an unreasonable one, though unformulable today in anything like their terms.

Unification problems

A last issue that was of great importance during the first cognitive revolution and that arises again today, though in a very different form, is the unification problem. This has two aspects. One has to do with the hardware–software relation (to adopt the metaphor): How do the computational procedures of the mind relate to cells and their organization, or whatever is the proper way to understand the functioning of the brain at this level? A second kind of unification problem is internal to the cognitive sciences. Is there a 'problem-solving' system, or a 'science-forming' system, as a component of the mind, and if so, are they distinct? Is there some kind of overarching unity?

For the first unification problem, a general faith in unity of science leads to the expectation that an answer exists, whether humans can find it or not. But the second need not have a solution. It could turn out there is no theory of 'mental organs' any more than there is an 'organ theory' for other components of the body: the kidney, the circulatory system, etc. Their fundamental building blocks are the same, but they may not fall together above the cellular level. If that is the case for cognitive systems, then there will be no cognitive science in any very useful sense of the phrase.

Let us turn to the first unification problem: finding the 'physical basis' for computational systems of the mind, to borrow the conventional (but as noted, highly misleading) terminology? There are several ways to approach the problem. The standard method of the sciences is to study each of these levels, try to discover their properties, and seek some kind of convergence. The problem arises constantly, and might be solved (if at all) in quite different ways. Reduction of one system to another is a possible outcome, but it may not be possible: the theory of electricity and magnetism is not reducible to mechanics, and the elementary properties of motion are not reducible to 'the mechanical worldview'. Consider chemistry and physics, long separated by what seemed to be an unbridgeable divide. Unification finally took place, though rather recently; in my lifetime, in fact. But it was not reduction of chemistry to physics. Rather, chemistry was unified with a radically altered physics, a step made possible by the quantum-theoretic revolution. What had seemed to be a gap was a real one. A few years later, parts of biology were unified with biochemistry, this time by genuine reduction. In the case of the mental aspects of the world, we have no idea how unification might proceed. Some believe it will be by means of the intermediate level of neurophysiology, perhaps neural nets. Perhaps so, perhaps not. Perhaps the contemporary brain sciences do not yet have the right way of looking at the brain and its function, so that unification in terms of contemporary understanding is impossible. If so, that should not come as a great surprise. The history of science provides many such examples.

This seems a perfectly reasonable way to address the first unification problem, though whether it can succeed, and if so how, we cannot know in advance, any more than in any other case.

There is also a different approach to the problem, which is highly influential though it seems to me not only foreign to the sciences but also close to senseless. This approach divorces the cognitive sciences from a biological setting, and seeks tests to determine whether some object 'manifests intelligence' ('plays chess', 'understands Chinese', or whatever). The approach relies on the 'Turing Test', devised by mathematician Alan Turing, who did much of the fundamental work on the modern theory of computation. In a famous paper of 1950 (Turing 1950), he proposed a way of evaluating the performance of a computer – basically, by determining whether observers will be able to distinguish it from the performance of people. If they cannot, the device passes the test. There is no fixed Turing test; rather, a battery of devices constructed on this model. The details need not concern us.

Adopting this approach, suppose we are interested in deciding whether a programmed computer can play chess or understand Chinese. We construct a variant of the Turing test, and see whether a jury can be fooled into thinking that a human is carrying out the observed performance. If so, we will have 'empirically established' that the computer can play chess, understand Chinese, think, etc., according to proponents of this version of artificial intelligence, while their critics deny that this result would establish the conclusion.

There is a great deal of often heated debate about these matters in the literature of the cognitive sciences, artificial intelligence, and philosophy of mind, but it is hard to see that any serious question has been posed. The question of whether a computer is playing chess or doing long division, or translating Chinese, is like the question of whether robots can murder or airplanes can fly – or people; after all, the 'flight' of the Olympic long jump champion is only an order of magnitude short of that of the chicken champion (so I am told). These are questions of decision, not fact; decision as to whether to adopt a certain metaphoric extension of common usage.

There is no answer to the question whether airplanes *really* fly (though perhaps not space shuttles). Fooling people into mistaking a submarine for a whale does not show that submarines really swim; nor does it fail to establish the fact. There is no fact, no meaningful question to be answered, as all agree, in this case. The same is true of computer programs, as Turing took pains to make clear in the 1950 paper that is regularly invoked in these discussions. Here he pointed out that the question whether machines think 'may be too meaningless to deserve discussion', being a question of decision, not fact, though he speculated that in fifty years, usage may have 'altered so much that one will be able to speak of machines thinking without expecting to be contradicted' – as in the case of airplanes flying (in English, at least), but not submarines swimming. Such alteration of usage amounts to the replacement of one lexical item by another one with somewhat different properties. There is no empirical question as to whether this is the right or wrong decision.

In this regard, there has been serious regression since the first cognitive revolution, in my opinion. Superficially, reliance on the Turing test is reminiscent of the Cartesian approach to the existence of other minds. But the comparison is misleading. The Cartesian experiments were something like a litmus test for acidity: they sought to determine whether an object has a certain property, in this case, possession of mind, one aspect of the world. But that is not true of the artificial intelligence debate.

Another superficial similarity is the interest in simulation of behavior, again only apparent, I think. As I mentioned earlier, the first cognitive revolution was stimulated by the achievements of automata, much as today, and complex devices were constructed to simulate real objects and their functioning: the digestion of a duck, a flying bird, and so on. But the purpose was not to determine whether machines can digest or fly. Jacques de Vaucanson, the great artificer of the period, was concerned to understand the animate systems he was modeling; he constructed mechanical devices in order to formulate and validate theories of his animate models, not to satisfy some performance criterion. His clockwork duck, for example, was intended to be a model of the actual digestion of a duck, not a facsimile that might fool his audience. In short, this was simulation in the manner of normal science: construction of models (in this case, mechanical models) to enhance understanding, not a confused attempt to answer a question that has no meaning.

Computer simulation of course proceeds in a similar way today: the approach to the theory of vision by David Marr and his colleagues, Robert Berwick's investigation of universal parsers, the study of robotics to determine how a person reaches for a cup, and so on. That is all perfectly sensible, and has often been very revealing as well. Also perfectly sensible is the development of robots for factories or expert systems. That is as legitimate as making bulldozers. But it would be of no interest to show that the performance of a bulldozer could be mistaken for that of a person, and a computer program that could 'beat' a grandmaster in chess is about as interesting as a bulldozer that can 'win' the Olympic weight-lifting competition.

Returning to the second unification problem, there is, as I mentioned, no particular reason to expect a solution. It has been assumed over a fairly broad range – from Skinner to Piaget in psychology, and very commonly in the philosophy of mind – that people (or perhaps organisms generally) have a uniform array of learning and problem-solving procedures that apply indifferently in all domains; general mechanisms of intelligence, or whatever (perhaps changing through childhood, as Piaget thought, but at each stage, uniformly applicable to any task or problem). The more we learn about human or animal intelligence, the less that seems likely. There are no serious proposals as to what such 'general mechanisms' might be. It seems that the brain is like other known biological systems: modular, constituted of highly specialized subsystems that have their particular character and domains of operation, interacting in all sorts of ways. There is a good deal to say about the topic, but I will have to leave the matter here.

Knowledge of language

Let me end with a few words about the kinds of questions that arise today in the study of language specifically, and the kinds of answers that can now be offered. Here things become interesting and intricate, and I will only be able to illustrate with a few examples.

Take some simple phrase, say, 'brown house'. What do we know about it? We know that it consists of two words; children have such understanding well before they can articulate it directly. In my speech, probably yours, the two words have the same vowel; they are in the formal relation of assonance. Similarly, 'house' and 'mouse' are in the fuller formal relation of rhyme. We know further that if I tell you about a brown house, I want you to understand that its exterior is brown, not necessarily its interior. So a brown house is something with a brown exterior. Similarly, if you see a house, you see its exterior. We cannot now see the building in which we are meeting, unless perhaps there were a window and a mirror outside reflecting its outer surface. Then we could see the building much in the way we can see the airplane in which we are flying if we can look out the window and see the surface of the wing.

The same is true of a very wide range of objects: boxes, igloos, mountains, etc. Suppose there is a lighted cave inside a mountain with a straight tunnel leading to it, so we can see into the cave when standing in the entrance to the tunnel. But we do not see the mountain in that case. If we are inside the cave, we cannot see the mountain, though we could if a mirror outside the entrance reflected its surface. Over a large range of cases, we think of an object somehow as its exterior surface, almost like a geometrical surface. This is even true of invented objects, even impossible ones. If I tell you that I painted my spherical cube brown, I intend you to understand that I painted its exterior surface brown.

But we do not think of a brown house just as a surface. If it were a surface, you could be near the house even if you were inside it. If a box were really a surface, then a marble in the box and another marble outside it at the same distance from the surface would be equidistant from the box. But they are not. So an object of this kind is at least an exterior surface with a designated interior.

A further look shows that the meanings of such terms are still more complex. If I say I painted my house brown, you understand me to mean that I painted the exterior surface brown; but I can say, perfectly intelligibly, that I painted my house brown *on the inside*. So we can think of the house as an interior surface, with the background circumstances complicated slightly. In technical jargon, this is called *marked* and *unmarked* usage; in the unmarked case, with a null context, we take the house to be the exterior surface, but a marked usage is allowed when the context provides the proper conditions. This is a pervasive feature of the semantics of natural language. If I say 'I climbed the mountain', you know that I went up – generally; I may at the moment be going down even if I am climbing the mountain, yet another fact about meaning that we know. But I can say 'I climbed *down* the mountain', adding extra information that permits the marked usage. The same holds quite generally.

Notice that my house is perfectly concrete. When I return to my house at night, I am returning to a concrete physical thing. On the other hand, it is also abstract: an exterior surface with a designated interior and a marked property that allows it to be an interior surface. We can refer to the house as simultaneously abstract and concrete, as when I say I painted my wooden house brown just before it was blown down by a tornado. And I can say that after my house blew down, leaving just rubble, I rebuilt *it* (my house) somewhere else, although it is no longer the same house; such terms of dependent reference as 'same', 'it', and 're-' function rather differently in this case, and differently still when we consider other objects. Take London, also both concrete and abstract; it can be destroyed by a fire or an administrative decision. If London is reduced to dust, *it* – that is, London – can be *re*-built elsewhere and still be the *same* city, London, unlike my house, which would not be the same house if it is reduced to dust and *it* is *re*-built somewhere else. The motor of my car is still different. If it is reduced to dust, it cannot be rebuilt, though if only partially damaged, it can be. If a physically indistinguishable motor is built from the same dust, it is not the same motor, but a different one. Judgments can be rather delicate, involving factors that have barely been explored.

These remarks only scratch the surface, but they perhaps suffice to indicate that there need be no objects in the world that correspond to what we talk about, even in the simplest cases, nor does anyone believe that there are. About all we can say at a general level is that the words of our language provide complex perspectives that offer us highly special ways to think about things – to ask for them, tell people about them, etc. Real natural language semantics will seek to discover these perspectives and the principles that underlie them. *People* use words to refer to things in complex ways, reflecting interests and circumstances, but the *words* do not refer; there is no word-thing relation of the Fregean variety, nor a more complex word-thing-person relation of the kind proposed by Charles Sanders Peirce in an equally classic work in the foundations of semantics. These approaches may be quite appropriate for the study of invented symbolic systems (for which they were initially designed, at least in the case of Frege). But they do not seem to provide appropriate concepts for the study of natural language. A word-thing (-person) relation seems as much of an illusion as a word-molecular motion (-person) relation, though it is true that each use of a word by a person is associated with a specific motion of molecules, and sometimes with a specific thing, viewed in a particular way. The study of speech production and analysis postulates no such mythical relations, but rather asks how the person's mental representations enter into articulation and perception. The study of the meaning of expressions should proceed along similar lines, I believe.

This does not mean that the study of meaning is the study of use, any more than the study of motor control is the study of particular actions. Usage and other actions provide evidence about the systems we hope to understand, as may information from other domains, but nothing more than that.

What we know about such simple words as 'brown', 'house', 'climb', 'London', 'it', 'same', etc., must be almost entirely unlearned. We are unaware of what we know without inquiry, and it could well turn out to be inaccessible to consciousness, so that we can learn about it only as we learn about circulation of the blood and visual perception. Even if experience were rich and extensive, it could not possibly provide information of the kind just barely sampled, or account for its uniformity among people with differing experience. But the question is academic, since experience is very limited. At the peak period of language acquisition, from ages two to six, a child is picking up words at an average of about one an hour, hence on a single exposure under highly ambiguous circumstances. Miracles aside, it must be that the child is relying on those 'parts of [its] knowledge' that are derived 'by the original hand of nature', in Hume's terms – on 'memory from an earlier existence', as reformulated within the framework of genetic endowment (in some as yet an unknown manner).

It is sometimes argued that genes do not carry enough information to yield such highly intricate results, but that argument is without force. One could say the same, with equal merit, about any other component of the body. Knowing nothing about the relevant physical–chemical constraints, one might be led to conclude (absurdly) that it takes infinite information to determine that an embryo will have two arms (rather than 11 or 93), so that it must be 'learned' or determined by the nutritional environment of the embryo. Just how the genes determine the specific number of arms, or the delicate structure of the visual system or the properties of human language, is a matter for discovery, not idle speculation. What seems evident from the most elementary observations is that interaction with the environment can have at most a marginally shaping and triggering effect. The assumption is taken for granted (virtually without direct evidence) in the case of development 'below the neck', metaphorically speaking. The conclusions should be no different in the case of mental aspects of the world, unless we adopt illegitimate forms of methodological dualism, which are all too prevalent.

Notice further that we learn little about these matters from dictionaries, even the most elaborate. The entry for the word 'house' will say nothing about what I just reviewed, a bare beginning. Until very recently, there was little recognition of the rich complexity of the semantics of words, though for accuracy, we should recall that there had been some penetrating discussion of the matter in the past, mostly forgotten. Even very elementary features of the meaning and sound of words are not presented in the most extensive dictionaries, which are useful only for people who already know the answers, apart from the further details that the dictionary provides.

That is not a defect of dictionaries; rather, their merit. It would be pointless – in fact, highly confusing – for a dictionary of English, Spanish, Japanese, or whatever to present the actual meanings of words, even if they had been discovered. Similarly, someone studying English as a second language would only be confused by instruction about the real principles of grammar; these they already know, being human. Though not by conscious design, dictionaries rightly focus on what a person could not know, namely superficial details of the kind provided by experience; not on what comes to us 'by the original hand of nature'. The latter is the topic of a different inquiry, the study of human nature, which is part of the sciences. Its aims are virtually complementary to those of the practical lexicographer. Dictionaries intended for use should – and in practice do – fill in gaps in the innate knowledge that dictionary users bring with them.

We expect that the basic semantic properties of words, being unlearned and unlearnable, will be shared with little variation across languages. These are aspects of human nature, which provides us with specific ways to think about the world, highly intricate and curious ones. That is clear even from the simplest cases, such as those just briefly reviewed.

When we turn to more complex expressions, the gap between what the speaker/hearer knows and the evidence available becomes a chasm, and the richness of innate endowment is still more evident. Take simple sentences, say, the following:

(1) John is eating an apple.
(2) John is eating.

In (2), the grammatical object of 'eat' is missing, and we understand the sentence on the analogy of (1), to mean (more or less) that John is eating something-or-other. The mind fills the gap, postulating an unspecified object of the verb.

Actually, that is not quite true. Consider the following brief discourse:
(3) John is eating his shoe. He must have lost his mind.

But the sentence (2) does not include the case of eating one's shoe. If I say that John is eating, I mean that he is eating in a normal way; having dinner, perhaps, but not eating his shoe. What the mind fills in is not an unspecified grammatical object, but something normal; that is part of the meaning of the constructions (though what counts as normal is not).

Let us suppose that this is roughly correct, and turn to a slightly more complex case. Consider the sentence (4):
(4) John is too stubborn to talk to Bill.

What it means is that John is too stubborn for him (John) to talk to Bill – he is so stubborn he refuses to talk to Bill. Suppose we drop 'Bill' from (4), yielding (5):
(5) John is too stubborn to talk to.

Following the principle illustrated by (1) and (2), we expect (5) to be understood on the analogy of (4), with the mind filling the gap with some (normal) object of 'talk to'. The sentence (5), then, should mean that John is too stubborn for him (John) to talk to someone or other. But it does not mean that at all. Rather, it means that John is too stubborn for anyone (maybe us) to talk to him, John.

For some reason, the semantic relations invert when the object of 'talk to' in (4) is deleted, unlike (1), where they remain unchanged. The same holds for more complex cases, as in (6):
(6) John is too stubborn to expect the teacher to talk to.

The meaning is that John is too stubborn for anyone (maybe us) to expect the teacher to talk to him (John). In this case, parsing difficulties may make the facts harder to detect, though the sentence is still a very simple one, well below average sentence length in normal discourse.

We know all of these things, though without awareness. The reasons lie beyond even possible consciousness. None of this could have been learned. The facts are known to people who have had no relevant experience with such constructions. Parents and peers, who impart knowledge of language (to the limited extent that they do), have no awareness of such facts. If a child made errors using such expressions, it would be virtually impossible to correct them, even if the errors were noticed (which is most unlikely, and surely rare to the point of non-existence). We expect that interpretations will be similar in every language, and so far as is known, that is indeed true.

Just as dictionaries do not even begin to provide the meanings of words, so the most elaborate multi-volume traditional grammars do not recognize, let alone try to explain, even elementary phenomena of the kind just illustrated. It is only in very recent years, in the course of attempts to construct explicit generative procedures, that such properties have come to light. Correspondingly, it has become clear how little is known of the elementary phenomena of language. That is not a surprising discovery. As long as people were satisfied that an apple falls to the ground because that is its natural place, even the basic properties of motion remained hidden. A willingness to be puzzled by the simplest phenomena is the very beginning of science. The attempt to formulate questions about simple phenomena has led to remarkable discoveries about elementary aspects of nature, previously unsuspected.

In the course of the second cognitive revolution, myriad facts of the kind just illustrated have been discovered in well-studied languages, and increasingly a fair sample of others; and more importantly, some understanding has been gained of the innate principles of the language faculty that account for what people know in such cases. The examples just given are simple ones, but it has been no trivial matter to discover the principles of universal grammar that interact to account for their properties. When we move on, complexities mount very quickly. As tentative answers have been developed, they have sometimes opened the way to the discovery of hitherto unknown phenomena, often very puzzling ones; and in not a few cases, new understanding as well. Nothing similar has happened in the rich tradition of 2500 years of research into language. It is an exciting development, with few parallels in the study of the mind, I think it is fair to say.

As I mentioned earlier, the conditions of language acquisition lead us to expect that in some fundamental sense, there must be only one language. There are two basic reasons. First, most of what we know must be 'pre-existent', in a modern version of Plato's insights; people lack evidence for even simple aspects of what they know. Furthermore, there is strong reason to suppose that no one is designed to speak one or another language. If my children were to have grown up in Japan, they would have spoken Japanese, indistinguishably from natives. The ability to acquire language is basically a fixed, uniform species property.

For such reasons, we expect all languages to be fundamentally alike, cast to the same mold, differing only in marginal ways that limited and ambiguous experience suffices to determine. We are now able to see how this might be so. It is now possible to formulate at least the outlines of a uniform, invariant computational procedure that assigns the meanings of arbitrary expressions for any language, and provides them with sensorimotor properties within a restricted range. At last, we may be approaching a period when the expectations of rational grammarians from Port Royal to Jespersen may be given a clear formulation and empirical support.

While this uniform procedure – in essence, THE human language – is common to all the specific manifestations of the human language faculty, it is not completely fixed. Variations at the periphery distinguish English from the Australian language Warlpiri, to take two cases that have been studied in considerable depth because they look so different on the surface. There are now some plausible hypotheses about where in the nature of language such differences reside. It seems (as we would anticipate) that they lie in restricted areas of language. One range of differences is in inflectional systems, as Jespersen suggested when he questioned the possibility of a universal morphology alongside a universal syntax. That is why so much of second-language learning is devoted to such morphological properties (in contrast, no Japanese-speaking student of English wastes time studying the properties of the words we looked at earlier, or the sentences (1)–(6)). An English speaker studying German has to learn about the case system, mostly lacking in English. Sanskrit and Finnish have a richer array, while Chinese has even more meager resources than English.

Or so it appears, on the surface. Work of the past few years suggests that these appearances may be illusions. The languages may have similar case systems, perhaps the same one. There may be a universal morphology after all. It is just that in Chinese (and mostly, in English) the cases are present only in the mental computations, not reaching the sensorimotor organs, while in German they partially reach these performance systems (and in Sanskrit and Finnish, still more so). The effects of case are seen in English and Chinese, even if nothing 'comes out of the mouth'. The languages do not differ much in inflection (if at all), but the sensorimotor systems access the mental computation at different points, so that there are differences in what is articulated. It may be that much of the typological variation of language reduces to factors of this kind.

Suppose we succeed in identifying the points of potential variation among languages – call them *parameters*, their values to be set by experience. Then it should be possible literally to deduce Hungarian or

Swahili or any other possible human language by setting the values of the parameters one way or another. And the process of language acquisition would be just the process of fixing those parameters – finding out the answers to a specific 'list of questions', in effect. It must be that these questions are readily answered, given the empirical conditions on language acquisition. A large part of the empirical study of language acquisition in varied languages has been framed in these terms in recent years, with encouraging progress, and plenty of new dilemmas.

If all of this turns out to be on the right track, it will follow that languages are learnable – a non-obvious conclusion, as noted. To discover the language of a community, the child has to determine how the values of the parameters are set. With the answers given, the full language is determined, lexicon aside. The properties of such sentences as 'John is too stubborn to talk to' need not be learned – fortunately, or no one would know them; they are determined in advance, as part of the biological endowment. As for the lexicon, it is unnecessary to learn properties of the kind discussed earlier – again, fortunately – because these too are determined in advance. Languages will be learnable, because there is little to learn.

What about the matter of usability? We know that parts of language are unusable, posing no problem for daily life because we keep to what is usable, naturally. But some recent work suggests that the unusability property may be more deeply rooted in the nature of language than previously suspected. It appears that the computations of language have to be optimal, in a certain well-defined sense. Suppose we think of the process of constructing an expression as selection of words from the mental lexicon, combining them, and performing certain operations on the structures so formed, continuing until an expression is constructed with a sound and meaning. It seems that some such processes are blocked, even if legitimate at each step, because others are more optimal. If so, a linguistic expression is not just a symbolic object constructed by the computational system, but rather an object constructed in an optimal fashion.

Those familiar with problems of computational complexity will recognize that there are dangers lurking here. Optimality considerations of the kind just sketched require comparison of computations to determine whether some object is a valid linguistic expression. Unless sharp constraints are introduced, the complexity of such computations will explode, and it will be virtually impossible to know what is an expression of the language. The search for such constraints, and for empirical evidence from varied languages that bears on them, raises difficult and intriguing problems, just recently being considered seriously.

If such optimality properties exist, and it seems they do, then still further questions arise: Can we show that the usable expressions do not raise problems of unfeasible computation, while unusable ones may do so – perhaps the source of their unusability? These are hard and interesting questions. We understand enough to formulate them intelligibly today, but not much more.

If language design has something like this character, then the unusability property may be rather deep.

Recent work also suggests that languages may be optimal in a different sense. The language faculty is part of the overall architecture of the mind/brain, interacting with other components: the sensorimotor apparatus and the systems that enter into thought, imagination, and other mental processes, and their expression and interpretation. The language faculty *interfaces* with other components of the mind/brain. The interface properties, imposed by the systems among which language is embedded, set constraints on what this faculty must be if it is to function within the mind/brain. The articulatory and perceptual systems, for example, require that expressions of the language have a linear (temporal, 'left-to-right') order at the interface; sensorimotor systems that operated in parallel would allow richer modes of expression of higher dimensionality.

Suppose we have some account of general properties P of the systems with which language interacts at the interface. We can now ask a question that is not precise, but is not vacuous either: How good a solution is language to the conditions P? How perfectly does language satisfy the general conditions imposed at the interface? If a divine architect were faced with the problem of designing something to satisfy these conditions, would actual human language be one of the candidates, or close to it?

Recent work suggests that language is surprisingly 'perfect' in this sense, satisfying in a near-optimal way some rather general conditions imposed at the interface. Insofar as that is true, language seems unlike other objects of the biological world, which are typically a rather messy solution to some class of problems, given the physical constraints and the materials that history and accident have made available. Evolution is a 'tinkerer', in the phrase of evolutionary biologist Francois Jacob, and the results of its tinkering may not be what a skilled engineer would construct from scratch to satisfy existing conditions. In the study of the inorganic world, for mysterious reasons, it has been a valuable heuristic to assume that things are very elegant and beautiful. If physicists run across a number like 7, they may assume that they have missed something, because 7 is too ridiculous a number: it must really be 2x+3, or something like that. A standard quip is that the only actual numbers are 1, 2, infinity, and maybe 3 – but not 79. And asymmetries, independent principles with much the same explanatory force, and other oddities that deface the picture of nature are viewed with a degree of skepticism. Similar intuitions have been reasonably successful in the study of language. If they are on target, it may mean that language is rather special and unique, or that we do not understand enough about other organic systems to see that they are much the same, in their basic structure and organization.

Possibly all of this is mere artifact; we are just not looking at things correctly. That would hardly be surprising. But the conclusions look reasonable, and if they are correct, they pose new mysteries to add to the ancient ones.

References

Descartes, R. (1645). Meditations on First Philosophy. In E.S. Haldane and G.R.T. Ross (trans.) *The Philosophical Works of Descartes*, Vol. 1, pp. 131–200.
Hume, D. (1748). *An Enquiry into Human Understanding*. L.A. Selby-Bigge (ed.), 3rd rev. edn by P.H. Nidditch. Oxford: Oxford University Press, 1975.
Leibniz, G. (1686). Discourse on metaphysics. In M. Morris and G.H.R. Parkinson (trans. and ed.) *Philosophical Writings*. London: Dent, 1973.
Turing, A. (1950. Computing machinery and intelligence. *Mind* 59, 433–460.

3
Hobbes's Challenge

Marcelo Dascal

Introductions to the cognitive sciences, in their excessively brief historical surveys, usually attribute to Thomas Hobbes (1588–1679) the merit of having been the first thinker to propose the 'computational theory of the mind'. Unfortunately, they overlook the details of Hobbes's proposal, the theoretical program it served, the intellectual context within which it was made, the reactions it provoked, and the issues it put in the agenda of seventeenth and eighteenth century thought. In this paper I will try to reconstruct the significance of Hobbes's proposal in the light of such contextual factors.

It will be apparent, from this reconstruction, how much of the current debate on central issues in the cognitive sciences addresses the problems raised by Hobbes's challenge and elaborates types of solutions adumbrated by himself and his contemporaries. Hobbes, then, can be credited not only with proposing the 'computational theory of the mind', but also with defining – along with his contemporaries – the problem-space within which present-day cognitive sciences still operate. Awareness of its historical roots may eventually help to tap hidden or forgotten potentialities in that space and/or to overcome its inherent limitations.

1. Verbalizing the mind?

Thomas Hobbes's exceptionally long life, ninety-one years, passed through one of the most turbulent periods in the history of England, the overthrow of the monarchy, Cromwell's dictatorship, and the restoration of the monarchy. Anyone with political interests was bound to end up on the wrong side of somebody in those years. In Hobbes's case, it was the parliamentarians. To avoid arrest and perhaps death, he exiled himself in France for eleven years. Hobbes's working years spanned the whole period of Descartes's productivity and he wrote a searching set of objections to Descartes's *Meditations*. His most influential work was *Leviathan*. It is best known for the social contract approach to political legitimation that it enunciates (one of the causes of Hobbes's troubles) but it also contains remarkable philosophy of mind and psychology.

The most frequently quoted passage in which Hobbes articulates his 'computational' picture of the mind comes in the first two paragraphs of Chapter 5 ('Of Reason, and Science') of Part I ('Of Man') of the *Leviathan*:

> When a man *reasoneth*, he does nothing else but conceive a sum total from *addition* of parcels, or conceive a remainder from *subtraction* of one sum from another; which (if it be done by words) is conceiving of the consequences of the names of all the parts to the names of the whole, or from the names of the whole and one part to the name of the other part. [...] In sum, in what matter soever there is place for *addition* and *subtraction*, there also is place for *reason*; and where these have no place, there *reason* has nothing at all to do.

> Out of all which we may define (that is to say determine) what that is which is meant by this word *reason*, when we reckon it amongst the faculties of the mind. For REASON, in this sense, is nothing but *reckoning* (that is, adding and subtracting), of the consequences of general names agreed upon for the *marking* and *signifying* of our thoughts; I say *marking* them when we reckon by ourselves, and *signifying*, when we demonstrate or approve our reckonings to other men. (*Leviathan* I, 5, 1–2)

Under the grip of the 'computational metaphor', we tend nowadays to be impressed by its forceful – albeit a bit too arithmetical perhaps – formulation in this passage, and to quickly see it as a forerunner of the 'physical symbol system' hypothesis. In so doing, we overlook its peculiarity, namely that the symbol system by means of which we perform our reasoning is claimed to be *linguistic*. Natural language itself, and not some sort of 'Mentalese', is the vehicle of mental reckoning.[1] And this

---

[1] Hobbes's 'reckoning' refers mainly to syllogistic deduction. It is not clear whether he relied upon an intensional or an extensional interpretation of the terms and quantifiers in the subject–predicate sentences out of which syllogisms are made. Each of them would allow for relatively straightforward readings of 'addition' and 'subtraction'. One should beware, however, not to employ set-theoretical tools – unavailable at the time – for such readings. Leibniz, presumably inspired by Hobbes, proposed several numerical calculi for syllogistic reasoning, thereby minimizing its *linguistic* aspect, emphasized by Hobbes. But he used the full range of arithmetical operations, rather than only addition and subtraction (cf. C 42–49, 70–77, 77–82, 84–89, etc.).

is stressed, in the last sentence, by pointing out that the very same 'names' are used in mental operations (as 'marks') and in communication (as 'signs').[2]

This was a far cry from the commonplace that language and reason, the two distinctive characteristics of humans and both forms of the Greek *logos*, should be somehow connected. Hobbes was claiming that language is directly involved in the process of reasoning and that without it reasoning cannot go very far, if it could at all exist. It was this intrusion of language in the *inner sanctum* of the mind and its consequences, rather than the 'computational' aspect of his thesis, that caught the attention of Hobbes's contemporaries and provoked violent reactions. His proposal was considered either ridiculously wrong (if people think with words, how can the thoughts of a Frenchman and an Englishman ever be the same? – asked Descartes and Arnauld) or else scandalously dangerous (since words are arbitrary, truth itself, resulting from mental manipulations of words, would be arbitrary).

Such reactions can be better understood against the background of the linguistic implications of the intellectual struggles that accompanied the rise of 'modern' philosophy and science in the first half of the seventeenth century. One should first recall the struggle against late medieval scholasticism, perceived by the new philosophers as a sterile form of manipulation of words, unable to advance our knowledge of the world. Renaissance thought was also seen as guilty of verbalism: on the one hand, for its excessive reliance on the authority of ancient texts and on futile hermeneutic exercises; on the other, for the widespread belief in language as a source of occult knowledge about the world – to wit the popularity of cabbalistic ideas up to the end of the seventeenth century. Reliance on words – whatever its source – was perceived as diametrically opposed to reliance on reason and observation – the only sure ways to achieve knowledge.

[2] In *De Corpore*, Hobbes elaborates upon the functional difference between marks (or 'notes', as he calls them here) and signs: the former are created for ourselves, the latter, for the others ['Notae ergo et signi differentia est, quod illa nostri, hoc aliorum gratia institutum sit' – *De Corpore* I, 2, 2]. He also somewhat restricts the mental role of the former: notes are said to have a mnemonic function and signs, a communicative one ['Notae ut recordari, signa ut demonstrari cogitationes nostras valeamus' – *De Corpore* I, 2, 3]. In principle, then, notes, being private, need not be identical to public signs. If this were the case, however, the thoughts they made accessible to an individual would be lost to humankind with his or her death. The advantage of using public signs for both functions was evident, for Hobbes. Furthermore, neither notes nor signs are 'natural', both being 'conventional' or arbitrarily 'instituted'.

Recall, further, the rise of the vernacular languages, which were replacing Latin as languages of culture. To be sure, in order to be broadly read and understood, authors had to write in these 'vulgar' languages, whose eloquence Dante Alighieri had long before praised. But, in addition to their lowly (and hence unreliable) origin, they had not yet achieved the stability, richness, and precision necessary for scientific and philosophical purposes. Montaigne, for instance, complained about the fluidity of the orthography, the rapid semantic changes and the lack of precision of the French of his time, and felt compelled to create a great number of new French words and expressions (cf. *Essais* II, 2 and III, 9). Similarly, Locke, nearly one century after Montaigne, introduced an estimated 500 new English words, expressions, or new senses for old terms (Hall 1976); and Leibniz, while emphasizing the advantages of German (a language more 'concrete' than those related to Latin), acknowledged its lack of philosophical terms (Schulenburg 1973).

Under these circumstances, the dangers of a language-based pseudo-science, of incomprehensible mumbo-jumbo passing for knowledge, and of relativism, were not merely remote possibilities. A critical attitude towards natural languages developed, which undertook to keep them strictly apart from the cognitive processes involved in the production of knowledge, and thereby to reduce its deleterious effects. Francis Bacon forcefully articulated this attitude early in the seventeenth century. For Bacon logic should supply to the intellect the tools necessary for overcoming the difficulties that endanger its endeavor to acquire and develop scientific knowledge. The art of detecting fallacies is one of such tools. The dangerous *idola* it helps to identify are 'false notions' which, being deeply entrenched in our thinking habits, distort our understanding of the 'nature of things' (NO I, 38, 41). Thereby they create a barrier for the formation of correct judgments. Among the idols, those of the 'market-place' are 'the most troublesome of all' (NO I, 59). They are the 'false appearances imposed upon us by words, which are framed and applied according to the conceit and capacities of the vulgar sort' (Sp III, 396), and thus 'follow those lines of division which are most obvious to the vulgar understanding' (NO I, 59). Therefore, they obstruct the way to scientific knowledge, for 'whenever an understanding of greater acuteness or a more diligent observation would alter those lines to suit the true divisions of nature, words stand in the way and resist the change' (*ibid.*).

Paradoxically, Bacon's critique of language led to an enhanced interest in language. For it suggested that only a better understanding of language and, eventually, its radical reform or even replacement could protect us from its dangers. The former suggestion led to the development of 'philosophical grammar' – the attempt to discover the principles underlying the variety of languages; the latter, to the projects of 'universal' or 'philosophical' languages. Such projects – which abounded in the second part of the seventeenth century (and were the object of Swift's sharp satire in *Gulliver's Travels*) – avoided natural language's problems simply by trying to create entirely artificial symbol systems (mostly only written). Furthermore, most of them accepted Bacon's assumption that language – whether natural or artificial – had no role to play in the production of knowledge, but at most in its transmission.[3] In fact, they presumed – like Descartes in his well-known reply to Mersenne (AT I, 76–82) – that the completion of science (at least in its foundations and basic categories) was not only totally independent of the availability of such languages, but also a precondition for their proper design.

Vis-à-vis this prevalent critical attitude towards language, Hobbes's claims were not only heterodox, but also appeared as regressive, for they seemed to promote a version of the old-fashioned verbalism every 'modern' thinker was trying to get rid of. Yet Hobbes himself *was*, as

---

[3] For a survey of such projects of universal language, see Knowlson (1975). Leibniz's projects, vis-à-vis those of his contemporaries, were sui generis, because he was interested in symbolic systems useful for the production of knowledge (*ars inveniendi*), and not only for its communication (cf. Dascal 1978; Pombo 1987).

Occasionally, Bacon's followers deviated from the two basic assumptions mentioned in the text, and lapsed into the beliefs of the previous era he most criticized. A case in point is John Webster. In his *Academiarum Examen* (1654), Webster proposed a reform of learning, largely inspired by Bacon, which purported to replace speculation by experimental philosophy – the 'philosophy of the Schools' by the 'philosophy of the furnaces'. Accordingly, he contrasted the library with the laboratory, and condemned verbalism. And yet, he freely combined these Baconian views with a good deal of *Renaissance Logosmystik*, by looking for that original 'language of nature' that 'still reveals itself in the great book of nature, in the inward signatures of things, in the language of animals, etc.' (quoted in Formigari 1988, 20). Our task, according to Webster, is to reconstruct our ability, lost in the Fall, to decipher this language, a task which is to be achieved by 'the recovery and restauration of the Catholique language in which lies hid all the rich treasury of nature admirable and excellent secrets' (Webster *ibid.*, p. 21). This cryptographic model of knowledge, rather than leading (as in Galilei) to an emphasis on the role of mathematics, takes hieroglyphs as the model for the 'Catholique language' to be restored/reinvented. Webster was sharply criticized by Seth Ward (1654), an influential member of the Royal Society, who condemned Webster's reliance on language mysticism as incompatible with Bacon's legacy and with the spirit of the new science.

much as Descartes, Bacon, Gassendi, Arnauld, Boyle, or Leibniz, a 'modern' philosopher/scientist. Like them, he adopted and contributed to the 'mechanization or the world view' – perhaps even more than them, insofar as he tried to extend it to the scientific study of the mind and of society. Like them he sought to develop a systematic model of scientific thought and practice. His heterodox proposal relating thought with 'linguistic computation' could not therefore be easily dismissed as retrograde. In fact, it forced his fellow moderns to ask fundamental questions they presumably would not have asked without his challenge. The ensuing sections spell out some of these questions.

2.   A new model for mental representation?

If you were to ask a seventeenth or eighteenth century thinker what are the basic units of thought processes, he would certainly reply: 'Ideas'. If you were to ask for a definition of this term, you would provoke puzzlement: 'why do you need a definition for such a simple and clear notion?'.[4] Puzzlement apart, the term 'idea' was carefully scrutinized and defined in quite different ways by different authors (and even by the same author) in the seventeenth and the eighteenth centuries, when its philosophical use peaked. Divergences about how to understand 'idea' gave rise to divergent philosophical 'schools' (e.g., rationalism vs. empiricism) and, within the same school, to bitter polemics (e.g., between Arnauld and Malebranche; cf. Dascal 1990a). After two centuries of intensive debates, Voltaire, for one, was skeptical about their yield: 'It is quite sad to have so many ideas, and not be able to know precisely the nature of ideas'.[5]

In spite of their divergences, all parties at the time were particularly interested in one type of idea, namely those endowed with the power to 'represent' something other than themselves. Their interest in these *representative* building blocks of thinking was, of course, derived from their interest in the question of how thinking can provide knowledge of, among other things, the world. For this particular kind of idea, the question 'how do ideas represent?' is fundamental. Its importance notwithstanding, surprisingly few alternative answers were seriously

---

[4] 'Le mot d'*Idée* est du nombre de ceux qui sont si clairs qu'on ne les peut expliquer par d'autres, parce qu'il n'y en a point de plus clairs et de plus simples', write Arnauld and Nicole in the first chapter of their influential *La Logique ou l'Art de Penser* (1683, 65).
[5] 'Il est bien triste d'avoir tant d'idées, et de ne savoir pas au juste la nature des idées'. In the entry *idée* (written in 1765), of his *Dictionnaire Philosophique* (Voltaire 1769, 224).

considered, and the most popular one cuts across the divergences mentioned above. Voltaire, in 1765, suggests this answer, in the characteristically implicit way it was presented in both the empiricist and the rationalist traditions: 'What is an idea? It is an image depicted in my brain'.[6] What this implies is that *ideas represent as images do*.

Images, for empiricists and rationalists alike, were (material) entities imprinted in the 'phantasy' or 'corporeal imagination'; as such, they are indeed 'depicted in certain parts of the brain';[7] in Hobbes's terminology, they are 'phantasms' formed in the imagination by a series of 'movements' beginning, usually, with sensorial stimuli.[8] Consequently, they were supposed to represent their objects by virtue of a physiological causal chain, i.e., as *indices* or traces of the latter – although it was widely assumed (and barely justified) that they were *iconic* representations too. On both counts, images are *natural* – as opposed to *conventional* – signs. By equating or comparing ideas with images, then, the former were also supposed to represent 'naturally'.

The empiricists tended to literally view ideas as images – thereby identifying the former as either sensorial or directly derived from sensorial images through simple processes such as 'association', 'fading', etc. But this identification posed for them the problem of how to account for those ideas that could not simply be equated with images or traced back to them, such as general ideas and the ideas corresponding to the operations of the mind (e.g., predication, conjunction, disjunction, implication), usually denoted by syncategorematic expressions.[9] What Hobbes

[6] 'Qu'est-ce qu'une idée? C'est une image qui se peint dans mon cerveau' (Voltaire, 1769, 223). What I am considering typical in Voltaire's answer is its use of 'image', not of 'brain'.

[7] '... images qui sont depeintes en la fantaisie; ... en la fantaisie corporelle, c'est à dire en tant qu'elles sont depeintes en quelques parties du cerveau ...' (Secondes Reponses; AT IX, 124).

[8] '... the immediate cause of sense perception consists in ... that the first organ of sense is touched and pressed; ... the pressure of the uttermost part proceeds from the pressure of some more remote body, and so continually, till we come to that from which ... we derive the phantasm or idea that is made in us by our sense' (*De Corpore* 4, 25; EW 1, 390). On Hobbes's psychology, see Gert (1996). A similar chain of transmission of 'movements' is described in detail by Descartes in his *Traité de l'Homme* (AT XI).

[9] Berkeley's criticism of Locke's 'general ideas' in the *Principles* is well known. He also called attention, in *Siris*, to the second kind of problematic cases, using the term 'notion' to distinguish the non-imagetic operations of the mind from *ideas* or images: 'There are properly no ideas, or passive objects, in the mind but what were derived from the sense: but there are also besides these her own acts or operations: such are notions' (*Siris* # 308).

was suggesting, in the footsteps of medieval nominalism, was a solution to this problem. The role of ideas, in the problematic cases in question, was to be fulfilled not by unavailable images but by words themselves.[10]

As for the rationalists, they obviously could not identify 'ideas' with physiological or physiologically derived phenomena, not only due to their adherence to mind-body dualism, but also because such a move would suppress the basis for their doctrine of necessary truths, making all knowledge contingent. So, when characterizing ideas as images they were bound to claim that this was only 'a way of speaking'. Thus, Descartes, who had said in the third *Meditation* that (representative) ideas are 'comme les images des choses' (AT IX, 29), quickly withdraws from this characterization in his reply to Hobbes's objection, and redefines idea as 'everything that is immediately conceived by the mind' (AT IX, 141).[11] Thus, ideas, properly speaking, are the products of the mental operation of 'conceiving'.

Although at first this operation was characterized in such a way as to eventually include also the products of the imagination,[12] it was later

---

[10] Hobbes, thus, is not claiming that all thought is verbal. He is only claiming that those mental processes where generality and orderly concatenation of thought are involved require the use of inner verbal means. 'General names' are mentioned in the long passage quoted in Section 1; as for syncategoremata, they are discussed, for example, in *Leviathan* (46, 16–17), as those words that 'serve to show the consequence or repugnance of one name to another', along with the suggestion that even languages such as Hebrew with 'no verb answerable to *est*, or is, or *be*)' actually express the appropriate relation of one name to another through the syntactic device of 'placing two names in order'.

[11] In his Fifth Objection to the *Meditations*, Hobbes points out (AT IX, 139–140) that the characterization of 'idea' as image implies that we can have no idea of God, since we cannot have an image of an invisible and immaterial thing. In line with his linguistic thesis, he suggests that we do not need to have an image of God in order to use significantly the name 'God', and to think about God. For this, he claims, it is sufficient that several trains of reasoning, beginning with this or that particular experience, lead us to conclude that there should be a being with such and such properties, to which we then attach the name in question. Descartes's reply (AT IX, 141) consists in withdrawing from his description of ideas as similar to images, so that the fact that we cannot have an image of God, no longer counts against our having an idea of God, provided God is 'immediately conceived' by our mind.

[12] 'On appelle *concevoir* la simple vue que nous avons des choses qui se présentent à notre esprit; comme lorsque nous nous représentons un soleil, une terre, un arbre, un rond, un quarré, la pensée, l'être, sans en former aucun jugement exprès. Et la forme par laquelle nous représentons ces choses, s'appelle *idée*' (Arnauld & Nicole 1683, 59).

on restricted to the intellect or understanding, and its products – 'concepts' – were, accordingly, sharply distinguished (e.g., by Kant) from the products of the imagination, be it reproductive or creative. The problem is that, whereas when ideas were equated or likened to images it was possible to rely on an implicit commonsensical explanation for how they represent and for the accuracy or correctness of such representation, once they became concepts this was no longer the case.

The rationalist way of tackling this problem consisted, for obvious reasons, in looking for intrinsic or 'formal' criteria for a concept's accurate representational power. Thus, Malebranche, drawing upon the Cartesian notions of 'immediacy' and 'clarity and distinction', characterizes an idea, in its more specific sense of 'concept', as an immediate object of the mind that represents clearly a thing, where a representation is clear when it permits one 'to discover by a simple inspection whether such and such modifications belong to it'.[13] Arnauld, following Descartes, was satisfied with a *psychological* interpretation of such criteria and, accordingly, viewed ideas as 'modifications of the mind' rather than as Malebranchean 'representative beings' (cf. Dascal 1990a). Malebranche and Leibniz (as well as Spinoza) considered such an interpretation insufficient because it is liable to subjectivism. Malebranche finally opted for a *Platonic* solution, equating our clear ideas/concepts with God's perfect knowledge of essences, without however spelling out in what precisely such a knowledge consists.[14] Leibniz, in a more practical spirit, sought to provide a clear-cut *logical* criterion for the existence of an idea. According to him we have an idea only if we are able

---

[13] Arnauld's (1683) criticism of his equivocal use of 'idea' led Malebranche to distinguish, in the *Eclaircissements*, three senses of this term, through the use of three properties – immediacy, representativity, and clearness – only ideas in the sense of concepts possessing all three: 'Ainsi ce mot, *idée*, est équivoque. Je l'ai pris quelquefois pour tout ce qui représente à l'esprit quelque objet, soit clairement, soit confusément. Je l'ai pris meme encore plus généralement pour tout ce qui est l'objet immédiat de l'esprit. Mais je l'ai pris aussi dans le sens le plus précis et le plus resserré; c'est-à-dire pour tout ce qui représente les choses à l'esprit d'une maniére si claire, qu'on peut découvrir d'une simple vue si telles ou telles modifications leur appartiennent' (Malebranche 1712, 822).

[14] This is his often mentioned but ill-understood theory of the 'vision in God'. For a brief but perceptive account of Malebranche's epistemological motives for such doctrine, see Popkin (1993, 322–324). Popkin felicitously compares Malebranche's ontological realism (*esse est concipi* = to be is to be conceived) to Berkeley's (*esse est percipi* = to be is to be perceived). In a sense, each draws the extreme consequences of the basic assumptions of rationalism and empiricism, respectively.

to prove its logical consistency; otherwise, all we have is a (psychological) 'notion', that may turn out to be devoid of representative content and hence, of epistemic value. We can speak and even think, say, of 'the greatest number', but we have no idea thereof, because we cannot give a *real definition* of this expression, i.e., a contradiction-free complete description of its content.

According to Leibniz, Hobbes was on the right track by pointing out the importance of words in thought and of their use according to precise definitions. But he created what Leibniz often refers to as 'the Hobbesian difficulty'[15] – namely, the alleged dependence of truth upon the arbitrariness of definitions – by overlooking the fact that *real* – as opposed, say, to mere *nominal* – definitions are not arbitrary insofar as they are subject to a powerful logical constraint.[16] The association of concepts with definitions was not restricted to those who, like Hobbes and Leibniz, admitted a role for words in thought. It loomed large also in authors who denied such a role – to wit, Bacon himself and, no less significantly, *Port Royal Logic*'s three chapters devoted to definitions. Such an association clearly indicates the acceptance of an implicit

---

[15] For example: 'De discrimine inter conceptus inadaequatos et adaequatos, sive definitionum nominalium et realium, ubi occurrendum Hobbesianae difficultati de veritate arbritraria, Cartesianae, de ideis eorum de quibus loquimur' (A VI, iv, 973). He also calls Hobbes's position 'super-nominalism', and contends that it is untenable: '... I confess that Hobbes seems to me to be a super-nominalist. For not content like the nominalists, to reduce universals to names, he says that the truth of things itself consists in names and what is more, that it depends on the human will, because truth allegedly depends on the definitions of terms, and definitions depend on the human will. This is the opinion of a man recognized as among the most profound of our century, and as I said, nothing can be more nominalistic than it. Yet it cannot stand. In arithmetic, and other disciplines as well, truths remain the same even if notations are changed, and it does not matter whether a decimal or a duodecimal number system is used' (L 128; GP IV, 158).

[16] '... a means of distinguishing between *nominal definitions*, which contain only marks for discerning one thing from others, and *real definitions*, through which the possibility of the thing is ascertained. In this way we can meet the view of Hobbes, who held truths to be arbitrary because they depend on nominal definitions, not considering that the reality of the definition does not depend upon our free choice and that not all concepts can be combined with each other. *Nominal definitions* do not suffice for perfect knowledge unless it has been established by other means that the defined thing is possible' (L 293; GP IV, 424–425). For Leibniz's theory of definitions, and its relationship to Hobbes's, see Dascal (1987, Chapter 4). As I point out there, Hobbes implicitly held some criterion of the 'correctness' of definitions, which prevented them from being purely a matter of the arbitrary 'imposition of names'.

'verbalization' of the notion of idea: if not straightforwardly identified with words themselves, ideas/concepts were conceived as language-like structured chains of components, closely corresponding to their verbal definitions – a far cry from the earlier view of ideas as similar to images. And this was not the only indication of the need for another – possibly verbal – model of mental representation. In fact, Descartes himself was not happy with the comparison between ideas and images. In the second *Meditation* he pointed out that the physiological chain producing images might induce subjectively convincing 'similarities', that were however objectively false. The sun, for example, appears small to us, whereas scientific reasoning proves it to be many times bigger than the Earth. In the *Dioptrics* (Chapter 4) he denounces the mistake of those philosophers who interpreted the visual metaphor too literally, leading to the belief that in order to feel, perceive, or think, the mind must 'contemplate images transmitted from the objects to the brain'. Thought, according to Descartes, need not rely upon such mistaken-prone *signs* of things. The naturalness of the representativity of ideas – which ensures their objectivity – must come exclusively from their intrinsic properties, not from extrinsic similarities. In criticizing once more, in his posthumously published treatise *The World* or *Treatise on Light*, the literal interpretation of the analogy idea/image, Descartes significantly appeals to words which, 'without having any similarity with the things they represent, nevertheless make us conceive them' – these very words which, he insists, 'signify something only by virtue of human imposition'.[17] And in the *Discours de la Méthode*, as well as in a letter to Henry More (5 February 1649), he proposed the ability to use language appropriately in changing and unexpected circumstances as a sort of Turing Test for differentiating animals (or automata) from humans.[18]

None of this means, of course, that Descartes and most of his contemporaries were prepared to endorse Hobbes's idea of actually making public language or any other public signs part and parcel of mental operations of

---

[17] 'Vous savez bien que les paroles, n'ayant aucune ressemblance avec les choses qu'elles signifient, ne laissent pas de nous les faire concevoir, et souvent même sans que nous prenions garde au son des mots ... Or, si les mots, qui ne signifient rien que par l'institution des hommes, suffisent pour nous faire concevoir des choses, avec lesquelles elles n'ont aucune ressemblance ...' AT, XI, 4).

[18] The relevant texts are in AT, VI, 56–57 and AT, V, 278. They have been highlighted by Chomsky (1966, 1968), who drew from them the wrong conclusion that, according to Descartes, 'language can serve as an instrument of thought' (1968, 11). For a discussion of this topic, see Dascal (1990b).

any kind. At most they would perhaps be willing to go along with something akin to the Fodorian hypothesis of a 'language of thought', i.e., of an innate (and therefore 'natural') language-like mental medium. Nevertheless, their qualms clearly indicate the need to elaborate an alternative model of mental representation. Unlike the ancient Aristotelian idea of thought as 'silent speech', which mysteriously allowed for the coexistence of a 'non-natural' account of words with a 'natural' account of thought-units, Hobbes's proposal forced his contemporaries to question such a dubious coexistence, regardless of whether they accepted or rejected his thesis of the actual intervention of public language in thought.

Hobbes's merit was to consider the linguistic model of mental representation as a serious alternative, and thereby to force everybody else to face its consequences, which raised far-reaching questions: (i) since the meaning of ideas is now to be modeled upon the meaning of words, linguistic semantics cannot be 'ideational' any more – a new theory of meaning for both words and ideas is required; (ii) if ideas, like words, do not represent 'naturally', does this entail the conventionality and presumably also the relativization of ideas and thought?; (iii) since language is typically a social phenomenon, should thought too be conceived as a public, rather than as a private affair?; (iv) what exactly does it mean to attribute to language and thought 'computational' powers?

If the new, 'verbal' model for mental representation was to take shape, *pace* Hobbes's opponents; if linguistic representation was to serve as a model for mental representation, both the nature and workings of language and mind had to be more carefully scrutinized and better understood. If, in addition, language was to be allowed to play any role in mental operations, Cartesian dualism should be reconsidered, giving way, eventually, to a new architecture of the mind and its functions.

3.   Mental computation: Linguistic, logical, mathematical

The questions raised by Hobbes's proposal were – intrinsically – of an interdisciplinary nature: they prompted reflection about the mind in the light of what was known about language (especially semantics) as well as logic and mathematics; and they benefited from the changes occurring in these areas at the time, and stimulated them as well.

Semantics had been concerned almost exclusively with the meaning of 'categorematic' words (nouns, adjectives, verbs), which it was easy and natural to relate to the ubiquitous 'ideas'. Locke's main semantic principle, thus, was that 'words, in their primary or immediate signification, stand for nothing but the ideas in the mind of him that uses them' (Locke, *Essay* III.2.2). However differently 'ideas' were understood by Locke and Descartes, they were for both what guaranteed – point by point – the meaningful use of language: 'Whenever I express something with words, when I understand what I say, it follows with certainty that I have in me the idea of the thing signified by my words'.[19]

This kind of 'ideational' semantics was directly correlated with an 'inspectionist' (cf. Reeves 1962, 11–12) conception of thought, according to which (a) the study of thought is the study of the elements of content which constitute it, (b) such elements are 'ideas', whose (c) successive 'presentation' to the mind in the course of cognitive processes is what cognition is all about. On this view, it is the constant inspection of ideas by the 'mind's eye' that ensures the validity of reasoning and the reliability of any mental process, especially those involving a measure of complexity.[20] For thinking is performed upon ideas themselves, not upon their (verbal or other) signs, and complex ideas or sustained reasoning must be captured by the understanding *uno intuitu* – at a glance – if their truth or validity is to be properly assessed. Thus, Descartes recommended, in his *Rules for the Direction of the Mind*, the use of a sort of 'mental gymnastics' whenever we are engaged in a complex mental task:

> ... if I have first found out by separate mental operations what the relation is between the magnitudes A and B, then that between B and C, between C and D, and finally between D and E, that does not entail my seeing what the relation is between A and E, nor can the truth previously learnt give me a precise knowledge of it unless I recall them all. To remedy this I would run them over from time to

---

[19] '... je ne puis rien exprimer par des paroles, lorsque j'entends ce que je dis, que de cela meme il ne soit certain que j'ai en moi l'idée de la chose qui est signifiée par mes paroles' (Secondes Reponses; AT IX, 124).

[20] The same assumption underlies *Port Royal Logic's* requirement to always replace in the mind a word by its definition: '... toutes les fois qu'on se sert du mot qu'on a défini, il faut substituer mentalement la définition à la place du defini; et avoir cette définition si présente, qu'aussitôt qu'on nomme, par exemple, le nombre pair, on entende précisément que c'est celui qui est divisible en deux également, et que ces deux choses soient tellement jointes et inséparables dans la pensée, qu'aussitôt que le discours en exprime l'une, l'esprit y attache immédiatement l'autre. Car ceux qui définissent les termes, comme font les Géomètres avec tant de soin, ne le font que pour abréger le discours ... mais ils ne le font pas pour abréger les idées des choses dont ils discourent' (Arnauld & Nicole 1683, 124).

time, keeping the imagination moving continuously in such a way that while it is intuitively perceiving each fact it simultaneously passes on to the next; and this I would do until I had learned to pass from the first to the last so quickly, that no stage in the process was left to the care of the memory, but I seemed to have the whole in intuition before me at the same time. This method will both relieve the memory, diminish the sluggishness of our thinking, and definitely enlarge our mental capacity. (*Rule 7*; AT X, 387–388; HR 19–20)

To be sure, Descartes also considers the possibility of employing abridging signs in order to render the above process more efficient. Such signs, preferably written, should be short, so that, after having distinctly examined each thing, one would be able to 'traverse them all with an extremely rapid movement of our thought and include as many as possible in a single intuitive glance' (*Rule 16*; AT X, 455; HR 67). But this use of signs is confined to a purely mnemonic function. They are useful only to evoke ideas, i.e., to place them before the mind's eye. The task of verifying the validity of a deduction or of actually drawing a conclusion from the premises of an argument is entirely left to the understanding itself. Descartes is suspicious of any attempt to formalize reasoning, for he does not trust the 'precepts of the dialecticians, by which they think to control the human reason' (*Rule 10*; AT X, 405; HR 32). In order to avoid the danger represented by blind obedience to such formal precepts, the only means is, for him, to employ at each step the watching eye of the understanding:

Wherefore as we wish here to be particularly careful lest our reason should go on holiday while we are examining the truth of any matter, we reject those formulae as being opposed to our project, and look out rather for all the aids by which our thought may be kept attentive ... (*Rule 10*; AT X, 406; HR 32).

Such an inspectionist model of mental computation is clearly opposed to Hobbes's suggestion of a mental manipulation of linguistic signs, just as it is very distant from the kinds of accounts we would associate today with the term 'computation', influenced as we are by formal logic, by Turing machines, and by Physical Symbol Systems. But it is worth pointing out that it was not entirely alien to Hobbes himself – as befits a citizen of his age. He too focused mainly on categorematic words, and his arithmetics of addition and subtraction can only work for subject–predicate sentences (where both subject and predicate are 'general names'), and under the presupposition of a given hierarchy of nouns according to their extension and/or comprehension.[21] Furthermore, he assumed a transducer model of speech, which presupposes a language-independent 'train of thoughts' or 'mental discourse', wherein the role of words as marks was restricted to 'fixing' (general) ideas and bringing them to the mind's attention.[22] And, like Descartes, he was wary of the scholastic allegedly vacuous use of words without referents, and considered the presence in the mind of the correctly defined 'ideas of things' corresponding to the words as the only possible guarantee against such abuses. This is why he was suspicious of algebra, whose 'symbols' were semantically empty symbols – to be viewed at most as useful abbreviations – and modeled his idea of mental computation upon the semantically interpreted signs of arithmetic (comparable to concrete geometric figures).[23]

It is algebra, however, that provides the clue – for Leibniz, Berkeley, and others – for a different approach to semantics and for a different model of mental computation, at odds with the inspectionist conception described above. Algebra is appealed to by Berkeley in the course of his argument against Locke's semantic principle – the 'received opinion

[21] 'By this imposition of names, some of larger, some of stricter signification, we turn the reckoning of the consequences of things imagined in the mind into a reckoning of the consequences of appellations' (*Leviathan* I.4.9).

[22] 'The general use of speech is to transfer our mental discourse into verbal, or the train of our thoughts into a train of words; and that for two commodities, whereof one is the registering of the consequences of our thoughts, which being apt to slip out of our memory and put us to a new labour, may again be recalled by such words as they were marked by. So that the first use of names is to serve for marks, or notes of remembrance' (*Leviathan* I.4.3).

[23] 'At symbolica, qua permulti hodie utuntur putantes esse analyticam, nec analyticam est nec synthetica, sed calculationum arithmicarum quidem vera, geometricarum autem falsa brachygraphia, ars quidem non docendi neque discendi geometriam, sed inventa geometrarum celeriter et compendio in commentarios redigendi. Nam etsi inter propositiones longe dissitas, facilis sit per symbola discursus, an tamen is discursus, cum fiat sine ipsarum rerum ideis, valde utilis existimandus sit, certe nescio' (*De Corpore III*, 20) [But the so-called 'symbolica', which is used by many scholars who believe that it is truly analytic, is neither analytic nor synthetic. It is merely an adequate abbreviation of arithmetical calculations, and not even of geometrical ones, for it does not contribute either to the teaching or to the learning of geometry but only to the quick and succinct compilation of what was already discovered by geometricians. Even though the use of symbols may facilitate the discourse about propositions which are wide apart from each other, I am not sure whether such a symbolic discourse, when employed without the corresponding ideas of things, is indeed to be considered useful].

that language has no other end but the communicating our ideas, and that every significant name stands for an idea':

> And a little attention will discover, that it is not necessary (even in the strictest reasonings) that significant names which stand for ideas should, every time they are used, excite in the understanding the ideas they are made to stand for: in reading and discoursing, names being for the most part used as letters are in algebra, in which, though a particular quantity be marked by each letter, yet to proceed right it is not requisite that in every step each letter suggest to your thoughts that particular quantity it was appointed to stand for (*Principles* Intro., 19).

To 'proceed right', Berkeley is suggesting, requires only the obedience to the 'procedural rules' that regulate mathematical operations, not the actual presence of contentful 'ideas'.

Leibniz went a step further, stressing the psychological impossibility of satisfying the inspectionist requirement. For him, in algebraic reasoning, the ideas underlying the symbols employed are not evoked or presented to the mind at each step. If this were to be done, he contends, algebraic reasoning would become impossible, for the mind would be permanently busy trying to get hold of the evoked ideas, with no capacity left to proceed with the business of reasoning itself. It is essential, on the contrary, that in this kind of reasoning the mind concentrates exclusively on the signs themselves and on the operations performed upon them, without caring to interpret them as it proceeds. In this sense, algebraic reasoning is viewed as nothing but the manipulation of signs, performed according to rules which guarantee the validity of its results (cf. Dascal 1987a, *passim*). He extends this observation to any thought process involving some degree of complexity, which essentially depends upon what he calls 'blind thought':[24]

> Similarly, nobody could follow a lengthy reasoning with his mind if certain signs or names had not been devised. Through them, a great number of things can be comprehended in such a way as to allow one to run through many of them very quickly; this would be impossible

[24] The notion of blind thought plays a central role in Leibniz's philosophy of signs as well as in his epistemology. It is first used in his early work *De Arte Combinatoria* (1666; A VI, i, 170), then in several intermediary papers, such as the one here quoted, to appear, finally, as a central piece of Leibniz's theory of knowledge, in his 'On knowledge, truth, and ideas' (1684; GP IV, 422–426; L 291–295), in the *Discourse on Metaphysics* (1684; GP IV, 427–463; L 303–330), etc.

if, suppressing the names and all equivalent signs, we should use the definitions instead of the defined. Thoughts of this kind I usually call *blind thoughts*, and there is nothing more common nor more necessary for men. Very few people, indeed, distinctly imagine all the units of the number nine, or the method of generating a hyperbola, when talking about them. If we were once conscious of ordering the words distinctly and constantly, then blind thoughts alone would be sufficient for distinct reasoning. This is why the modern Analysis Symbolica [i.e., algebra], in spite of Hobbes's criticism, is so useful for quick and sure reasoning (A VI, ii, 481; trans. in Dascal 1987a, 149).

Algebra's use of letters for 'unknown quantities', along with the new 'procedural' mathematics embodied in the calculus, which allowed it to deal with infinite magnitudes without the need to refer to entities called 'infinitesimals',[25] further supported the emerging alternative – a non-inspectionist model of cognition – by demonstrating the possibility of performing computations with non-interpreted symbols. Reasoning, within this perspective, can be accounted for in 'formal' terms, i.e., through a system of operational rules that defines the relevant 'formal' properties of the symbols, and spells out their 'valid' sequences, independently of their interpretations. In such a system, computation viewed as a manipulation of symbols, as that 'playing with characters' in which 'blind thought' consists, could thus indeed 'go far, very far' – as Leibniz says in a note (cf. Dascal 1987a, vii). For the 'cashing out' of the meanings of the symbols in terms of their referents, be they 'ideas', 'things', or other kinds of 'content', could be in fact postponed indefinitely until the end of the game, as suggested by Berkeley in his dialogue *Alciphron:*

Words, it is agreed, are signs: it may not therefore be amiss to examine the use of other signs, in order to know that of words. Counters,

[25] Berkeley, as is well known, was critical of the new calculus, on the grounds that it made not explicit what kind of entities or ideas it was referring to. In fact, many of Berkeley's assertions, especially in the *Philosophical Commentaries*, were incompatible with the nominalism he expresses in his praise for algebra and in other passages quoted in the text. For example, he says that no reasoning about things of which we have no idea – hence no reasoning about infinitesimals – should be allowed (PC 354) and he affirms that one should not use any word without an Idea (PC 356) as well as that all signifying words represent Ideas (PC 378). For Berkeley's 'semantic classicism', see Brykman (1993, 202–209) and for a discussion of its inconsistency with his nominalism, in the context of his philosophy of mathematics, see Robles (1993, Chapters 2 and 5).

for instance, at a card-table, are used, not for their own sake, but only as signs substituted for money, as words are for ideas. Say now, Alciphron, is it necessary every time these counters are used throughout the progress of a game, to frame an idea of the distinct sum of value each represents? ... From hence it seems to follow, that words may be significant, although they should not, every time they are used, excite the ideas they signify in our minds; it being sufficient that we have it in our power to substitute things or ideas for their signs when there is occasion (*Works* III, 291–292).

Just as the circulation of goods, made possible by the replacement of gold and silver by banknotes, cheques, and letters of credit, is what matters for a healthy economy, so too the cognitive economy of the mind depends, on the non-inspectionist view, upon the regular and reliable *circulation* of contents – which it achieves by replacing the problematic 'ideas' by symbols which can be easily grasped by the senses and whose 'exchanges' can be formally regulated in a precise and public way.[26]

The development of the notion of formalization in mathematics and logic was concomitant with a closer interest in the notion of linguistic form (cf. Land 1974; see also Aarsleff 1982). This implied a shift of attention from the word to the sentence as the basic unit of meaning, and from the categorematic to the syncategorematic words – those 'particles' (a term that included affixes and suffixes) that structure the sentence (and even larger linguistic units).[27] Leibniz, here too, was a pioneer. (Most of his texts on linguistic matters remained unpublished until the beginning of this century, and some of them are still waiting for publication.) The dominant trend was represented, for instance, by the *Port Royal Grammar* (Arnauld and Lancelot 1676), which, consonant with the prevalent view that favored the direction of explanation mental → linguistic, sought to explain linguistic 'deep structure' in terms of 'universal logical structure'. Leibniz, instead, tried to define a level of

[26] The comparison between language and money was – and still is – a popular topos. For a book-length study, see Shell (1982). For a specific study of the role of language in thought as expressed in the simile, linking words with counters, tokens, or *Rechenpfennige*, as employed by Bacon, Hobbes, and Leibniz, see Dascal (1987a, Chapter 1).

[27] In his *Real Character*, an artificial language for the purposes of scientific communication, commissioned by the Royal Society, Wilkins (1668) focuses on representational words, and his treatment of particles, which 'do not have objective referents' is very problematic. Dalgarno's *Ars Signorum* (1661), on the other hand, devotes much more attention to this formal part of language.

'rational grammar' which, although underlying all languages, was not to be equated with 'logic'. It is at such a level that a specific notion of 'linguistic form', hence, of 'linguistic computation', could be defined. And Leibniz's detailed comparative analyses of the 'particles' were intended to provide the 'meat' for this formal characterization of linguistic structure.[28] Like the logico/mathematical notion of form, which permitted one to ignore the *local* arbitrariness of the individual signs chosen by focusing on the structural non-arbitrariness of larger units and of the system of rules as a whole,[29] so too at the level of their shared 'rational grammar', languages could be viewed as non-arbitrary in spite of their surface differences.[30] This made them fit for overcoming 'Hobbes's difficulty' and playing a role in cognition.

In David Hartley's (1749) classification of four types of words, (1) Such as have Ideas only; (2) Such as have both Ideas and Definitions; (3) Such as have Definitions only; (4) Such as have neither Ideas nor Definitions, the close relation of the mathematical and linguistic developments described above is made apparent. Words of the first class are compared to 'propositions purely geometrical, i.e., to such as are too simple to admit of Algebra' (e.g., the equality of the base angles of an isosceles triangle). Those of the second class are analogous to 'that part of Geometry, which may be demonstrated either synthetically or analytically; either so that the Learner's Imagination shall go along with every Step of the Process painting out each Line, Angle, etc. according to the Method of Demonstration used by the ancient Mathematicians; or so that he shall operate entirely by algebraic Quantities and Methods, and only represent the Conclusion to his Imagination'. Those of the third class are like 'Problems concerning Quadratures, and Rectifications of Curves, Chances, Equations of the higher Orders, etc. as are too perplexed to be treated geometrically', requiring the use of signs for

---

[28] See Dascal (1990b). For a comparison between Leibniz's and the Cartesians' presumed anticipation of the notion of 'generative grammar', see Dascal (1987, Chapter 7), and for a broader comparison between Leibniz's and Descartes's cognitivist paradigms, see Dascal (1988).

[29] See the final sentence of the second text quoted in note 15.

[30] Leibniz's rationalism abhorred arbitrariness of any kind. Accordingly, he attempted to show, through elaborate etymological and comparative analyses, that even individual words were not in fact 'arbitrary', insofar as their roots could be shown to be in correspondence across languages and to be related to basic emotional and behavioral human reactions to shared circumstances. See, for example, his text 'On the connection between words and things' (trans. in Dascal 1987a), as well as Gensini (1990, 1991) and Dascal (1998a).

unknown quantities. And those of the fourth class 'answer to the algebraic Signs for Addition, Subtraction, etc., to Indexes, Coefficients, etc.; these are not algebraic Quantities themselves; but they alter the Import of the Letters that are; just as Particles vary the Sense of the principal Words of a Sentence, and yet signify nothing of themselves' (Hartley 1749, 277–280; quoted in Land 1974, 149–150). It is apparent from these quotations that, from Hartley's vantage point, the recent history of mathematics provided a convenient model for distinguishing between different kinds of mental computations in terms of which linguistic expressions were to be classified – a model where the inspectionist and formal approaches did not exclude each other but could be viewed as complementary.

The *rapprochement* between language and mathematics tended to favor a reading of 'computation' that emphasizes the logically formalizable aspects of natural languages at the expense of other aspects – e.g., those sometimes lumped under the label 'rhetoric'. Such an emphasis naturally leads to texts such as Condillac's *Langue des Calculs* (1798), which is not just a treatise on algebra but an attempt to construct a model of a completely formalized non-arbitrary language for scientific thought and communication.[31] Although coming from a declared empiricist, such a project corresponds to what Auroux (1992) calls 'maximalist rationalism', which holds a conception of language that not only seeks to develop a formal theory of language but equates language itself with a formal calculus.[32] A somewhat milder version of this idea is epitomized in his claim that the art of reasoning is nothing but a well-formed language, which was enthusiastically adopted by Lavoisier and his colleagues as the ideology underlying their major reform of chemical notation at the end of the eighteenth century (cf. Crossland 1978, Chapter 5).

This tendency is no doubt the one stimulated by Hobbes's talk of reasoning as computation, while at the same time demanding strict adherence to definitions, proscribing metaphor, and – generally – conducting

---

[31] As pointed out by Rieu (1982, 37–39), Condillac's mathematical models changed from his early *Essai sur l'origine des connaissances humaines* to his posthumously published *Langue des Calculs*, from geometry, through arithmetic, to algebra – an evolution that parallels Hartley's classification of words. For the influence of Condillac on the development of linguistic thought in the eighteenth century, see Aarsleff (1982).

[32] Auroux quotes Richard Montague as expressing clearly this view: 'I reject the contention that an important theoretical difference exists between formal and natural language' (Montague 1974, 188).

his theoretical discussion of language and speech within the framework of his methodology of science (cf. Jesseph 1996). But there was also another strand of reflection about language in Hobbes, which emerges in other parts of his work. He was also concerned both with language's daily uses and with its theological and political abuses, where feelings, emotions, ambiguities, and their linguistic expression cannot be overlooked. In fact, most of the *Leviathan* is devoted to these kinds of linguistic phenomena. True, here too Hobbes wishes to provide a *scientific* account of society and to denounce superstition that passes for true religion only thanks to obscure and imprecise language. Nevertheless his approach to language here is notably more flexible: he withdraws from a rigid semantics of definitions, admits plausible metaphorical interpretations of the Scriptures (and provides guidelines for producing them), analyzes a variety of speech acts other than assertions, and calls attention to the role of context (e.g., the addressees' opinions, the situation of utterance, the historical circumstances, the possibly different stages of linguistic evolution) in determining meaning. He thus addresses themes that traditionally belonged to rhetoric, and adumbrates others that would later become central to pragmatics.[33]

These pragmatic and rhetorical aspects of language surely had nothing to do, in Hobbes's mind, with its computational cognitive role. But since they cannot be excised from the use of natural language, no matter how carefully one tries to purge it from them, why insist that it is *in* natural language rather than in some artificial symbolism that we perform our mental computations? Hobbes had no clear answer to this question. But Condillac, at least prior to his 'formal turn', had. And it was a genetic answer, namely that natural language is, both ontogenetically and phylogenetically, our first 'computational' tool. For it is through the acquisition of language that we acquire the capacity of *analysis*, without which our sensations would remain forever holistic, a situation that would not allow us to have any definite ideas nor to articulate them (cf. Dascal 1983). Natural language plays an essential role in thought, according to Condillac, because, prior to its advent, 'lacking any source of organization, the thinking subject must rely entirely upon language in order to structure the representations themselves' (Formigari 1992, 181). Natural language may not be the most perfect computational tool for reasoning, but without it better tools could not

---

[33] Hobbes published a summary of Aristotle's rhetoric under the title *A Briefe of the Art of Rhetorique* (1637).

be developed.[34] It has the further advantage of being the first such tool acquired by the untutored child so that it is the cognitive tool every person is familiar with and can handle most naturally. Still, for Condillac's school the cognitively valuable, 'analytic' powers of natural language had virtually nothing to do with its rhetorical and pragmatic uses, which were considered to be rather a disposable nuisance from the cognitive point of view.[35]

It is customary to associate the re-valuation of these rejected aspects of language with the rise of romanticism in the nineteenth century, i.e., with the decline of cognitivism. A refreshing and somewhat surprising exception to this view can be found in the Scottish philosopher Dugald Stewart (1753–1828) who was aware of the cognitive value of such features of natural language as vagueness, ambiguity, context dependence, and the unending need of interpretive efforts – all of which were shunned by the cognitivists. Stewart argued that Leibniz and Condillac overlooked

... the essential distinction between mathematics and the other sciences ... In the former science, where the use of an ambiguous word is impossible, it may be easily conceived how the solution of the problem may be reduced to something resembling the operation of a mill – the conditions of the problem, when ones translated from the common language into that of algebra, disappearing entirely from the view; and the subsequent process being almost mechanically regulated by general rules, till the final result is obtained. In the latter, *the whole* of the words about which our reasonings are conversant, admit, more or less, of different shades of meaning; and it is only by considering attentively the relation in which they stand to the immediate context, that the precise idea of the author

---

[34] Some of these later developed tools, e.g., arithmetical notation, actually are nothing but imitations or extrapolations of grammatical and lexical rules, as pointed out in detail by Condillac's follower Destutt de Tracy (1817, Chapter 16), who insists that 'les règles grammaticales font juste le même effet que les règles du calcul'; ibid., p. 340).

[35] The rhetorical tradition in the eighteenth and nineteenth centuries generally accepted this view, confining itself mainly to the study of what it considered to be the 'ornamental' effects of language use. Only in the twentieth century, a return to the Aristotelian view of rhetoric as concerned with argumentation, and hence as having cognitive value, was undertaken, mainly through the work of Chaim Perelman and his associates. On some of the dividends of this approach, see Dascal (1998b) and Dascal and Gross (1999).

in any particular instance is to be ascertained. In these sciences, accordingly, the constant and unremitting exercise of the attention is indispensably necessary to prevent us, at every step of our progress, from going astray (Stewart 1854/1860; III, 106; quoted in Land 1974, 113).

Are we returning here to the Cartesian mental gymnastics? I do not think so. For, unlike Descartes, Stewart does not deny language's role in cognitive processes. Nor does he propose to bypass it through 'direct inspection' of sequential logical processes. Quite on the contrary, he highlights the special nature of the logical-cognitive processes underlying language use in all sciences except pure mathematics, where

... the mind must necessarily carry on, along with the logical deduction expressed in words, another logical process of a far nicer and more difficult nature, – that of fixing, with a rapidity which escapes our memory, the precise sense of every word which is ambiguous, by the relation in which it stands to the general scope of the argument ... The improvements which language receives, in consequence of the progress of knowledge, consisting rather in a more precise distinction of these meanings in point of number, the task of mental induction and interpretation may be rendered more easy and unerring; but the necessity of this task can never be superseded, till every word which we employ shall be as fixed and invariable in its signification as an algebraical character, or as the name of a geometrical figure (Stewart 1854/1860; III, 107; quoted in Land 1974, 121).

I am tempted to say that Stewart anticipates some of Peirce's central ideas as well as of present-day pragmatic theory. He is telling us that only a broader notion of computation can do justice to the wealth of computational processes operative in natural language use, many of which involve operations that cannot be 'mechanically regulated by general rules' for they depend upon heuristic roles, fuzzy logic, non-monotonic logic, abduction, and similar 'soft' procedures that do not fit 'hard' computationalism. Nonetheless, these are definitely cognitive as well as computational processes, in the sense that they are inferential in nature (cf. Dascal and Gross 1999). We might perhaps say that Stewart's position represents, in Auroux's (1992) terminology, a 'minimal rationalist' position, which only claims that 'computation has a role in linguistic activity' – provided 'computation' is understood in the broad sense just mentioned.[36]

4. The ontological challenge

Hobbes's linguistic computation thesis, we should not forget, was part and parcel of his metaphysical onslaught on Cartesian dualism.[37] The mental is not a separate substance (Hobbes lists 'immaterial substance' as an example of a nonsensical expression); the senses and the imagination – both continuous with the understanding – are also continuous with material movement; hence, the sounds or written marks of language are, essentially, 'of the same stuff' as the components of our mental life – ideas, judgments, beliefs, and desires. If reasoning is nothing but linguistic computation, he politely suggests to Descartes, then 'le raisonnement dépendra des noms, les noms de l'imagination, et l'imagination peut-être (et ceci selon mon sentiment) du mouvement des organes corporels; et ainsi l'esprit ne sera rien autre qu'un mouvement en certaines parties du corps organique' (Hobbes's fourth Objection; AT IX-1, 138).

This use of the linguistic computational thesis to support monistic materialism was, for Descartes, a further – perhaps the most powerful – reason not to grant to language any foothold whatsoever in the realm of the mental. This, regardless of the fact that he had no explanation for the interaction between the physical and semantic sides of linguistic phenomena, between which stood the unsurmountable barrier separating two entirely different substances- body and mind. Hobbes's materialism seemed to overcome smoothly such a difficulty, by simply removing the barrier. But it remained largely programmatic, 'explaining' the interplay between linguistic and mental phenomena, as well as, generally, that

[36] Like in all 'prehistoric' work of this kind, I have perhaps read more cognitive science prehistory in Stewart's text than is actually there.

[37] In his objections to the second *Meditation*, Hobbes contends that Descartes is wrong in inferring from 'I am a thinking [being]' that I am a spirit, a soul, an understanding, a reason, i.e., that I am a non-material being. According to him, Descartes's proof does not allow him to draw this conclusion: for all we know, the kind of being I am, the kind of being that does the thinking, may well be corporeal. He adduces further reasons to transform this possibility into a categorical statement to the effect that a being that thinks is material, rather than immaterial (AT IX-1, 134–135). Descartes's elaborate reply reiterates that 'intellectual acts have no affinity whatsoever with corporeal acts', and ultimately appeals, question beggingly, to our having formed 'two clear and distinct concepts of these two substances'(AT IX-1, 137).

between body and mind, only in the most general terms available to the incipient 'mechanical physiology' of the time.

Perhaps the most challenging aspect of Hobbes's legacy for cognitive science is the materialistic research programme. While at first strongly opposed, with only a few courageous adepts such as La Mettrie (1709–1751) and Cabanis (1757–1808), the assumption that the mind has no other ontological substrate than the body became, in the twentieth century, virtually unquestionable among scientists and philosophers alike, to the point that hardly anyone would question the following principle:

> [The anti-Cartesian principle] There can be no purely mental beings (for example, Cartesian souls). That is, nothing can have a mental property without having some physical property and hence without being a physical thing (Kim 1996, 11),

and perhaps also this one:

> [Mind-body supervenience] The mental supervenes on the physical in that any two things (objects, events, organisms, persons, etc.) exactly alike in all physical properties cannot differ in respect of mental properties. That is, physical indiscernibility entails psychological indiscernibility (*ibid.*, p. 10).

The challenge, of course, consists in finding out the relevant physical properties and the kinds of relations the 'corresponding' mental properties hold with them.

In the history of the attempts to cash out this materialist programme, language has loomed large, ever since Hobbes – sometimes providing arguments on its behalf, sometimes raising problems for it. Broca's discovery of a brain location associated with speech provided for the first time concrete evidence for the belief that higher cognitive functions can be investigated by finding their neural correlates, possibly neatly packed in 'modules'. But up to this day brain scientists struggle with the task of finding exactly what corresponds, in the brain, to mental states, mental contents, and mental functions – including the alleged components of the 'language organ'. Behaviorism, in its early Watsonian form, considered it possible to reduce all mental activity to sub-vocal speech. But its later, Skinnerian, account of verbal behavior, in order to come to

grips with the basic psycho-linguistic phenomenon of 'semantic gener-
alization', had to posit 'covert' stimuli and responses, in addition to
their physical, observable counterparts. Philosophers of mind and of
language such as Searle or Fodor, who adhere to the materialist program
and see in the ability to explain linguistic behavior the touchstone for
its success, provide elaborate arguments that show that such notions as
'intentionality' or 'content' occupy a special explanatory niche, which
prevents their explanation in terms of the physical properties of linguistic symbols. Artificial Intelligence pioneering projects, which
assumed the significance of the Turing Test, preferred to employ a simple transducer view of language use of the Cartesian type, and to model
intelligent thought as occurring in a purely logical symbol space,
underestimating the problems involved in 'translating' public language
utterances into that space.[38] In all these cases it is as if language resisted
a straightforward materialist account, leaving room for some sort of
dualism (albeit not avowedly ontological) to silently creep in. It is, nevertheless, a tribute to Hobbes that he insightfully picked up what is both
the most difficult and also the most promising phenomenon for the
implementation of the materialist programme.

In all likelihood, Hobbes's suggestion that the most distinctive form
of human thinking, reasoning, is nothing but linguistic computation is
not directly responsible for all the developments discussed in this
paper. Nevertheless, it set in motion, in the seventeenth and eighteenth centuries, a research programme – to which these developments
belong – which culminated with a conception of language and mental
life quite different from the one prevalent in Hobbes's time. The
change was so radical that, instead of Descartes's surprise and scorn at
the mere suggestion that language might have any direct role in thinking, by the end of the eighteenth century, it is Kant's silence about this
intensively debated question that causes puzzlement (cf. Dascal and
Senderowicz 1992). The twentieth century's impressive achievements
in the study of language, cognition, mathematics, logic, and brain sciences have certainly provided new empirical and conceptual tools for
pursuing this debate. But Hobbes's challenge remains, as yet, unsolved.

---

[38] I am referring here to Newell and Simon (1972), among others. For a critique
of this approach, see Dascal (1987b, 1992). It should be said that more recently
Newell and his associates have revised the SOAR architecture, acknowledging a
role for natural language in the inner workings of the model (see Lehman,
Newell, Polk and Lewis 1993). For a critique of the representational assumptions
underlying much of AI research, see Dascal (1989).

References

Sources

Arnauld, A. (1683). [= *Oeuvres*] *Des Vrayes et des Fausses Idées, contre ce qu'enseigne l'auteur de la Recherche de la Vérité*. In Oeuvres de A. Arnauld, G. du Pac de Bellegarde (ed.), vol. 38. Cologne: N. Schouten.

Arnauld, A. and Lancelot, C. (1676). *Grammaire Générale et Raisonnée* (3rd edn). Paris: Pierre le Petit.

Arnauld, A. and Nicole, P. (1683). *La Logique ou l'Art de Penser* (5th edn), L. Marin (ed.). Paris: Flammarion, 1970.

Bacon, F. (1620). *Novum Organum* [= NO]. [quoted from *The English Philosophers from Bacon to Mill*, E.A. Burtt (ed.), New York: The Modern Library, 1939].

Bacon, F. (1864/1874). [= Sp]. *The Works of Francis Bacon*, J. Spedding, R.E. Ellis and D.D. Heath (eds).

Berkeley, G. (1710). *A Treatise Concerning the Principles of Human Knowledge* [Quoted from *The English Philosophers from Bacon to Mill*, E.A. Burtt (ed.). New York: The Modern Library, 1939].

Berkeley, G. (1948/1957). *The Works of George Berkeley*, A.A. Luce and T.E. Jessop (eds).

Berkeley, G. (1976). [= PC]. *Philosophical Commentaries*, G.H. Thomas (ed.). Alliance, Ohio: Mount Union College.

Cabanis, P.-J.G. (1823/1825). *Oeuvres*, P.J.G. Thurot (ed.). Paris.

Condillac, E.B. de. (1798). *La Langue des Calculs*, A.M. Chouillet (ed.). Lille: Presses Universitaires de Lille [1981].

Condillac, E.B. de. (1947/1951). *Oeuvres Philosophiques*, G. Le Roy (ed.). Paris: Presses Universitaires de France.

Descartes, R. [= AT]. *Oeuvres de Descartes*, C. Adam and P. Tannery (eds). [Paris: Vrin. Nouvelle Edition, 1967–1975].

Descartes, R. (1964). [= HR]. *The Philosophical Works of Descartes*, E.S. Haldane and G.R.T. Ross (trans.). Cambridge: Cambridge University Press.

Dalgarno, G. (1661). *Ars Signorum*. London.

Destutt de Tracy, A. (1817). *Eléments d'Idéologie*, vol. 1: *Idéologie proprement dite* (3rd edn). Paris: Courcier [reprint, Henri Gouhier (ed.), Paris, Vrin, 1970].

Hartley, D. (1749). *Observations on Man, His Frame, His Duty, and His Expectations* [Gainesville, Florida, reprint 1966].

Hobbes, T. (1637). *A Briefe of the Art of Rhetorique*. In *The Rhetorics of Thomas Hobbes and Bernard Lamy*, J. T. Harwood (ed.). Carbondale and Edwardsville, IL: Southern Illinois University Press (1986).

Hobbes, T. (1651). *Leviathan or The Matter, Forme and Power of a Commonwealth Ecclesiastical and Civil*, E. Curley (ed.). Indianapolis: Hackett [1994].

Hobbes, T. (1665). *De Corpore*. In *Thomas Hobbes Opera Philosophica quae Latina scripsit*, W. Molesworth (ed.). London [1839/1845].

La Mettrie, J.O. de. (1745). *L'Homme Machine*. Paris.

La Mettrie, J.O. de. (1748). *Histoire Naturelle de l'Ame*. Leyden.

Leibniz, G.W. (1684) Discourse on Metaphysics. In R. Ariew and D. Garber (eds), *G.W. Leibniz: Philosophical Essays*. Indianapolis: Hackett, 1989.

Leibniz, G.W. [= A]. *Sämtliche Schriften und Briefe*. Berlin: Deutschen Akademie der Wissenschaften, 1923.

Leibniz, G.W. |= C|. *Opuscules et Fragments Inédits*, L. Couturat (ed.). Paris, 1903 (Hildesheim: G. Olms, reprint 1966).

Leibniz, G.W. |= D|. *Gothofredi Guiliemi Leibnitii Opera Omnia*, L. Dutens (ed.). Genéve, 1767.

Leibniz, G.W. |= GP|. *Die philosophischen Schriften von G. W. Leibniz*, C.I. Gerhardt (ed.), Berlin, 1875–1890 (Hildesheim: G. Olms, reprint 1965).

Leibniz, G.W. |= L|. *Philosophical Papers and Letters*, L.E. Loemker (ed.) (2nd edn). Dordrecht: Reidel, 1969.

Locke, J. (1690). *An Essay Concerning Human Understanding*. J. Yolton (ed.). New York/London, Everyman's Library |1965|.

Malebranche, N. (1712). *De la Recherche de la Vérité, 6éme éd. revue et augmentée de plusieurs Eclaircissements.* |In Malebranche, Oeuvres, vol. 1, G. Rodis-Lewis (ed.). Paris: Gallimard, 1979|.

Montaigne, M.E. de. (1922). *Les Essais de Michel de Montaigne*, P. Villey (ed.). Paris: Alcan.

Stewart, D. (1854/1860). *The Collected Works of Dugald Stewart*, W. Hamilton (ed.). Edinburgh.

Voltaire. (1769). *Dictionnaire Philosophique*. Paris: Garnier-Flammarion |1964|.

Wilkins, J. (1668). *An Essay towards a Real Character, and a Philosophical Language.* London.

Studies

Aarsleff, H. (1982). *From Locke to Saussure: Essays on the Study of Language and Intellectual History*. Minneapolis: University of Minnesota Press.

Auroux, S. (1992). La tradition rationaliste dans la philosophie du langage. In Dascal, M., Gerhardus D., Lorenz, K. and Meggle, G. (eds) (1992/5), *Philosophy of Language – An International Handbook of Contemporary Research*, 2 volumes. Berlin/New York: De Gruyter, pp. 184–197.

Brykman, G. (1993). *Berkeley et le Voile des Mots*. Paris: Vrin.

Chomsky, N. (1966). *Cartesian Linguistics*. New York: Harper & Row.

Chomsky, N. (1968). *Language and Mind*. New York: Harcourt, Brace & World.

Crossland, M.P. (1978). *Historical Studies in the Language of Chemistry*. New York: Dover.

Dascal, M. (1978). *La Sémiologie de Leibniz*. Paris: Aubier.

Dascal, M. (1983). Signs and cognitive processes: Notes for a chapter in the history of semiotics. In A. Eschbach and J. Trabant (eds), *History of Semiotics*. Amsterdam: John Benjamins, pp. 169–190.

Dascal, M. (1987a). *Leibniz. Language, Signs and Thought*. Amsterdam: John Benjamins.

Dascal, M. (1987b). Language and reasoning: Sorting out sociopragmatic and psychopragmatic factors. In J.C. Boudreaux, B.W. Hamill and R. Jernigan (eds), *The Role of Language in Problem Solving 2*. Amsterdam: Elsevier, pp. 183–197.

Dascal, M. (1988). Leibniz vs Descartes: Competing paradigms for cognitive science. In *Leibniz: Tradition und Aktualitaet* (Proceedings of the Fifth International Leibniz Congress). Hannover: Leibniz Gesellschaft, pp. 189–196.

Dascal, M. (1989). Artificial intelligence and philosophy: The knowledge of representation. *Systems Research* 6(1): 39–52.

Dascal, M. (1990a). The controversy about ideas and the ideas about controversy. In F. Gil (ed.), *Controvérsias Científicas e Filósoficas*. Lisboa: Editora Fragmentos, pp. 61–100.

Dascal, M. (1990b). Leibniz on particles: Linguistic form and comparatism. In De Mauro, T. and Formigari, L.(eds) (1990), *Leibniz, Humboldt, and the Origins of Comparativism*. Amsterdam: John Benjamins, pp. 31–60.

Dascal, M. (1992). Why does language matter to artificial intelligence?. *Minds and Machines* 2(2): 145–174.

Dascal, M. (1995). The dispute on the primacy of thinking or speaking. In Dascal, M., Gerhardus D., Lorenz, K. and Meggle, G. (eds) (1992/5), *Philosophy of Language – An International Handbook of Contemporary Research*, 2 volumes. Berlin/New York: De Gruyter, pp. 1024–1041.

Dascal, M. (1998a). Language in the mind's house. *Leibniz Society Review* 8: 1–24.

Dascal, M. (1998b). Types of polemics and types of polemical moves. In S. Cmerkova et al., *Dialogue in the Heart of Europe*. Tubingen: Niemeyer.

Dascal, M. and Gross, A. (1999). The marriage between pragmatics and rhetoric. *Philosophy and Rhetoric* 32(2): 107–130.

Dascal, M., Gerhardus D., Lorenz, K. and Meggle, G. (eds). (1992/5). *Philosophy of Language – An International Handbook of Contemporary Research*, 2 volumes. Berlin/New York: De Gruyter.

Dascal, M. and Senderowicz, Y. (1992). How pure is pure reason? Language, empirical concepts, and empirical laws in Kant's theory of knowledge. *Histoire, Epistemologie, Langage* 14(2): 129–152.

De Mauro, T. and Formigari, L. (eds). (1990). *Leibniz, Humboldt, and the Origins of Comparativism*. Amsterdam: John Benjamins.

Formigari, L. (1988). *Language and Experience in 17th-Century British Philosophy*. Amsterdam: John Benjamins.

Formigari, L. (1992). The empiricist tradition in the philosophy of language. In Dascal, M., Gerhardus D., Lorenz, K. and Meggle, G. (eds) (1992/5), *Philosophy of Language – An International Handbook of Contemporary Research*, 2 volumes. Berlin/New York: De Gruyter, pp. 175–184.

Gensini, S. (1990). Vulgaris opinio babelica: sui fondamenti storico-teorici della pluralita delle lingue nel pensiero di Leibniz. In De Mauro, T. and Formigari, L. (eds) (1990), *Leibniz, Humboldt, and the Origins of Comparativism*. Amsterdam: John Benjamins, pp. 61–84.

Gensini, S. (1991). *Il naturale e il Simbolico: Saggio su Leibniz*. Roma: Bulzoni.

Gert, B. (1996). Hobbes's psychology. In Sorell, T. (ed.) (1996), *The Cambridge Companion to Hobbes*. Cambridge: Cambridge University Press, pp. 157–174.

Hall, R. (1976). John Locke's new words and uses. *The Locke Newsletter* 7: 11–39.

Jesseph, D. (1996). Hobbes and the method of natural science. In Sorell, T. (ed.) (1996), *The Cambridge Companion to Hobbes*. Cambridge: Cambridge University Press, pp. 86–107.

Kim, J. (1996). *Philosophy of Mind*. Boulder, CO: Westview.

Knowlson, J. (1975). *Universal Language Schemes in England and France 1600–1800*. Toronto: University of Toronto Press.

Land, S.K. (1974). *From Signs to Propositions: The Concept of Form in Eighteenth-Century Semantic Theory*. London: Longman.

Lehman, J.F., Newell, A., Polk, T. and Lewis, R.L. (1993). The role of language in cognition: A computational inquiry. In G. Harman (ed.), *Conceptions of the*

Mind: Essays in Honour of George Miller. Hillsdale, NJ: Lawrence Erlbaum (reprinted in H. Geirsson and M. Losonsky, (eds), *Readings in Language and Mind*; Oxford: Blackwell, pp. 489–507 [1996]).

Losonsky, M. (1993). Passionate thought: Computation, thought and action in Hobbes. *Pragmatics & Cognition* 1: 245–266.

Montague, R. (1974). *Formal Philosophy*, R. Thomason (ed.). New Haven, CT: Yale University Press.

Newell, A. and Simon, H.A. (1972). *Human Problem Solving*. Englewood Cliffs, NJ: Prentice-Hall.

Pombo, O. (1987). *Leibniz and the Problem of a Universal Language*. Munster: Nodus.

Popkin, R. (1993). *The High Road to Pyrrhonism*. Indianapolis: Hackett.

Reeves, J.W. (1969). *Thinking about Thinking*. London: Methuen.

Rieu, A.-M. (1982). Le complexe nature-science-langage chez Condillac. In J. Sgard (ed.), *Condillac et les Problémes du Langage*. Genéve/Paris: Slatkine, pp. 27–46.

Robles, J.A. (1993). *Las Ideas Matemáticas de George Berkeley*. México: Universidad Nacional Autónoma de Mexico.

Schulenburg, S. von der. (1973). *Leibniz als Sprachforscher*. Frankfurt: Klostermann

Shell, M. (1982). *Money, Language, and Thought: Literary and Philosophic Economies from the Medieval to the Modern Era*. Berkeley: The University of California Press.

Sorell, T. (ed.) (1996). *The Cambridge Companion to Hobbes*. Cambridge: Cambridge University Press.

4
Doing It His Way: Hume's Theory of Ideas and Contemporary Cognitive Science

Anne Jaap Jacobson

Introduction

In two of his most frequently read works, the *Treatise of Human Nature* and the *Enquiry Concerning Human Understanding*, David Hume, the eighteenth-century Scottish philosopher, describes himself as building a science of human nature.[1] In each work, the very first step in the construction is his theory of ideas. The judgment of the history of philosophy has not been kind to the theory. Friends of Hume and foes alike have agreed that the theory is inherently skeptical, leading to implausible and self-defeating conclusions (example, friend: Baier 1991; example, foe: Flew 1986).

Twentieth century developments in cognitive science can give Hume's readers a fresh perspective on his theory of ideas, and enable us to see important positive elements in it. Hume's science of human nature anticipates some of our most interesting issues. Our investigation supports the view that taking twentieth century concerns with cognitive science back to the eighteenth century is not anachronistic.

In what follows, we will first briefly consider Hume's status as a historical figure. We will then turn to the central features of his theory of ideas. Once we have the elements in place, we can see that Hume has interesting views on the operations of the imagination in what we take to be reasoning. Together with his conception of ideas as lacking language-like structure, the theory of the imagination becomes a new

---

[1] Citations are from Hume (1975) and Hume (1978). Page numbers for the *Treatise* refer to page numbers of the correlative passage in P.H. Nidditch's 1978 revision of Selby-Bigge's edition. Page numbers for the *Enquiry* refer to Hume (1975).

theory of reasoning and of knowledge. Further, it is one which can easily be placed in the context of some of our most interesting debates. We will look for the skeptical element in Hume's philosophy through two lenses. One concerns the ubiquitous appeal today to mental representations, the other a persistent picture of human rationality that has been severely challenged, though it continues to be invoked in interpretations of past philosophers.

Hume in the history of philosophy

David Hume (1711–1776) lived most of his life in Edinburgh, though he spent some years in France, indeed wrote the *Treatise* there. Hume was one of the most precocious figures in the history of philosophy or psychology; the *Treatise,* his biggest and most important work, appeared before he was thirty. Disappointed by how his work was received, he turned to history later in life. Because he was considered (probably falsely) to be an atheist, he never held a university appointment.

Hume is a puzzling figure in the history of philosophy. On the one hand, he is widely considered to be the greatest philosopher to have written in the English language. To sympathetic readers his work reveals a profound mind, one which brings fresh arguments and views into play on page after page, and more so than any other English-speaking philosopher. On the other hand, for many other readers, he appears to be a really rather silly man, a perverse critic who has rightly been a target for generations of philosophers. So read, Hume does not just question everything; he also rejects everything, from our knowledge of our surroundings and unobserved matters of fact to our knowledge of our own selves and our rationality. As Boswell tells us, Goldsmith said that 'David Hume was one of those, who seeing the first place occupied on the right side, rather than take a second, wants to have a first in what is wrong' (quoted by Box 1990, p. 4). Many historians of philosophy have seen Hume as a thinker whose genius consisted largely in revealing the deep errors in the theory of ideas sketched out by Descartes, and filled in by Locke and Berkeley.

Hume's reputation has been changing recently. One recent correction to the very negative picture has been made by seeing Hume's science of human nature as intimately related to his moral philosophy.[2] The ethical writings present us with a philosopher clearly engaged on a positive project, one which pictures us as unavoidably social beings. When

---

[2] Many Hume scholars have made this point. Most think that Smith (1941) originated it.

we read Hume's ethical writings, it becomes much more difficult to see him as merely working out the implications of a wrong-headed theory of ideas.

A second correction is made by a more careful reading of the texts. For example, the view that Hume argues for the skeptical thesis that all science is impossible appears to ignore an obvious feature. Hume explicitly presents himself as developing a science of the mind, a project which, he assures us, can have significant successes. Whatever else is true, he cannot *simply* be a skeptic. And a third correction has been made possible by the rise in naturalism in our time. Philosophers have begun to realize that an understanding of what knowledge is may be better achieved by looking at how we do proceed, rather than imposing *a priori* conceptions of how we ought to proceed (see, for example, Quine 1969 and Goldman 1986).

Despite their role in securing his greatly more positive reputation, a number of Hume's recent friends have also rejected his theory of ideas on his behalf. According to these recent commentators, what appear to be skeptical arguments are really his attempts to reduce the theory of ideas to absurdity (at least as it is presented in the works we will be looking at), thus motivating us to reject it. Are they right?

The theory of ideas

Hume's science of human nature starts with a theory of the understanding and the theory of the understanding starts with his theory of ideas. The theory of ideas is, to use Hume's terminology, a theory of *perceptions*. Perceptions include sensations, passions, and emotions. The intense feeling of heat had near a fire is a sensation. Desire for water or anger at rudeness are also examples of sensations. Such perceptions, which Hume thinks of as particularly vivid and forceful, are *impressions*.

There is another class of perceptions. In addition to feeling heat, we can think about being hot. We can make plans about the best way to survive during a hot spell. Or we can remember the heat we felt on some occasion before. Or we can imagine being hot in the future. In such cases, Hume maintains, we have faint images of impressions. These fainter images are called *ideas*.

Impressions come either from sensation or reflection, the latter including passions, desires, and emotions. Hume singles out two particular sources of ideas: memory and imagination. The imagination plays a very important role in Hume's philosophy, though its introduction in the theory of ideas does not really prepare us for this. Hume starts simply by remarking that the ideas of the imagination are less lively and strong than those of the memory and that the imagination, unlike the memory, is at liberty to transpose and change its ideas.

Hume's distinction between impressions and ideas is an explicit amendment of Locke's theory of ideas, which does not attempt a corresponding distinction. Hume does not tell us much at all about how to draw the distinction or decide a problem case, though he thinks that, in a few cases, we can have ideas nearly as vivid as impressions or impressions nearly as faint as ideas. Nonetheless, he thinks the distinction is in general quite obvious and thus it is not 'very necessary to employ many words in explaining [it]' (*Treatise*, 1)

Having introduced impressions and ideas, Hume gives us a distinction which applies to both categories. Both impressions and ideas can be *simple* or *complex*. Hume tells us that 'simple perceptions or impressions and ideas are such as admit of no distinction nor separation' (*Treatise*, 2). As first examples Hume gives the color, taste, and smell of an apple.

Hume's simple–complex distinction allows him both to attempt to explain the creative powers of the human mind and to hold at the same time that in some sense all our ideas are derived from impressions. Hume is well aware of at least some of the creative powers of the human mind:

> To form monsters, and join incongruous shapes and appearances, costs the imagination no more trouble than to conceive the most natural and familiar objects. ... What never was seen, or heard of, may yet be conceived; nor is anything beyond the power of thought, except what implies an absolute contradiction.
>
> (*Enquiry*, 18; *Treatise*, 19)

Hume explains our ability to form complex ideas which are not directly derived from impressions as the ability to compound, transpose, augment, or diminish the materials of experience (*Enquiry*, 19; *Treatise*, 19). He tells us that we can analyze our thoughts or ideas, however compounded or sublime, into simple ideas; each complex idea is composed of simple ideas which are and must be derived from impressions. Thus, *simple* ideas are basic ingredients for the fictions of the imagination, among other things. Hume's distinction between simple and complex and his view that simple ideas are the ingredients for all complex ideas makes thought compositional. On Hume's account, thought is compositional just because, and only because, the content of a thought is a function of the content of its components and a largely unexplained relation of uniting.

Hume's opening distinction between impressions and ideas is quite different from those many theorists would make today, and it is important in understanding him to see why. Many recent theorists begin with a distinction between propositional attitudes and qualia. See, for example, the following recent introduction to cognitive science and the philosophy of mind:

> First, we may distinguish those mental phenomena that involve *sensations:* pains; itches ... Second, there are mental states that are standardly attributed to a person or organism by the use of that-clauses ...
> (Kim 1996, p. 13).

The first items are qualia; the second class of mental states is composed of the propositional attitudes, the text tells us. The idea of propositional attitudes as inner states introduces very early on the question of the possible linguistic structure of our inner states. What could make it true that we have such states?

We will look at Hume's answer to this question below. For now we need to notice that the basic categories in Hume's theory of ideas are highly sensory. To use today's terminology, Hume's basic categories are more like qualia than anything else. The first, the impressions, are sensory experiences themselves, broadly understood to include both the taste of chocolate and a craving for it. The second, the ideas, are faint copies of these in our thinking, as when we imaginatively conjure up the taste of chocolate or remember having had some yesterday.

It is a cliché, and a questionable one, to say that Hume was trying to be the Newton of the mind. But Hume's theory of ideas is certainly intended to give us a theory about the mind's contents and the laws of working that the mind has. In doing this, Hume sees himself as fulfilling one criterion of success which preceded his presentation of the theory and going considerably toward meeting a second and loftier aim.

> And if we can go no farther than this mental geography, or delineation of the distinct parts and powers of the mind, it is at least a satisfaction to go so far ....
> (*Enquiry*, 13; *Treatise*, 17–25)

Further,

> But may we not hope, that philosophy, if cultivated with care, and encouraged by the attention of the public, may carry its researches still farther, and discover, at least in some degree, the secret springs and principles, by which the human mind is actuated in its operations?
> (*Enquiry*, 14; *Treatise*, 14)

The principles are the principles of association. And here the imagination has its most important role. We associate together ideas of objects which are in certain relations; namely, similarity, contiguity or causation. For example, the sight of the vase falling will be associated with – bring to mind – an idea of the vase's breaking, since the first is the kind of thing to cause the second. In Hume's account the imagination is also at work in ways which lead us to see our world as more unified and less diverse than it actually is. The imagination, for example, tends to take very similar impressions to be in some ways the same impression. This second kind of operation can lead to comforting but somewhat less felicitous results. Though we will not be looking at how it does it, we should note that the imagination is in large part responsible for the ordinary person's problematic belief in the external world.

Hume's theory has another important feature. He sees himself as working with categories which are easily available to common sense. In part, he is simply relying on our bringing a good grasp of what he regards as the basic categories with us. The difference between thinking and feeling, he assumes, is clear to all of us. But something more is going on. Hume joins Locke in being among the first in the modern era to provide a theoretical place for the terms of our ordinary psychological discourse. In Hume's philosophy, 'belief', 'memory', 'anger' and so on, become natural kind terms in a science of the mind. This approach has been incalculably influential in today's cognitive science. Both those who think cognitive science can retain the terms of our ordinary psychological discourse, and those who do not, assume that these terms are effectively natural kind terms. As natural kind terms, they are taken to denote uniform essences alike at least to the extent of sharing causal or functional properties.[3] The idea that ordinary psychological discourse provides natural kind terms is one of the features of contemporary cognitive science (at least in the philosophy quadrant) which comes almost directly from the eighteenth century. The transference is not completely direct since the idea was sidetracked for a short while by some philosophers of the 1940s and 1950s. (See, for example, Ryle 1949 and Wittgenstein 1953.)

---

[3] Stich (1996, p. 108) takes this view to be entirely uncontroversial. Stich's book is also an excellent source for an update on the controversy to which this view has led. More recently, Griffiths (1997) has argued that since the psychological term 'emotion' does not denote a natural kind, there are no emotions.

Thought and propositional structure

How, on Hume's model, does thought get its propositional structure? Is not 'Jane believes that the cat is on the mat' true because of an internal item with syntactical structure? Hume's response is negative. He is quite explicit about this:

> We may here take occasion to observe a very remarkable error ... [which] consists in the vulgar division of acts of the understanding, into *conception, judgment* and *reasoning* ... Conception is defin'd to be the simple survey of one or more ideas: Judgment to be the separating or uniting of different ideas ... Taking them in a proper light, they all resolve themselves into the first ... .
>
> (*Treatise*, 96 Fn)

For Hume, then, our impressions and ideas do not have propositional structure. Does this mean that we cannot attribute beliefs to ourselves? To echo the definitions of propositional attitudes, is it ever correct on Hume's account to attribute to us states with propositional content? Can statements like 'Jane believes that the dog is happy' be literally true?

Given that Hume thinks that ideas do not have syntactic complexity, he is committed to claiming that correct belief ascriptions do not depend on there being syntactically complex inner contents in us. Further, Hume's theory can accommodate recognition that the language used to describe the contents of our thoughts may have semantic features not present in our thought. His treatment of abstract ideas is a case in point. He thinks that there are abstract words, and he allows that 'All triangles have three sides' is about all past, present, and future triangles. That is, he wants to maintain that the statement has the implications we standardly believe it has. However, Hume does not think we have abstract ideas, such as ideas of triangles which are of no specific sort of triangle (T 1.1.7; SBN 17–25). Our sensory-based ideas are very particular. Having argued that we cannot have abstract ideas, Hume proceeds to give us an account of how we can nonetheless use language with abstract terms, and be correctly said to believe that all triangles have three sides.

In the example of abstract ideas, Hume offers us something that could be made into a strategic reply to charges that his theory of ideas is defective because it cannot account for the many descriptions that impute language-like characteristics to our thought. Hume's strategic reply would be to locate the features in a shared language and then to use his theory of ideas to give an account of how we are able to use language with such features. Generalizing this strategy on his behalf, we can see Hume as a participant in a very recent argument about whether there is a language of thought. It is fair, if simplifying, to see this debate as a debate over whether a theory which posits merely associationist connections can explain our use of language (see Garfield 1997). Those who see our thought as possessing syntax argue that it must do so in order to account for our use of language. The classic source for this thesis is Fodor (1975). Proponents of connectionist models who are engaged on this topic tend to reject the idea that only syntactically structured thought can account for our ability to produce syntactically structured utterances. It is not too much of an exaggeration to say that Hume's philosophy anticipates one of our most interesting debates.

Interestingly enough, the sides also disagree on an issue which is dear to Hume. The connectionist/associationist side of the debate stresses our continuity with the non-language speaking animals, while the other side insists on language and logic as characterizing deep features of our thought. Proponents of the second view portray human reasoning as employing a language of thought.

Hume, it must be said, does not give us a good discussion of all the issues involved. He does not recognize sufficiently the explanatory debt he takes on when he posits ideas without language-like structure. For example, it is difficult to see how Hume is going to treat negation. Suppose we accept the idea that the belief that John is in the kitchen is simply a vivid image of the kitchen with John in it. What will it be like to believe that John is *not* in the kitchen? The idea of an empty kitchen will not suffice. The idea of a kitchen without anyone in it is also an idea of a kitchen without Bill in it, without Jill in it, and so on. The idea of the empty kitchen does not match the semantic content of 'John is not in the kitchen' which is entirely uncommitted as to the rest of one's friends. Thus, it is not obvious that one can explain negation without invoking items with syntactic complexity.

To summarize: Hume does not attempt to explain how we use human languages by positing that our thought has linguistic features such as abstractness or grammatical complexity. Rather, in at least one case, that of abstract ideas, he tries to explain how we can operate with a language which contains features which our thought does not. It is to be regretted that he did not attempt more in this vein. The most important implication of our discussion so far is the fact that, on Hume's model, lacking logical structure, our thought does not unfold in accordance to logical rules. Rather, our thought unfolds according to principles of association.

Naturalized epistemology

The fact that our thought unfolds according to the principles of association points to one of the most startling characteristics of Hume's theorizing. Hume's theory leads to a very distinctive theory of knowledge. The products of our thought are judged according to new standards, as we are about to see.

One merit claimed for theories which attribute to us a syntactically complex 'language of thought' is that they explain why human thought has a deep conformance to logical rules. For example, it is claimed, someone who believes that a young woman is a feminist bank teller will believe that she is a feminist and that she is a teller. And this is so because, on the theory in question, thought has the linguistic structure which underlies the logical rule that 'P and Q' entails both 'P' and 'Q'.[4]

What we get from Hume is a theory in which thought does not necessarily obey such logical rules. Rather, he has a new theory of human knowledge, one which takes good human reasoning to be at least very often not a matter of thought conforming or attempting to conform to logical principles. As we have seen, it is here that the imagination has its great role in Hume's philosophy. The imagination leads us to make associations which give us knowledge when reason cannot provide it. For example, if Hume is right, there can be no good argument for 'the future resembles the past'. However, we proceed as though that were true because of the principles of association, which result in an association between, for example, an impression of the cause and an idea of the effect. One can know, for example, that the clock will strike the hour, just as it has in the past. To know this, one's thought does not have to take a detour through general principles about the future resembling the past. Rather, one's knowledge is a matter of one's thinking of the striking as the large hand approaches twelve and doing so because in the past that sort of sight has been accompanied by the striking. One projects one's past experience onto the future. And if one's thinking of the striking is a quite vivid idea, then it just does count as a belief. Beliefs, for Hume, are just such vivid ideas related to sensory impressions.

[4] Using the well-known feminist-teller example, Kahneman (2002) describes in his Nobel Prize lecture the fact that human beings are prone to committing the 'conjunction fallacy', which takes 'P and Q' as more likely than either 'P' or 'Q'. The importance of such biases in human thinking arises at the end of the present essay.

What Hume is giving us here is a 'naturalized epistemology' (Quine 1969; Goldman 1986). Epistemology is the theory of knowledge. Naturalized epistemologies emphasize the importance of the ways in which we do in fact acquire beliefs. On such accounts, the task of epistemology is quite different from that of standard epistemologies. Standard epistemologies tend to seek to justify our claims to knowledge by appealing to logically sanctioned arguments that we could use to support the claims. Standard epistemologies, then, tend to work to silence the skeptic (who ironically enough is often Hume). A naturalized epistemology takes it for granted that we do in fact have knowledge and develops an account of justification based on how we normally acquire such knowledge.

Part, though not all, of Hume's reputation as a skeptic comes from the fact that his new theory of knowledge was read originally as entailing that we could not have knowledge on the standard model and nothing more. What his readers did not realize was that he is also claiming that we do have such knowledge, much of it anyway. Even though Hume argues that we cannot construct good arguments for the claim that the future resembles the past, he claims, at least initially, that we nonetheless know that it will because of the correct operation of instinct in us. [5]

Much of Hume's work is the very careful and insightful struggle to explain how we have and work with the large conceptions which are of great importance to us. How much sense can we make of the seeming notion that one thing can make another occur? How do we manage to form and trust our expectations? What does our conception of ourselves as the originators of our actions really amount to? What about us makes it possible for us to be moral? In all these important human phenomena, the imagination is at work, Hume tells us.

Optimism and skepticism

In both the *Treatise* and the *Enquiry*, Hume's initial presentation of the theory of ideas is marked by its optimism. For example, he tells us with regard to his principles of association that 'The more instances we examine, and the more care we employ, the more assurance shall we acquire, that the enumeration, which we form from the whole, is complete and entire' (*Enquiry*, 24; *Treatise*, 24). To say this really is to endorse the idea that there is a community of learners who can share knowledge.

[5] (*Enquiry*, 35–55; *Treatise*, 94–97). I have argued (Jacobson 1987) that Hume identifies an underlying metaphysical problem which reintroduces skepticism, indeed, a skeptical problem worse than the one usually attributed to him.

However, in neither volume is this optimism entirely maintained. In each case, the final section of the work contains thoughts much more in line with the traditional picture of Hume as exceedingly negative. For example, in the final section of the *Enquiry* he says,

Thus the first philosophical objection to the evidence of sense or to the opinion of external existence consists in this, that such an opinion, if rested on natural instinct, is contrary to reason, and if referred to reason, is contrary to natural instinct, and at the same time carries no rational evidence with it, to convince an impartial enquirer.

(*Enquiry*, 155; *Treatise*, 155)

This is Hume as traditionally conceived, Hume the skeptic. What has happened? What role does the theory of ideas have in the genesis of this transition from optimism to pessimism? More generally, how are we to fit the negative passages into our picture of Hume's thought?

Hume's strategy is to examine both the ordinary person's [the vulgar] belief in an external, mind-independent world and the philosophers' response to that belief. Both views will be displayed as radically defective. Hume does not give us any attractive alternatives to these two.

We ordinarily think that many of the objects in our environment have a complete independence of our thought. For example, one thinks that the shape of a car parked across the street is independent of what one thinks it to be. According to Hume, ordinary people have a very powerful instinct to believe in an independent world outside our minds. However, the beliefs of ordinary people are radically defective. This is so because the ordinary beliefs fail to meet the ambitions of their possessions; our beliefs fail in reaching any such world. Rather, reflection shows us that ordinary people, when they talk about a seemingly mind-independent world, are actually talking about their altogether mind-dependent perceptions. Hence, their powerful instinct leads them to believe something false. '... [T]he opinion of external existence consists in this, that such an opinion, if rested on natural instinct, is contrary to reason ...' (*Enquiry*, 155; *Treatise*, 155). Hume tells us that for ordinary folk, 'Those very sensations which enter by the eye or ear are with them the true objects, nor can they readily conceive that this pen or paper, which is immediately perceived, represents another which is different from, but resembling it' (*Treatise*, 202).

Philosophers, for whom the slightest reflection reveals the absurdity in the ordinary beliefs, develop a double existence view: they distinguish between mind-dependent perceptions and mind-independent objects which cause the perceptions. For the philosophers, the perception of a mind-independent object consists in having a perception caused by such an object with the perception resembling the object.

Hume rejects the philosophers' beliefs. First of all, the philosophers' account contains a causal statement: the world causes resembling perceptions. There is never any way, according to Hume, to reach around our perceptions and check up on this causal story. In addition, the philosophers' double existence view lacks the backing of instinct. Hence, the opinion of external existence, 'if referred to reason, is contrary to natural instinct, and at the same time carries no rational evidence with it, to convince an impartial enquirer' (*Enquiry*, 155; *Treatise*, 155).

Hume's summary in the *Treatise* is telling:

> I begun this subject with premising, that we ought to have an implicit faith in our senses, and that this wou'd be the conclusion, I shou'd draw from the whole of my reasoning. But to be ingenuous, I feel myself *at present* of a quite contrary sentiment, and am more inclin'd to repose no faith at all in my senses, or rather imagination ... [The beliefs of ordinary folk contain] a gross illusion ... [while the philosophers' view] is liable to the same difficulties; and is over-and-above loaded with this absurdity, *that it at once denies and establishes the vulgar supposition* ... Philosophers ... have so great a propensity to believe [what the vulgar believe] that *they arbitrarily invent a new set of perceptions*, to which they attribute these qualities ... [For] this skeptical doubt ... carelessness and in-attention alone can afford us any remedy.
>
> (*Treatise*, 217–218; my emphasis)

As this passage makes clear, the vulgar belief is unacceptable and philosophers both rely on it and are unable to construct an acceptable alternative to it.

The philosophers' theory needs a name. We will call it the 'Representational Theory of Perception' (RTOP). It is clear that Hume does not endorse it. He thinks that this theory gets developed when philosophers try to correct the problems of the ordinary view of perception, but that RTOP relies on that view.

Humean ideas and the representational theory of mind

We need to contrast a Representational Theory of Perception with a Representational Theory of Mind. The latter endorses a theory of inner, mental representations, but it does not suppose that these representations form some sort of veil that is between us and the external world. Hence, it might seem, a Representational Theory of Mind can avoid the skeptical problem that Hume fails to solve. Richard Rorty in effect contrasts the former, the RTOP, with the latter. His views, according to Peter Dlugos, imply that 'Since we know objects through our ideas of them [according to some figures in early modern philosophy], these ideas play a mediating role in cognition. The mediating role of ideas, not their metaphysical status, is the essential presupposition of veil of ideas skepticism' (Dlugos 1996).

On the other hand, Rorty praises Jerry Fodor, a leading figure in the development of a Representational Theory of Mind in our time, for undertaking the right sort of task (Rorty 1979). This is ironic because Fodor can embrace much in an RTOP. The mere presence of inner representations does not entail skepticism. Or, if it does, that has yet to be argued.

Fodor has recently argued that Hume holds a Representational Theory of Mind (Fodor 2003). However, that theory, as Fodor and most recent philosophers understand it, has an underlying feature that Hume's lacks. Fodor's theory of mental representations takes these inner ideas to have intentional content. Nothing is easier than for the mind to think about the world beyond itself; that is because, possessing intentional states, the mind can be directed outward toward something beyond itself.

It is a problem with such a picture that we entirely lack any generally accepted account of what makes states of the mind intentional states. In our time, philosophy of mind eschews any ontology which includes anything immaterial, and so mental representations are assumed to be brain states or in some way intimately related to brain states. It is not easy to see how some activity in the brain might be directed toward, for example, the bed in the next room. Of course, we can think about the bed in the next room, but to advance the thesis that we do so because we have inner states that are directed toward that bed is simply to provide a location for the aboutness, and not to explain it.

The absence of any generally agreed-upon explication of the mind's supposed intentionality is certainly not for lack of trying. Giving an account of mental representations is one of the major enterprises in today's philosophy of mind. The central problem that needs to be solved, it is generally agreed, is to account for a normativity that comes with intentionality. That is, such states represent things and they can do so well or badly.

Many philosophers would agree that the best candidate for capturing the normativity is given by 'teleosemantics', an account of intentionality that appeals to some sort of selectivity. To put it very roughly, inner states can be about an external world if they were selected for that role. Here the agent of selection is evolution.

A prominent theorist has recently made it clear, however, that teleose-mantics has yet to solve major problems (Neander 2004). In addition, the theory appears to rely upon a controversial adaptationist view about the role of evolution in the shaping of the mind. In contrast, crucially, apparently representing states of the mind might in fact be coincidental effects of our neural architecture (Corballis 2003 makes a related point).

A recent conviction that the mind has inner mental states with inten-tional content has led us to neglect an alternative model that has been prevalent in philosophy for centuries. It originates with Aristotle and it is found in the medieval philosopher, Thomas Aquinas. Its influence can be seen in Descartes and it arguably impacted the schools of Locke's and Hume's time. In fact, a strong case can be made for saying that Hume was influenced by it, and once that case is made, it is relatively easy to see how the theory becomes skeptical in Hume's hands.

Act or object? Being similar or being about?

According to Thomas Reid, a near contemporary of Hume, one of the few virtues of Hume's philosophy is that it makes clear the deep involvement of the 'ideal philosophy' with skepticism (Reid 1756, 1786). For Reid, the ideal philosophy dominates all Western philosophy and is given a partic-ular boost with Descartes, as a consequence of which it is espoused by the most notable philosophers of the seventeenth and eighteenth centuries. Reid tells us that these philosophers take ideas to be *objects*, and accord-ingly are contributing to an inherently skeptical project.

Reid is right about the prevalence of theories of ideas, at least in the seventeenth and eighteenth centuries, but wrong to maintain that every such theorist holds that ideas are objects. Rather, whether ideas are acts or objects was a controversy in that period. However, the ques-tion which concerns us is not about the accuracy of Reid's diagnosis, but about the theoretical satisfactoriness of the key terms of the debate in enabling us to understand Hume.

According to a view present in Western philosophy since Aristotle, the mind is not so much directed outward as the outward gets into the mind.[6] This view is clearly present in philosophy that affected the Early Modern philosophers. Thus, John Yolton (1984) has brought to bear the Thomistic account of perception in his interpretation of some of these philosophers.

---

[6] I have argued that this model also gives us a better picture of many uses of 'representation' in recent cognitive neuroscience than the classic picture (Jacobson 2003). The neuroscientist does not, of course, appeal to scholastic sub-stantial forms. She appeals to abstract relations such as isomorphism.

According to this account, in a completed perception of, say, a cat, the existing essence or form of the cat is abstracted from its matter and realized in our intellects.[7] The idea is *not* that one literally has a cat in one's mind or brain, since the form of a cat realized in one's mind is exemplified in an entirely different way from how it occurs in the world outside our minds. Nonetheless, catness does get realized and we get a surrogate of cats in our minds. Yolton sees this view in Arnauld, and more controversially uses it in his interpretations of Descartes and Locke.

There are obviously severe difficulties in taking this view to Hume. Hume rejects the thesis of multiply instantiated forms or essences in a way that is connected to his discussion of abstract terms. While Hume allows abstract terms, he disallows both abstract ideas and abstract things. A theory of the essence existing in each cat will, for Hume, be a theory of an abstract kind of thing. Since his theory provides no room for multiply instantiated essences, Hume is committed to the rejection of this account of perception. He rejects the metaphysics which makes it possible to think in terms of a form of a cat being in someone's mind in some way. In this sense, he denies that ideas are acts.

Nonetheless, there is a crucial element of the Aristotelian–Thomistic account present in Hume. The result of realizing an essence of a cat in the mind is a surrogate for cats, and it is not itself about cats. It stands in for cats somewhat in the way that one might stand in for one's family in a ceremony. One represents one's family but one is not oneself about one's family or somehow directed toward one's family. The representing is not done by the possession of intentional content. Similarly, one might use a color swatch to represent the color of a room's walls. Here again, the swatch is not about the room; it informs us of a feature of the walls of the room not by possessing intentionality, but rather, in this case, by possessing some of the same features.

One fact that Hume is completely clear about is that ideas represent their impressions by copying them. And in copying them, ideas acquire the very same features as impressions have, with the exception of force and vivacity. This is a point that he makes time and again:

> The first circumstance, that strikes my eye, is the great resemblance betwixt our impressions and ideas in every other particular, except their degree of force and vivacity. The one seems to be, in a manner, the reflection of the other; so that all the perceptions of the mind are

---

[7] On this theory, we can see material objects as having 'substantial forms'. A substantial form is the existing essence of the object and makes it the kind of thing that it is.

double, and appear both as impressions and ideas. When I shut my eyes, and think of my chamber, the ideas I form are exact representations of the impressions I felt; *nor is there any circumstance of the one, which is not to be found in the other.* In running over my other perceptions, I find still the same resemblance and representation. Ideas and impressions appear always to correspond to each other.

(*Treatise*, 2–3; my emphasis)

We can now see how Hume's theory of ideas ends up with skeptical implications. Our perceptions, while we have them, cannot instantiate the features that would give the objects of the senses their mind-independence:

Thus to resume what I have said concerning the senses; *they give us no notion of continu'd existence,* because they cannot operate beyond the extent, in which they really operate. *They as little produce the opinion of a distinct existence,* because they neither can offer it to the mind as represented, nor as original.

(*Treatise*, 191; my emphasis)

The senses cannot give us a notion of an existent that continues when not sensed, because they do not present what is not sensed. Neither can they give us a notion of an entity distinct from our perceptions. What this means is that the senses fail to give us the resources to think about distinct and continuing objects. But reason and imagination do not fill in this sort of gap in sensory impressions. Accordingly, because we cannot have an impression instantiating 'continued and distinct', we will not have an idea of that either.

The consequence is that ordinary thought cannot reach an external world, or, to put it alternatively, that aspect of the world cannot make its way into the mind. The philosophers really do not have a hope of doing better, since they do not have any resources for ideas that the ordinary folk lack. Accordingly, Hume ends his discussion of our knowledge of the external world on a clear note of skepticism.

To say this is not to say that Hume is overall a skeptic. Too much in his philosophy depends on our having knowledge of an external world. His claiming we have it, however, requires carelessness and inattention (*Treatise*, 217–218).[8]

[8] This interpretation of Hume could be compared to those in Pears (1990) and Garrett (1997).

Hume and the cognitive architecture of the mind

Could it possibly be the case that a philosopher of Hume's greatness escapes skepticism solely through carelessness and inattention? Could he really just assume sometimes that there is an external world and at other times hold that our thought cannot reach such a world? To say this is the case would be to say that Hume's philosophy is inconsistent. Further, the inconsistency would be so noticeable that he must have been aware of it.

The idea that Hume is knowingly inconsistent is not itself a popular idea. Since its appearance in *Feminist Interpretations of David Hume* (Jacobson 2000; see also my contribution to Read & Richman 2000), several commentators have attempted to refute it (Garrett 2004 and in Jacobson 2000), one going so far as to claim that such a thesis is the sort of thing that gives feminist philosophy a bad name (Mason 2001). But the idea that any good philosopher would be consistent employs a picture of the architecture of the mind that is now thoroughly in question.

It is easy to think of us as having a system of beliefs that is rather like an essay on a word processor. Things get entered and deleted quite easily; the rules of logic and good evidence are employed in the process. If the mind worked that way, consistency would be too easy for a good thinker to disregard its demands. But the evidence against the picture has been mounting for decades.

The central challenge to this picture has been the growing mass of data that show that the human mind employs a variety of heuristics; these 'rules of thumb' introduce systematic biases in our thought. As Murray Clarke points out (2004), we now have thirty years of research deconstructing the idea that the mind operates with an underlying Russellian psycho-logic. Whether or not the mind is actually composed of self-contained modules that operate in relative isolation, as some theorists have posited, our beliefs tend to cluster in units with much less oversight and accessibility than the essay model suggests.

Further, cognitive scientists have come to realize that the fact that the mind operates with heuristics is a very good thing in a number of ways. We are creatures of action; we cannot afford the time needed to shift through all the evidence and check up on all possible logical implications. Indeed, the logical rationality so beloved still by philosophers, appears to be a very imperfect guide for human lives, and very fallible in its operations. We can find very much the same point in Hume being made regarding our ability to predict effects:

> [A]s this operation of the mind, by which we infer like effects from like causes, and vice versa, is so essential to the subsistence of all human creatures, it is not probable, that it could be trusted to the fallacious deductions of our reason, which is slow in its operations; appears not, in any degree, during the first years of infancy; and at best is, in every age and period of human life, extremely liable to error and mistake. It is more conformable to the ordinary wisdom of nature to secure so necessary an act of the mind, by some instinct or mechanical tendency, which may be infallible in its operations, may discover itself at the first appearance of life and thought, and may be independent of all the laboured deductions of the understanding.
>
> (*Enquiry*, 55; *Treatise*, 55)

Paul Griffiths (1997) characterizes the questionable philosophers' picture of mind as holding that we have 'a single stock of beliefs [which] combines with a single stock of goals in accordance with a set of logical principles modeled on formal decision theory'. As he argues, 'Classical logic makes it natural to impose consistency under at least simple deductive operations on both the beliefs and the goals. After this process of idealization it becomes much harder to handle inconsistent thoughts or the use of different information to control different processes'. Accordingly, it is, relative to recent research, a *defect* of a view if it makes logical inconsistency surprising.

We are considering new views about the mind that have won a Nobel Prize for one of its two originators, Daniel Kahneman (2002). Though the work is very new, one can see Hume as very clearly anticipating it. Kahneman's picture of a dual process model of the mind, with specific 'intuitions' or modes of thought operating on sensory input and an occasionally employed lumbering formal reason invoked to make corrections is very close to Hume's general view, according to which 'carelessness and inattention' may secure for us some of our most important beliefs, and reason is too slow and fallible to rely on for much.

It is not too much of an exaggeration to think of the new model of the mind as a modernization of Hume's view. It has unfortunately not yet impacted the community of Hume scholars. As a consequence, Hume is more cutting edge than many of his recent commentators are prepared to allow.

References

Baier, A. (1991). *A Progress of Sentiments: Reflections on Hume's Treatise*. Cambridge, MA: Harvard University Press.

Box, M.A. (1990). *The Suasive Art of David Hume*. Princeton, NJ: Princeton University Press.

Clarke, M. (2004). *Reconstructing Reason and Representation*. Cambridge, MA: MIT Press.

Corballis, M.C. (2003). From mouth to hand: Gesture, speech, and the evolution of right-handedness. *Behavioral and Brain Sciences*, 26, 199–260.

Dlugos, P. (1996). Yolton and Rorty on the veil of ideas in Locke. *History of Philosophy Quarterly*, 13(3), 317–329.

Flew, A. (1986). *David Hume, Philosopher of Moral Science*. Oxford, New York: Basil Blackwell.

Fodor, J.A. (1975). *The Language of Thought*. New York: Crowell.

Fodor, J.A. (2003). *Hume Variations*. Oxford: Oxford University Press.

Garfield, J.L. (1997). Mentalese not spoken here: Computation, cognition and causation. *Philosophical Psychology*, 10(4), 413–435.

Garrett, D. (1997). *Cognition and Commitment in Hume's Philosophy*. New York: Oxford University Press.

Garrett, D. (2004). Hume as 'man of reason' and 'women's philosopher'. In L. Alanen & C. Witt (eds), *Feminist Reflections on the History of Philosophy* (pp. 171–192). Dordrecht, Boston: Kluwer Academic Publishers.

Goldman, A.I. (1986). *Epistemology and Cognition*. Cambridge, MA: Harvard University Press.

Griffiths, P.E. (1997). *What Emotions Really are: The problem of Psychological Categories*. Chicago, IL: University of Chicago Press.

Hume, D. (1975). *Enquiries Concerning Human Understanding, and Concerning the Principles of Morals* (3rd edn). L.A. Selby-Bigge & P.H. Nidditch (eds). Oxford: Clarendon press.

Hume, D. (1978). *A Treatise of Human Nature* (2nd edn), L.A. Selby-Bigge & P.H. Nidditch (eds). Oxford: Clarendon Press.

Jacobson, A.J. (1987). The problem of induction: What is Hume's argument? *Pacific Philosophical Quarterly*, 68(3,4), 265–284.

Jacobson, A.J. (2000). *Feminist Interpretations of David Hume*. University Park, PA: Pennsylvania State University Press.

Jacobson, A.J. (2003). Mental representations: What philosophy leaves out and neuroscience puts in. *Philosophical Psychology*, 16(2), 189–203.

Jacobson, A.J. (2004). The psychology of philosophy: Interpreting Locke and Hume. In L.W. Alanen & C.E. Witt (eds), *Feminist Reflections on the History of Philosophy*. Dordrecht; Boston: Kluwer Academic Publishers.

Kahneman, D. (2002). Maps of bounded rationality. A perspective on intuitive judgment and choice. In T. Frangsmyr (ed.), *Les Prix Nobel 2002*, 416–499.

Kim, J. (1996). *Philosophy of Mind*. Boulder, CO: Westview Press.

Mason, M. (2001). Review of Ann Jaap Jacobson (ed.) Feminist interpretations of David Hume. *Hume Studies*, 27(1), 181–185.

Neander, K. (2004). Teleological Theories of Mental Content. In E. Zalta (ed.) *The Stanford Encyclopedia of Philosophy* (*Summer 2004 Edition*), http://plato.stanford.edu/archives/sum 2004/entries/content-teleological.

Pears, D.F. (1990). *Hume's System: An Examination of the First Book of his Treatise.* Oxford; New York: Oxford University Press.

Quine, W.V. (1969). *Ontological Relativity, and Other Essays.* New York: Columbia University Press.

Read, R.J., & Richman, K. (2000). *The New Hume Debate.* London, New York: Routledge.

Reid, T. (1756). *Philosophical Orations of Thomas Reid, delivered at Graduation Ceremonies in King's College, Aberdeen, 1753, 1756, 1759, 1762,* D.D. Todd (ed.). Carbondale: Southern Illinois University Press, 1989.

Reid, T. (1786). *Essays on the Intellectual Powers of Man.* Dublin: Printed for L. White.

Rorty, R. (1979). *Philosophy and the Mirror of Nature.* Princeton: Princeton University Press.

Ryle, G. (1949). *The Concept of Mind.* New York: Barnes & Noble.

Smith, N.K. (1941). *The Philosophy of David Hume.* London: Macmillan.

Stich, S.P. (1996). *Deconstructing the Mind.* New York: Oxford University Press.

Wittgenstein, L. (1953). *Philosophical Investigations.* Oxford: Blackwell.

Yolton, J.W. (1984). *Perceptual Acquaintance: From Descartes to Reid.* Minneapolis: University of Minnesota Press.

5
Kant and Cognitive Science

Andrew Brook

Introduction

Immanuel Kant (1724–1804) has a serious claim to be the single most influential figure in the pre-twentieth century history of cognitive research. His influence continues to be so deep-running that in many respects he is the intellectual grandfather of contemporary cognitive science. Consider the widely held view that sensory input has to be worked up using concepts or concept-like states, or the conception of the mind as a system of functions that lies behind the view. Kant originated the first view and worked the second up into something more than a sketch for the first time (the basic idea can be found in Aristotle, Descartes and Hobbes). Both views were central to Kant's model of knowledge and mind and they came to contemporary cognitive science from him by a direct line of descent. In Section 2, we will explore these influences.

Some great thinkers of the past may now be merely cultural artifacts, intriguing, and historically significant but long since superseded. In one of the most patronizing comments ever made about a philosopher, William James expressed just that attitude about Kant:

> Kant's mind is the rarest and most intricate of all possible antique bric-à-brac museums, and connoisseurs and dilettanti will always wish to visit it and see the wondrous and racy contents. The temper of the dear old man about his work is perfectly delectable. And yet he is really ... at bottom a mere curio, a 'specimen'
>
> (James 1907, p. 269)].

Kant is more than a cultural artefact, however. If the Kantian cast of much of contemporary cognitive science is striking, what cognitive science has not assimilated from Kant's work is equally striking.

As well as the ideas just mentioned about the relation of concepts to sensory input and the functional nature of the mind, Kant also held that processes of synthesis, mental unity, and consciousness are central to cognition as we know it and he had some highly original views about self-consciousness. Until recently, these ideas have played no role in cognitive science (what might turn out to be related ideas are now beginning to appear in some quarters). Far from Kant's work being superseded by work in the past half-century on cognition, much of what Kant has to offer has not even been assimilated by it, to its detriment. What cognitive science has not taken over from Kant's work on cognition will be the topic of Sections 3 and 4.

1. Biography and Writings

Kant was the last great thinker of the German Enlightenment. As was true of most Enlightenment thinkers, he took the human individual and his or her experience of self and world to be the fundamental unit of analysis. Kant was born in 1724 and lived a very long life, dying just before his eightieth birthday in 1804. Though one-quarter Scottish (it is said that 'Kant' is a Germanization of 'Candt'), he lived his whole life in Königsberg in what was then East Prussia. (The area is now called Kaliningrad and is an autonomous region of Russia located just below Lithuania.) He was a devoutly religious man, though hostile to many forms of conventional religious observance, and came from a very humble background. By the time of his death, he had been rector of the University of Königsberg and was virtually the official philosopher of the German-speaking world.

Until middle age, he was a prominent rationalist in the tradition of Leibniz and Wolff. Then recollection of David Hume (probably Hume's *Enquiry*), 'interrupted my dogmatic slumbers', as he put it (*Prolegomena to Any Future Metaphysics*, Ak. IV,260).[1] He called the new approach that ensued Critical Philosophy. One of its fundamental questions was,

[1] Except for references to the *Critique of Pure Reason*, references to Kant's work in the text follow the practice of using the volume and page number of the twenty-nine volume German edition begun in 1902 by the Preussischen Academie der Wissenschaften and still not completed. References to the *Critique of Pure Reason* is in the pagination of the first two editions, usually called the 'A' and the 'B' editions. (These were the only two editions that Kant prepared himself.) Translations are from Norman Kemp Smith's 1929 translation, *Immanuel Kant's Critique of Pure Reason*. If a reference is to only one edition, the passage does not appear in the other one.

What must we be like to have the experiences that we have? The view of the mind that Kant developed in the course of answering this question framed all subsequent cognitive research until the advent of connectionism and dynamic systems theory.

Philosophy of mind and knowledge were by no means the only areas in which Kant made seminal contributions. He founded physical geometry. (Since it is said that he never travelled more the fifty kilometres from Königsberg in his whole life, fieldwork was clearly not important. Kant had a wide circle of sea-faring friends whose company he preferred to the company of academics; apparently Kant learned his physical geography from his many, many discussions with them.) His work on political philosophy grounds modern liberal democratic theory. And his deontological approach to the justification of ethical beliefs put ethics on a new footing, one that remains influential to this day. (Deontology is the approach of deducing ethical propositions from more general, factual propositions about the nature of the person, or the requirements of rationality, or some other factor that far transcends the specific domain of ethical thought.) He taught mechanics, theoretical physics, algebra, calculus, trigonometry, and history, in addition to metaphysics, ethics, and physical geometry, an almost unimaginable range of topics for anyone now.

Kant's most famous work is the *Critique of Pure Reason*, which discusses perception, science, and the mind, among other things. He was already fifty-seven when it was published in 1781 (his Humean awakening came relatively late in life). In addition to this work, he wrote two further *Critiques*, the *Critique of Practical Reasoning* (1788) on moral reasoning and the *Critique of Judgment* (1790), a work devoted to a number of topics including reasoning about ends, the nature of judgment, and aesthetics. The three *Critiques* are only a tiny portion of his corpus. He wrote books on natural science, cosmology, history, politics, geography, logic – the list is long. For our purposes, the two most important books are the *Critique of Pure Reason* just mentioned and a small book that he worked up from lecture notes and published only when he became too old to lecture any longer, *Anthropology from a Pragmatic Point of View* (1798).

By the time the Critical Philosophy reached full maturity in the *Critique of Pure Reason* (hereafter the first *Critique*), Kant aimed to do two principal things with it:

1. Justify our conviction that mathematics and especially physics are a unified body of necessary and universal truth.
2. Insulate morality and religion from the corrosive effects of this very same science.

The reason for (2) was that for Kant there was not the slightest doubt that moral responsibility and God exist but, as he also thought, the universal causal determinism and mechanism of science would undermine both morality and religion if scientific evidence and argument were relevant to them. If so, morality and religion can survive modern science only if the truth of the propositions of science is irrelevant to the truth of the propositions of morality and religion. This Kant attempted to show, primarily by arguing as follows: (1) science is about how things appear to us, morality and religion are about how things are; (2) we can never know that the mechanism and determinism that we find in things as they appear to us reflects their real nature; therefore, (3) we are free to form our views about how things really are on the basis of factors other than scientific evidence, the latter being merely evidence concerning how things appear to us.

It was the pursuit of the first aim, the aim of putting mathematics and science on a secure footing, that led Kant to his views about the mind. This came about in the following way. Kant approached the foundations of mathematics and science by asking: What are the necessary conditions of experience? Now such conditions could be found in two places – in what our experience and the objects of our experience must be like, and in what *we* must be like to have such experience. It was in the former that Kant uncovered the foundations for mathematics and physics that he sought, in particular in the conditions of our experience having objects at all, but Kant went after the conditions of our *experience* having object via the latter: What must *we* be like to experience objects? Though this question is, as Kant once put it, strictly speaking inessential to his main task (A xvii), it led him to his discoveries about the mind.

From the point of view of contemporary cognitive science, two things about Kant's approach are interesting. The first is this. Like contemporary cognitive science but radically unlike other philosophies of his own time, Kant was blithely unconcerned about the great questions about knowledge of the external world, skepticism, solipsism, etc. His target is human knowledge, that is to say, objectively valid perception and belief, and he was a successor to Descartes, Berkeley, and Hume. However, his concerns are strikingly different from theirs. Unlike the tradition but like contemporary cognitive science, he simply took it for granted that we have knowledge: *a priori* knowledge about conceptual structures and perceptual knowledge of the world of space and time. What interested him is how these various types of knowledge hang together. In any case, as he argued, our access to ourselves is neither better nor worse than our access to the spatiotemporal world, so the contrast at the centre of, for example, Descartes's account of knowledge between the access we have to ourselves and the access we have to things elsewhere in space does not obtain. (We will return to this point below.) Kant had concerns that go beyond those of contemporary cognitive science, of course, in particular his negative interest in showing that knowledge has limits in order to make room for faith (B xxx). Nevertheless, his positive interest in knowledge is strikingly like the interest of contemporary cognitive science.

This brings us to the second point about Kant's approach. If Kant's interest in knowledge was like contemporary cognitive scientists', his methods were utterly different in one crucial respect: unlike virtually all cognitive researchers now, Kant held that an empirical science of psychology is impossible. As he argues in a famous passage in *The Metaphysical Foundations of Natural Science*, 'the empirical doctrine of the soul ... must remain even further removed than chemistry from the rank of what may be called a natural science proper' (Ak. IV, 471). (Kant's notorious remark about chemistry was made before it had been reduced to a single quantified theory.) First, mental states have only one universal dimension, namely distribution in time, so their contents cannot be quantified; this make a mathematical model of them impossible. Second, there is no objective basis for deciding where one mental state stops and the next ones starts. Third, these items 'cannot be kept separate' in a way that would allow us to connect them again 'at will', by which Kant presumably means, 'according to the dictates of our developing theory'. Fourth, each person can study the mental states of only one person, namely, him- or herself. Finally, 'the observation itself alters and distorts the state of the object observed'. (Little did Kant know how big an issue that would become!)

How then can we study the mind? For Kant, the answer was: by *a priori* reasoning – we study what the mind *must* be like and what capacities it *must* have to represent things as it does. He called this the transcendental method; as we will see, it came to have a huge influence on the research programme of cognitive science, its nonempirical roots notwithstanding.

Everything I have just said about Kant's hostility to the idea of an empirical science of psychology is true but it may also be misleading. Kant did not mean by 'psychology' what we mean by it. For him, psychology is the study of what we can be aware of in ourselves via introspection. What we would now call psychology, largely the study of behavior and the causal context of behavior, he gave the name 'anthropology'. To see the contrast, we need to return to a work mentioned earlier, *Anthropology from a Pragmatic Point of View*. In this unjustly neglected work, Kant tells us that anthropology is the study of human beings from the point of view of their behavior, especially behavior toward one another, and of the things revealed in behavior. Anthropology in this sense contrasts with what Kant understood as empirical psychology, namely the introspective observations of our own mental states. Kant's rejection of introspection and turn to behavior have a very contemporary feel to them. (For more on Kant on introspection, see Brook 2004.)

The *Anthropology* is important for other reasons, too. In particular, it illuminates many things in Kant's picture of cognition. To make sense of behavior, character, etc., Kant urges early in the work, we must know something of the powers and faculties of the human mind: how it gains knowledge and controls behavior. Thus, before we can study character, etc., we must first study the mind. In fact, this study of the mind (Anthropological Didactic, he calls it) ends up being three-quarters of the book. In it, Kant discusses many topics more clearly than anywhere else. In one amusing passage, Kant indicates that he was, if anything, even more hostile to the use of introspection to understand the mind than I have indicated. Introspection, he tells us, can be a road to 'mental illness' (Ak. VII,161). Strangely enough, Kant never seems to have asked whether anthropology in his sense could be a science.

2.   Where Kant influenced cognitive science

Kant's influence on cognitive science was via a direct line of descent through nineteenth century cognitive researchers such as Herbart and Helmholtz, to turn-of-the-century thinkers such as Freud and James (even though James ridiculed Kant, his model of the mind is still quite Kantian) and on to contemporary researchers such as Fodor and the classical symbolic cognition model of classic cognitive science, 1970's-style.

Of the ideas about cognition that came down to cognitive science from Kant, probably the best known is the doctrine that representation, much of it at any rate, requires concepts as well as percepts – rule-guided acts of cognition as well as deliverances of the senses. This doctrine has become as orthodox in cognitive science as it was central to Kant. Its origins in Kant are well known; as he put it, 'Concepts without intuitions are empty, intuitions without concepts are blind' (A 51=B 74). The idea, put in more contemporary terms, is that to discriminate anything from anything, we need information on which to base the discrimination; but for information to be of any use to us, we must also bring capacities to discriminate to it.

Second, Kant's central methodological innovation, the method of transcendental argument as he called it, has become a major, perhaps the major, method of cognitive science. One way to describe the role of transcendental arguments is to say that they attempt to infer the conditions necessary for some phenomenon to occur. Other ways include: they are used to infer the constraints on any such phenomenon occurring, and, they are used to infer what must be true of a system which could contain that phenomenon. This method is important in cognitive science because it provides a toehold on which to climb from observable behavior to unobservable psychological antecedents. Transcendental arguments are a way of identifying constraints on what the unobservable antecedents could be like. So closely linked is this method to Kant that Flanagan, for example, evens calls it the method of transcendental deduction, Kant's term for his most important form of analysis (1984, p. 180).[2]

Here is a simple example: in an early experiment aimed to tease out how memory works, subjects were asked to memorize a short list of random items (letters of the alphabet or whatever). They were then asked if a given letter occurred in the list. Researchers then reasoned as follows. If it takes subjects less time to find the target letter when it is near the beginning of the list than near the end, memory must work by serial search starting at the beginning of the list. If it takes the subject the same length of time no matter where the target item occurs, they must be doing an exhaustive search. If, on the other hand, reaction times vary but unsystematically, then it is likely that subjects are searching only til they find the target item but entering the list at randomly varying points. And so on. We do not need to describe the whole range of possibilities to see the Kantian point: what researchers *actually*

---

[2] Flanagan's choice of this name for transcendental argumentation is curious, the intention to honor Kant notwithstanding. Kant himself used the term 'transcendental deduction' for something quite different, namely the kind of analysis used to *deduce* that use of certain concepts is necessary for representations to come to have objects. Kant used transcendental arguments in the course of this deduction, of course, but they are still different things. Nevertheless, Flanagan is quite right to pick Kant out as the originator of the method of transcendental argumentation. Given that Kant urged that empirical psychology (= introspective psychology) is impossible and never pursued the question of whether an empirical science of anthropology in his sense is possible, it might seem paradoxical that the main method behind his nonempirical, purely *a priori* work on cognition should become the methodological basis for current empirical theory-building about cognition but that is what happened

observed was reaction times. They then *inferred* something about underlying mechanisms as causes of the observed behavior. This is precisely the method of transcendental argument as Kant described it.

Third, even Kant's general conception of the mind and what we can and cannot capture in our models of it has been taken over by cognitive science and philosophers associated with it, at least in a general way. In the light of what cognitive science has not taken up in Kant's model of the mind, this may seem a bit strange, so let us explore the matter further. In cognitive science at the moment, functionalism, specifically the functionalist version of the representational model of the mind, is virtually the official philosophical view of the mind, eliminativist antagonists such as P.M. Churchland (1984) and P.S. Churchland (1986) notwithstanding. The basic idea behind functionalism is this. The way to model the mind is to model what it does and can do, that is to say, to model its functions (in the words of one slogan, 'the mind is what the brain does'). In representational models, the basic function of a mind is to shape and transform representations. Kant too held a representational model of the mind and he too viewed the mind as a system of functions for applying concepts to percepts.

The three tenets of Kant's model of the mind are as follows: (i) Most or all representation is representation of objects; such objects are the result of acts of synthesis. (ii) For representations of objects to be anything to anyone, they must 'belong with others to one consciousness' (A 116); for this, the mind must synthesize its various objects of representation into what I will call the *global object* of a *global representation* (these terms are defined in Section 3). (iii) Synthesis into either individual or global objects requires the application of concepts. – These are the central elements of the model. All three tenets describe either functions or conditions on functions operating (unified consciousness, for example). Kant even called them functions (A 68=B 93, A 94 and elsewhere). In general, like functionalism, Kant's approach to the mind is centered on how it works, as opposed, for example, to how such a system might be physically constituted. He even shared functionalism's lack of enthusiasm for introspection.

Functionalism now comes in many flavors – that mental content can only be specified by its relationship to other mental content (plus, perhaps, the environment and the subject's history); that explanation of mental functioning is a special sort of explanation (focusing on reasons for action); that explanation of mental functioning must be conducted in the language of psychology; that this vocabulary and the style of explanation conducted by using it have 'autonomy' (cannot be reduced to nonpsychological explanation); that this autonomy stems from such explanation being holistic in certain ways; and perhaps others. Kant had no notion of such variation, of course. Kant's functionalism was of a rather general sort. Nevertheless, I think it is fair to view his model of the mind as a precursor of functionalism.

The thought that Kant was a functionalist *avant le mot* is not new. Sellars (1970) was perhaps the first to read Kant as a functionalist or protofunctionalist; more recently Dennett (1978), Patricia Kitcher (1984), Meerbote (1989), Powell (1990), and others have joined him. (Sellars, 1968, also offers an early version of functional classification, and in a Kantian context.) It is less often noticed that Kant was committed to a vital negative doctrine of functionalism, too, the dictum that function does not determine form.

About the relation of function to form, functionalists maintain two things: (i) mental functioning could be realized in principle in objects of many different forms; and, (ii) we know too little about the form or structure of the mind at present to say anything useful at this level in any case, except that mental functions will never be straightforwardly mapped onto any forms that may be associated with them. Kant accepted a variant of both these positions. Concerning (ii), Kant maintained not just that we know little about the 'substrate' (A 350) that underlies mental functioning but that we know nothing about it. This is his doctrine of the unknowability of the noumenal mind. If the noumenal mind is unknowable, however, (i) immediately follows; the mind as it is has to be able to take different forms. Otherwise, how it functions would tell us how it is. Indeed, function imposes so few constraints on form that, so far as we can infer from function, we cannot determine even something as basic as whether the mind is simple or complex (A 353). In short, Kant not only accepted the notion that function does not dictate form, but accepted a very strong version of it.

Indeed, his doctrine of the unknowability of the noumenal mind is little more than a strong version of that idea, at least on some readings. And noumenalism is no mere personal fancy in his system. On the contrary, the doctrine was absolutely vital to him. The very possibility of free will and immortality hang on it, and our belief in freedom and immortality are two of the three great practical beliefs whose possible truth Kant wrote the whole first *Critique* to defend (B xxx). (The third was belief in God's existence; the possibility of its truth depends on noumenalism, too, but noumenalism about the world, not the mind.) The first *Critique* has other goals too, of course – more positive, theory justifying goals. But noumenalism is vital to the work's practical goals.

In short, three of Kant's most central insights have been embraced by cognitive science:

- his epistemological insight into the interdependence of concepts and percepts in experience;
- his main method, the method of transcendental argument; and,
- his general picture of the mind as a system of concept-using functions whose task is to manipulate representations.

Indeed, some workers in cognitive science have even explored the implications of more specific aspects of Kant's model of the mind for their work, Martindale (1987), for example.

Let us turn now to ideas of Kant's that have not been taken up by cognitive science so far.

3.   Ideas of Kant's that have not been taken up by cognitive science

If some of Kant's ideas have been taken over by cognitive science, came down indeed via a direct line of descent, others have not been taken up by cognitive science at all, not from Kant and not from anywhere else either. Before we begin our investigation of the latter, it would be helpful to say a word about the general nature of what cognitive science has and has not taken over from Kant. There are some systematic differences between the two groups of ideas.

Begin with the commonly accepted point that cognitive science has made better progress with mental content (information bearing states of certain kinds) and the processing of content (cognition) than it has with consciousness. This obtains, most would agree, whether it is consciousness of external objects of which we are speaking or consciousness of self. It would be natural to expect that what has been taken over from Kant and what has not would split along the same fault line. That would be only partly true. Until very recently, cognitive science has certainly not paid much attention to consciousness, neither of objects nor of self, but it has paid equally little attention to other aspects of the mind that Kant emphasized, one kind of synthesizing power that we have and the mind's unity in particular. Nor has the explosion of writing on consciousness since about 1985 changed things with respect to either topic. What makes this absence so peculiar is that no feature of cognition and consciousness is more obvious than that we tie the various elements of our experience together, and that what results is a single, unified representation of the world.

Kant held that cognition of the sort that we have requires two kinds of synthesis. The first ties the raw material of sensible experience together into objects. The second ties these individual representations together into what I will call *global representations* (to be introduced shortly).

The first kind of synthesis is to be found in contemporary research in the form of the notion of binding (in the psychological, not the linguistic sense). It has been the object of considerable attention. However, the second has hardly received any attention at all. Here is one standard picture of binding. Colors, lines, shapes, textures, etc., are represented in widely dispersed areas of the brain. These dispersed representations have to be brought into relation to one another if they are to become parts of a single representation of an object.

Interestingly, one influential current model of binding even parallels Kant's in important ways, namely, the model developed by Treisman and her colleague (1980). Though they do not indicate any awareness of the parallel, like Kant they hold that three stages of visual processing are involved. First, the content of feature modules are applied to the input of the senses, next the result of this application of stored features to sensible input is located on a map of locations, and then the result of both processes is recognized via a recognition network and object files. Kant too had a three-stage model of synthesis of objects and Treisman's stages parallel his stages of apprehension, reproduction, and recognition in concepts very closely.

Binding is only one of the two forms of activity to which Kant gave the name synthesis, however. The other is the activity of tying multiple representations together into a global representation. What is special about a global representation is the unity that it displays. It is a single representation, and it is single by virtue of connecting the representations that are its parts to one another in such a way that to be aware of any part of the representation is to be aware of other parts of it, too, and of the collection of them as a single group. Let us try to capture the unities we are discussing more formally.

The unities all begin with the activity of forming multiple representations into what we might call a global representation. We can define a global representation as follows:

> A global representation =*df.* a representation that a number of objects or contents of representation, and usually a number of ways of representing, as its single global object.

We can then define 'single global object':

> A single global object =df. an intentional object that consists of a number of intentional objects such that to be aware of any of these objects and/or their representation is also to be aware of other objects and/or their representation and of the collection of them as a single group.[3]

As a very simple example, each person reading this chapter is aware of the words I have written, the page of the book, the surrounding room, various bodily sensations, thoughts about what I have written ('why is he taking me through this silly exercise?'), and so on. And each of us is aware of these various things not individually but all together, as the single complex object of a single representation.

Kant thought that the capacity to form global representations is absolutely essential to both the kind of cognition that we have and the kind of consciousness that we have. One of the interesting aspects of Kant's work on synthesis is that he tried to unite the two kinds of synthesis he distinguished in a single theory, something that no other theorist to my knowledge has done.

The two kinds of synthesis can be viewed as operating on two different levels. Here is an example. As a result of having bad handwriting, I am all too often in the position of not being able to recognize a word I wrote earlier. If, however, I take a careful look at what I scrawled and then go and do something else for a while, I will eventually recognize what I wrote. The word 'marginalized' was a recent example. (If the brain is a neural network, that is about what one would expect; a neural network needs time to settle on a solution.) All of this happens without any apparent recourse to complex reasoning and quite outside of consciousness. However, at the end of this process of nonconscious interpretation, a second level of activity commences; I form a representation of the word, recognize it, and set out to do whatever I choose to do with it.

Much of the work of cognitive science so far has focused on the first level, the transformation of the meaningless scrawl into a recognizable word and similar kinds of processing. Where cognitive science is Kantian, it is Kant's ideas about processing at this level that it displays: ideas about the synthesis (or binding as it is now called) of diverse sensory information into representations of single objects, ideas about

---

[3] The notions of a global representation and global object and the rest of the ideas discussed in this chapter are considered further in Brook (1994).

the functional nature of minds able to do such synthesizing, and so on. Where cognitive science has not assimilated ideas of Kant's, on the other hand, it is generally ideas that he had about what is going on at the second level, ideas about broader and more complex processes of synthesis, about the unity of minds able to perform these more complicated kinds of synthesis, and about the consciousness involved in recognition of representations and in consciousness of self. Looked at in the light of this distinction between two quite different levels of cognitive processing, the contrast between what cognitive science has taken over from Kant and what it has not begins to look quite interesting.

Earlier I said that cognitive science has neglected more than consciousness in Kant and that is true. However, it *has* neglected what he had to say about consciousness. Indeed, the unity found in global representations is also the feature of consciousness that most interested Kant. Global representations need not be conscious, certainly not conscious of themselves and perhaps not even conscious of objects. This is an important point and one on which Kant is widely misunderstood. It is equally important, however, that when representations are conscious, they display the same unity as global representations generally.

In fact, this unity is a feature not just of global representations and of consciousness. It is also a feature of *recognition* of representations – we recognize them as single representations. We can pull these points together in a single definition:

The unity of representation, recognition, consciousness =*df*.

- a single act of representation, recognition, consciousness, in which,
- a number of objects of representation and, often, the representing of them are combined in such a way that to represent, recognize, or be conscious of any of these items is also to be conscious of at least some of the other items, as the object of a single representation.

As this definition makes clear, the kind of unity in question is more than just being one representation, one object of recognition, one object of consciousness. All three are not just singular but also combine a multiplicity of representational items into one representation. This latter is what their unity consists in.

Unity on the side of representations also requires unity on the side of the thing doing the representing, the mind. Though Kant dealt with this topic quite briefly, he left us at least the outline of a theory that unified global representations are the result of unifying acts of synthesis, and/or recognition and/or consciousness, and that to perform such unifying acts, the actor must be a single, unified mind. None of these claims about the unities crucial to cognition has played any significant role in contemporary cognitive science.

The ideas about synthesis, consciousness, and the mental unity underlying them that cognitive science has not taken over from Kant have a common feature. They all concern the mind as a whole and are about functions that can draw on information in a great many subsystems of the mind, functions that Fodor (1983, p. 107) calls isotropic. Another way to put the point is to say that they are all relatively holistic features of the mind. Now, some cognitive scientists have paid attention to properties of the mind as whole. Here I am thinking of the work on production systems such as Newell's (1973, 1990) Soar, Anderson's (1983) ACT, and Minsky's (1985) society of mind. There is also relevant work in metacognition theory and in philosophy, for example, the work of Patricia Churchland and others (1986, 1991) on connectionist models and large-scale integration of data and Dennett's (1991) multiple drafts model of consciousness. However, none of this work takes up the unities that interested Kant.

That Kant's insights into the various unities central to cognition have been neglected in cognitive science heretofore is due in part, I think, to the way recent philosophers of mind have dealt with issues closely related to mental unity.

It seems obvious, *prima facie*, that the most interesting and cognitively central unities are synchronic: the representing or recognizing or being aware of a number of things *at the same time*. Synchronic unity was the form of mental unity that most interested Kant (of the many passages that indicate this, A 100, A 103, A 108, and A 352 are especially relevant). Yet when contemporary philosophers of mind talk about mental unity at all, they almost always take up only unity *across* time – even when they are discussing Kant! Kitcher (1990) is a good example: she always interprets Kant's talk about mental unity to be about diachronic unity. Of course, diachronic unity, the representing or recognizing or being aware of earlier representations and combining them with current ones, is vital to many cognitive activities. But it is not the only or even the most important form of mental unity.

The way many philosophers have linked unity to personal identity exacerbates the problem. (When philosophers use the term 'personal identity', they mean 'being one person', usually over time. What they mean by the term is thus very different from what clinical psychologists mean.) Philosophers, including most commentators on Kant, tend to tie the two closely together, taking it to be obvious that mental unity requires personal identity, that a number of representations can be unified into one global representation only if they are all the representations of a single person or mind. Since cognitive scientists have generally not been much interested in personal identity, I suspect that the philosophers' way of linking unity and identity may be have helped to turn cognitive scientists away from questions of unity. Whatever, the neglect is a shame; mental unity is central to our kind of mind.

Moreover, the linkage between unity and identity is looser than these philosophers hold. Again, there is both a synchronic and a diachronic question. Synchronically, the link may be close; if a number of representations are combined in one global representation, it is plausible to think that that will be enough to make them the representations of a single mind. (The possibility of the link here makes it, if anything, even more strange that philosophers have typically ignored the synchronic forms of both unity and identity.) When we turn to diachronic unity and identity, however, the link is anything but close. There seems to be no reason in principle why a mind could not combine earlier representations had by another mind with his or her current representations. All it would take is the right kind of memory access to the earlier representations. (Of course, what the right kind of access *is like* might be tricky to specify.) Moreover, and this is what makes the standard treatment of Kant on the subject so surprising, Kant was well aware of this possibility. In a famous footnote to A 363, he entertains the possibility of minds so structured that 'one [mind] communicates representations together with the consciousness [memory] of them' to another one, and so on in a chain. Clearly, both for Kant and in fact, mental unity across time can be and should be distinguished from personal identity.

4. Kant's claims about consciousness of self

Contrary to what is often said, Kant did not consider consciousness to be essential to all forms of unified cognition, not consciousness of self at any rate. To the contrary, he spoke of cognitive systems that are not aware of themselves at all a number of times. (Whether simple consciousness of objects is required is a more complicated matter; on one view, consciousness of objects simply *is* a synthesized, unified global representation of them.) Nevertheless, Kant was well aware that consciousness of self is at least a prominent feature of cognitive systems as we find them in people and he had some interesting things to say about it.

Indeed, Kant made both positive and negative contributions to our picture of consciousness of self. His negative contributions are contained in his attack on rationalist pretensions to infer fundamental facts about minds from concepts and an appeal to consciousness of self alone. Descartes, Leibniz, and maybe Reid were the prime targets; Kant called their reasoning paralogisms and his attack on it is found in the well-known chapter called 'Paralogisms of Pure Reason' in the first *Critique*. The key inferences are that the mind or soul is simple and that it has some form of strict and absolute persistence. Kant's attack is devastating but it had no enduring influence because the ideas under attack had no enduring influence, thanks in part to Kant's attack. So we will not consider it further.

By contrast, some of Kant's positive contributions are not well known at all. They address six topics.

1. How many kinds of self-consciousness there are. Most theorists of self-consciousness, whether they are working in the terminology of self-consciousness as most philosophers do or the terminology of metarepresentation as is more common among cognitive psychologists, treat it as all being much alike. Kant did not. He distinguished between two kinds, consciousness of one's representational states and consciousness of oneself as the subject of these states. In the latter, I am aware of myself as myself, the common subject of my representations. In the former, I am aware of particular psychological states and activities, states and activities that are in fact mine, though I may or may not be aware of that. It seems obvious that there are these two quite different kinds of consciousness of self, indeed that it should be fundamentally important to distinguish them, yet few theorists have followed Kant in doing so.

2. The cognitive and semantic machinery used to obtain consciousness of self as subject. Here Kant made a major discovery: we use a very special kind of referential apparatus to become aware of ourselves as ourselves, as the subject of our representations. Kant says that when we refer to ourselves in this way, we 'denote' but do not 'represent' ourselves (A 382) or we designate ourselves 'only transcendentally', without noting in ourselves 'any quality whatsoever' (A 355). What Kant is isolating here anticipates Frege's and other work on indexicals and bears a striking resemblance to Shoemaker's (1968,[4] p. 558)

---

[4] Among commentators on Kant, Strawson (1966) came closest to seeing that Kant spotted something similar to what Shoemaker later labelled 'reference to self without identification'. Strawson's name for the phenomenon, 'criterionless self-ascription' (p. 165), obscures more than it reveals, however. What is in question is not ascription but reference.

notion of reference to self without identification. Compare Kant's last remark to this statement of Shoemaker's:

> My use of the word 'I' as the subject of [statements such as 'I feel pain' or 'I see a canary'] is not due to my having identified as myself something [otherwise recognized] of which I know, or believe, or wish to say, that the predicate of my statement applies to it
>
> (1968, p. 558).

That is to say, I am aware of myself, as myself, without inferring this from any other feature of myself. If so, that the referent is myself is something I know independently of knowing anything else. If so, I must be able to refer to myself as myself independently of 'noting any quality' in myself, just as Kant said. Let us call this *nonascriptive reference to self.* Shoemaker attributes the core of the idea to Wittgenstein but it goes all the way back to Kant.

3. How we appear to ourselves when we are aware of ourselves as subject. When we are aware of ourselves as subject, Kant thought that the way we appear to ourselves has important peculiarities. As we appear to ourselves here, 'nothing manifold is given' to ourselves (B 135). As well as explaining the peculiarities of self-reference without identification, the theory of the universality of the representational base of consciousness of self explains this peculiar lack of content, too.

4. The representational base of consciousness of self as subject. Kant had an explanation for the peculiarities of this form of reference to self. He never laid this theory out fully in any one place, so it is easy to miss it, but it is there. The fundamental idea is this. To become aware of a representation of X, usually we do not need any representation other than the representation of X (we also need some general cognitive skills). In the same way, virtually any representation can make us aware of ourselves as its subject. It is this universality that opens the way to reference to self without ascription. (The details are complicated. I discuss them in Brook 1994, Chapter 4 and Brook 2004.). No cognitive theorist has ever developed a general explanation of the peculiar semantics of reference to self that is better than Kant's. Most theorists do not even try.

5. The unity in our consciousness of ourselves as subject. When we are aware of ourselves as subject, we are aware of ourselves as the 'single common subject' of a number of representations (A 350). And this representation is itself unified. Both these instances of unity strongly resist explication by the resources of any existing theory of

mental contents, and may be a main source of the tenacity of the problem of the homunculus.

To reveal the power of this notion of the unity of consciousness of self as subject, let us apply it to that old saw of anti-functionalism, the mind whose 'neurons' are the population of China. As an objection to functionalism, the story goes as follows: 'If what defines a mind is functional organization, then size is irrelevant. If so, then the people of China could be one mind. All that would be required is that they be hooked up to one another so as to exhibit the right functional organization. And that is absurd'. It is interesting to reflect on how Kant might have reacted to this claim.

Perhaps along the following lines. To find out whether the population of China could be a single mind, we need to determine two things. First, could the information realized in the relationships among the members of this population, some of it at least, be integrated so as to become a single object of a global representation? Second, could we imagine the spread-out entity composed of this population becoming aware (i) of such an object, (ii) of the global representation of this object, and (iii) of itself, and *as* itself, the common subject of the elements of this representation? I do not know how to answer these questions and I am not sure what Kant's answer would have been but he does give us the right questions. His notions of the unity of experience, the unity of consciousness, and the consciousness of oneself as the common subject of one's representations clarify the issue of what the Chinese population *would have to be like* to be a mind.

6. When I am aware of myself as subject, of what am I aware? Here the question is: am I aware of myself? That is to say, does nonascriptive reference to self give me epistemic access to the thing that I am, or is consciousness of self, so-called, just consciousness of another representation, in this case a representation of myself? Such a representation would presumably be as concept-laden and doctored by the mind as all other representations are. All cognitive theorists in Kant's time and most since have simply taken it for granted that nonascriptive reference to self gives us consciousness of ourselves, not just of another representation. Even among contemporary theorists, the Churchlands are among a rare few who think otherwise. Kant is the only pre-twentieth century theorist that I know of who rejected the idea; he would have been firmly on the side of the Churchlands. We 'know even ourselves only through inner sense, and therefore as appearance ...' (A 278; see B 153–154). However, there is a twist to Kant's rejection. He certainly thought that we have no *knowledge* of ourselves as we are but he may

have thought that we do have a 'bare consciousness' of ourselves as we are, a 'consciousness of self [which is] very far from being a knowledge of the self' (B 158). This twist is enough by itself to make his version of the 'no direct consciousness of self' thesis more subtle than, for example, the Churchlands' version.

As has been indicated, not one of Kant's six ideas about consciousness of self has been taken up by cognitive science. Even when parallel ideas have appeared in recent work, as with Shoemaker's reference to self without identification and the Churchlands' denial that we have direct, unmediated consciousness of self, the authors of the idea do not seem to know that Kant beat them to it over two hundred years ago. As a general theorist of the mind, Kant is no mere cultural artifact.

Final comments

In this chapter we have explored ideas of Kant's that have been incorporated into contemporary cognitive science and ideas that have not. The latter concern his claims about synthesis, about the unity of representation, consciousness and mind, and about the peculiarities of consciousness of self as subject.

The topic that we have discussed do not exhaust Kant's ideas about cognition. In particular, he had a complex, sophisticated model of representation in space and time. I have not discussed it because, unlike his claims about synthesis, unity, consciousness, etc., his views on cognition in space and time have been almost universally rejected (Kitcher 1990 and Falkenstein 1995 are excellent treatments; for my thoughts on Falkenstein, see Brook 1998). There are also some important questions about Kant. One of the more intriguing is the one raised by Dascal at the end of his chapter in this volume: Why did Kant care so little about language? It was not as though he was not exposed to sophisticated theorists about language, Herder for example. Since there is not much to be said by way of an answer to this question, I have not taken it up.

I thank Rob Stainton for his helpful comments on a draft of this chapter.

References

Anderson, J. (1983). *The Architecture of Cognition.* Cambridge, MA: Harvard University Press.
Brook, A. (1994). *Kant and the Mind.* New York: Cambridge University Press.

Brook, A. (1998) Critical Notice of L. Falkenstein, *Kant's Intuitionism: A Commentary on the Transcendental Aesthetic*, *Canadian Journal of Philosophy* (forthcoming).

Brook, A. (2004) Kant's View of the Mind and Consciousness of Self. *Stanford Electronic Encyclopedia of Philosophy*. http://plato.stanford.edu/entries/kant-mind/.

Churchland, P.S. (1986). *Neurophilosophy*. Cambridge, MA: MIT Press/Bradford Books.

Churchland, P.S. and Sejnowski, T.J. (1991). *The Computational Brain*. Cambridge, MA: MIT Press/Bradford Books.

Dennett, D. (1978). *Brainstorms*. Montgomery, VT: Bradford Books.

Dennett, D. (1991). *Consciousness Explained*. Boston: Little, Brown and Co.

Falkenstein, L. (1995). *Kant's Intuitionism: A Commentary on the Transcendental Aesthetic* Toronto: University of Toronto Press.

Flanagan, O.J. (1984). *The Science of the Mind*. Cambridge, MA: MIT Press/Bradford Books.

Fodor, J. (1983). *Modularity of Mind*. Cambridge, MA: MIT Press/Bradford Books.

James, W. (1907) *Pragmatism*. Cambridge, MA: Harvard University Press.

Kant, I. (1781/1787). *Critique of Pure Reason*. Translated by N. Kemp Smith as *Immanuel Kant's Critique of Pure Reason*. London: Macmillan, 1929.

Kant, I. (1783). *Prolegomena to Any Future Metaphysics that will be able to come Forward as a Science*. P. Carus (trans.), rev. with intro. by L.W. Beck. Indianapolis, IN: Library of the Liberal Arts.

Kant, I. (1786). *The Metaphysical Foundations of Natural Science*, J. Ellington (trans. and intro.). Indianapolis: Library of Liberal Arts, 1970

Kant, I. (1798) *Anthropology from a Pragmatic Point of View*. Mary Gregor (trans.). The Hague: Martinus Nijhoff, 1974.

Kitcher, P. (1984). Kant's real self. In A. Wood (ed.), *Self and Nature in Kant's Philosophy* (pp. 111–145). Ithaca, NY and London: Cornell University Press.

Kitcher, P. (1990). *Kant's Transcendental Psychology*. New York: Oxford University Press.

Martindale, C. (1987). Can we construct Kantian mental machines?. *The Journal of Mind and Behaviour* 8, 261–268.

Meerbote, R. (1989). Kant's functionalism. In J.-C. Smith (ed.), *Historical Foundations of Cognitive Science*. Dordrecht, Holland: Reidel.

Minsky, M. (1985). *The Society of Mind*. New York: Simon and Schuster.

Newell, A. (1973). Production systems: Models of control structures. In W.G. Chase (ed.), *Visual Information Processing*. New York: Academic Press.

Newell, A. (1990). *Unified Theories of Cognition*. Cambridge, MA: Harvard University Press.

Powell, C.T. (1990). *Kant's Theory of Self-Consciousness*. Oxford: Oxford University Press.

Sellars, W. (1968). *Science and Metaphysics*. New York: Humanities Press.

Sellars, W. (1970). "... this I or he or it (the thing) which thinks ...'. *Proceedings of the American Philosophical Association* 44, 5–31.

Shoemaker, S. (1968). Self-reference and self-awareness. *Journal of Philosophy* 65(20), 555–567.

Strawson, P.F. (1966). *The Bounds of Sense*. London: Methuen.

Treisman, A. and Gelade, G. (1980). A feature-integration theory of attention. *Cognitive Psychology* 12, 97–136.

Part II   Innovations in the Nineteenth Century

6

The Early Darwinians, Natural Selection and Cognitive Science

Don Ross

About twenty years ago, when the (then) 'new' connectionists were launching their revolt against symbol-processing approaches in artificial intelligence (AI), they promoted a particular narrative about the postwar history of cognitive science.[1] Just a few years later this narrative was picked up and amplified by the pioneers of 'artificial life' in (mainly) Santa Fe.[2] The dramatic core of the story is that cognitive science paid insufficient attention to biological considerations for about twenty years following the late 1960s, during which time a kind of Cartesian rationalism encouraged by early AI dominated the field. Since this story was told by and for revolutionary heroes, it then described the pendulum swinging back, to the point where considerations deriving from biology were taking on paramount importance in research.

This account was not false; but, like most simple narratives mainly motivated by interest in the (then) present, it involved exaggeration and foreshortening, and glossed over some important distinctions. In particular, it often obscured the difference between merely treating *biological* data as important to cognitive science – which, of course, it is – and efforts to use knowledge of *evolutionary* processes and history to constrain hypothesis formation about the nature of mind and behavior. In what follows, I will begin by recapitulating the standard story – and the one to which it reacted – and then go on to suggest a number of important nuances that render that story more accurate, and accord a set of historical figures, the first two generations of Darwinian theorists, not only the credit they are due, but credit in the right place.

---

[1] To catch this story at its moment of crystallization, see a number of the papers in Graubard (1988).
[2] See Langton (1989).

Where should the history of cognitive science begin? Plato, Aristotle, medieval philosophers, Descartes and the early empiricists and sensationalists all speculated, and often empirically studied, the nature of mind. Hume, famously, aimed at being 'the Newton of psychology', and, recognized, as did virtually all of his serious immediate successors in this enterprise, that a central question for any such science was the extent to which some behavioral responses are, to speak anachronistically, hard-wired, and the extent to which others are the products of interaction between native dispositions and changing environments. As Richards (1987) has painstakingly demonstrated, struggles with the legacy of sensationalism were a major part of the intellectual background in which Darwin found himself, and these struggles on the part of pre-Darwinian biologists such as Erasmus, Lamarck, and Cuvier were by no means as crude as popular accounts often lead one to suppose. Were these people doing cognitive science? The answer is surely 'yes'; given the issues that preoccupied them, they should not be denied the honorific merely because, for a few decades during the twentieth century, their concerns were given less relative emphasis than that placed on internal information-processing mechanisms.

Standard histories of cognitive science before the connectionist revolt, however, either tended to depict cognitive science as being born with Turing and von Neumann, or featured Hume and the sensationalists of the succeeding century as proto-behaviorists. Then these tales told of a 'cognitive revolution'[3] against prevailing behaviorist orthodoxy, the prime manifesto of which was Chomsky's famous 1959 review of Skinner's *Verbal Behavior*. This approximately coincided with the dawn of AI, which resembled Chomsky's program in linguistics in two respects, one obvious and somewhat superficial, and one that has deeper implications. The obvious parallel was that both programs posited complex, internal information-processing algorithms in place of simple associative mechanisms.[4] To whatever extent calling this a 'revolution' requires assenting to a caricature of behaviorism, few would now dispute the claim that it represented a major shift of intellectual emphasis. Although few behaviorists actually denied the reality of internal mental processes, there is no doubt that as a group they carried reluctance to

[3] This element of the story is explicit in the title of a volume of papers by major figures associated with cognitivism, including Chomsky: *Reassessing the Cognitive Revolution* (Johnson and Erneling, 1996).
[4] Of course, the standard story, being a standard story, often exaggerates the extent to which the mechanisms posited by behaviorists were necessarily simple. For a discussion of what is wrong *and* right in the general behaviorist research program, see Dennett (1978, Chapter 4).

posit particular such processes beyond what a mere commitment to Occam's Razor warranted. More interesting for present purposes, however, is the relationship between the so-called cognitive revolutionaries and the complex issue of nativism.

According to the pre-connectionist story, biological *details* ceased to be immediately relevant to cognitive science once McCulloch and Pitts (1943) provided a possibility proof that groups of neurons could compute some Turing-computable functions. Thereafter, it was the task of AI to actually produce programs that could, in fact, compute the functions that apparently, given behavioral evidence, must somehow be processed in human brains. To the extent that such programs were successful, they constituted abstract descriptions, based on so-called *functions in extension*, of the computations that biological systems evidently perform. A function in extension is simply a mapping from some objectively described input to an objectively described output, abstracting from specific details of implementation and from aspects of the information-processing path that might be internally accessible to the system itself. Describing organisms' behavioral patterns in terms of functions in extension thus leads attention away from considerations of biological plausibility. This is a point to which Marr (1982) is more sensitive than most researchers in traditional AI (henceforth, following Haugeland 1985 and many of his successors, 'GOFAI' for 'good old-fashioned artificial intelligence'). Beginning with extensionally described functions mapping contingencies to behavior put early AI researchers in the role of reverse engineers, a point that has been repeatedly emphasized by Dennett (1995 and elsewhere). Their ideal paradigm of procedure – though not, as noted above, the paradigm that was consistently respected – was made explicit by Marr. The first task of the researcher is to individuate the cognitive task that is performed; the second is to specify an algorithm whose execution would constitute computation of the function from the input constraints to the behavioral output (here is the function in extension); but the third is to write a program that computes the function in question, in plausible real time. To the extent that someone thinks that some specific consequences of our evolutionary history are crucial for computational capacities *like ours* (in some specific sense or other) one might also think that 'real time plausibility' should incorporate 'plausibility in evolutionary and other biological terms'.

In principle this research approach is agnostic on the question of nativism. A successful program, with respect to the approach described above, could simply be offered as a possibility proof where actual biological instantiation is concerned, after the fashion of the accomplishment of McCulloch and Pitts. However, there is a major difference between the two sorts of proof. Had a proof of the 1943 sort eluded us, we would remain baffled, at a *very* fundamental level, about how brains could *conceivably* work. However, once we know that brains can function as computers, we are unlikely to be impressed – at least, as cognitive scientists – by any particular abstract, extensional description of one of the brain's already established computational capacities unless we have at least *some* evidence that the constraints governing the individuation of the computational task are in fact biologically realistic. As I have noted, Marr himself, in his work on vision, is sensitive to this issue, but it can hardly be disputed that many AI researchers, particularly during the 1960s, were not. Dennett (1984) argued that this problem was the basic cause of the emergence in AI of the frame problem: that is, the problem that in the design of a program for accomplishing a task that is not restricted to a closed domain, it is fiendishly difficult for the programmer to anticipate all and exactly the information that the system should consider when faced with any specific instantiation of the task, or, more pointedly, to design a program that could generate this sensitivity to relevance on its own. Failure in this area creates programs that are said to be 'brittle': they may perform nicely within the constrained toy domains relative to which their tasks are specified, and spectacularly stupidly and inflexibly, relative to human standards, in environments which vary slightly from those imagined by their designers.

This problem relates to the issue of nativism in the following way. As Hume (1748/1977) recognized, no system to which purposes can be assigned can be entirely without native dispositions; in their absence, the system would have no wedge into any action which merits appellation of 'behavior'. But dispositions can be more or less general. The more a system is loaded with highly task-specific generalizations not malleable by learning, the more brittle it will be. In this respect, AI programs which cannot function outside of their toy domains resemble insects, a point emphasized by Hofstadter (1985), who coined the term 'sphexishness', in honor of some famous ethological studies of the sphex wasp,[5] to describe a measurement index for cognitive brittleness. Since no system can be possessed of infinite learning capacities, all cognitive systems

---

[5] The sphex displays apparently cunning behavior in preparing a paralyzed insect or spider meal for the offspring that will eventually emerge from her abandoned eggs. However, the cunning is all to evolution's credit and none to the wasp's; the slightest perturbation in normal environmental circumstances, such as a genuinely cunning ethologist's moving the paralyzed prey while the wasp inspects her nest, will set the insect into a pointless behavioral loop, which fails to be infinite only because the wasp is not.

will display *some* degree of sphexishness. Human minds, however, are the least sphexish systems of which we are aware. AI systems crippled by the frame problem, on the other hand, are as sphexish as the most cognitively humble creatures. Henceforth, I will mean here by 'innate knowledge' dispositions that are produced by sphexish reflexes rather than through the deployment of some degree of cognitive plasticity. Put another way, innate knowledge is gathered by Mother Nature, rather than by organisms themselves.

I have argued elsewhere (Ross 1995) that, while the frame problem was not GOFAI's only problem, it was its *terminal* problem. Despite the continuing existence of Lenat's heroic CYC project (Lenat and Guha 1990), which thrives on the hope that possession of a sufficiently large set of brute data will prove sufficient for something approaching the human degree of sphexishness, the research thrust in AI has undergone a clear and large-scale shift away from the idea that human designers can hope to anticipate and build into artificial systems solutions to most of the problems with which a complex environment will confront an autonomous mind. This recognition has indeed been reflected, just as the revolutionaries emphasized, in the rise of Artificial Life (AL) – attempts to construct whole artificial organisms by taking cues from nature's designs (Langton 1989; Langton, Taylor, Farmer and Rasmussen 1992) – and in the explosion of interest in connectionist and neural network models of cognition that followed the propagation by Rumelhart and McClelland et al. (1986) of a family of general learning algorithms and techniques for implementing them in simulated systems which bear at least an architectural resemblance to biological brains. Comparative discussion of these two research programs will lead into the promised reflections on the distinction between generically biologically inspired contributions to cognitive science, and more specifically *Darwinian* contributions.

Connectionist models abandon the nativism (in the sense discussed above) of conventional AI systems by severely restricting the amount of knowledge of contingent description of environmental regularities that is pre-loaded as input. The connectionist modeler sorts the data over which the system computes into more or less crude input features; generic and highly powerful learning algorithms then discover relationships among these features that permit the accomplishment of various tasks. Of course, these systems are not *tabulae rasae*; their learning rules, and the feature-sets that constitute data for them, and the foundation from which their implicit representational ontology is constructed, are innate. But this is a variety of dispositional innateness that is biologically plausible in the sense that CYC's level of innate knowledge, for example, is not. Most of the excitement generated in the 1980s by the development of multi-layer connectionist systems rested on this affinity to the biological. (Their crude architectural similarity to brains, by contrast, is of little interest because it is *so* crude.)

However, connectionist research in cognitive science has been heavily focused on two main problems, both of which tend to lead it away from, rather than toward, biological considerations as Darwin and his near-contemporaries understood them. The first is the problem of interpretation: at least in the case of connectionist systems which employ genuinely distributed representations,[6] the internal operations of the system are often opaque to descriptions at the conceptual level; in such cases, it is difficult to say just what the system has learned, beyond the ability to *somehow or other* compute the functions necessary for execution of the tasks on which it has been trained. In this sense, the accomplishments of connectionist systems are no more informative to the biologist than are those of most GOFAI systems. The second problem, and the one more relevant to present concerns, is the over-generality of standard connectionist learning rules; they are in a sense *too* powerful, in that if there *is* a projectible pattern to be found in the data, it is guaranteed that a multi-layered network using one of these rules will sooner or later find it.[7] As Clark (1987) has forcefully argued, this is *not* a plausible *general* property of brains, for reasons to which I shall return.

Superficially, connectionism appears to be a Darwinian research program, since it offers models of gradual design improvement in functional structures by an iterative, mechanical process, but in other, perhaps more important, regards, it is not a genuinely Darwinian turn in cognitive science because all the research program does, most fundamentally,

---

[6] Let us say, somewhat glibly for the sake of brevity, that a system employs distributed representations if the data it stores (where 'storage' refers to dispositions rather than hard-coded data) cannot be mapped onto the activity of particular subsets of nodes in the network. For proper discussions of the notion, see Hanson and Burr (1990) and van Gelder (1991).

[7] Malcolm Forster points out that this claim requires an important codicil: once a connectionist system finds *a* solution to a task problem, the way in which such systems are trained will prevent them from seeking more *unified* solutions (in the sense familiar to philosophers and historians of science), even if these exist. Forster's Problem, described in general terms in Forster and Sober (1994), concerns the parameters on task-individuation to which the concept of a 'solution' is necessarily relative; it is thus *not* equivalent to the problem of learning systems settling into locally minimal equilibria *given* a well-defined task-space, which was anticipated and dealt with by the pioneers of connectionism.

is (massively) extend the possibility proof of McCulloch and Pitts. McCulloch and Pitts showed that neural networks, of which biological brains are a very special instance, can compute; contemporary connectionist researchers have shown that neural networks can also learn, and have thereby helped to relieve anxieties, caused by the frame problem (and other more impressionistic hunches), to the effect that AI might be in principle impossible. (For an example of such anxieties, see Fodor 1983; for a rejoinder, see Ross 1990.) But connectionist models, like their GOFAI predecessors, are designed by foresighted engineers; brains were not. The importance of this fact about the development of the organ of intelligence, especially in the context of debates over the conceptual and substantive nature of claims about nativism, was the great preoccupation of Darwin and of his contemporary critics and supporters following the publication of the *Descent of Man, and Selection in Relation to Sex* (1871). As I shall go on to discuss, such recognition is crucial to understanding the importance of natural selection to cognitive science. Before returning to the contemporary scene, however, it is time to dip back into what this volume calls' 'the prehistory' of cognitive science.[8]

The overly simple standard story about the history of cognitive science finds a parallel in the history of evolutionary thinking. This story rightly emphasizes that the idea of natural selection was Darwin's great accomplishment, and that this idea supplanted Lamarckian ideas about the inheritance of acquired characteristics as the engine of evolution. Despite the fact that the debate between Darwinians and Lamarckians occurred in the absence of knowledge of the mechanisms of inheritance, the Darwinians won the argument for the most respectable of scientific reasons: Lamarckian theses fared poorly in the laboratory. As was established before Darwin's death, for example, mice whose tails have been cut off do not produce tailless offspring. Lamarckians attempted to minimize the significance of such experiments by arguing that changes due to *use* might be different from other acquired changes. Logically, their point was sound, but in the circumstances it constituted special pleading. By the time of Darwin's death his thesis was clearly becoming the consensus view among professional biologists – at least where sphexish dispositions were concerned.

This last qualification is one which the post-Darwinian tendency to *identify* evolutionary accounts in general with Darwinian accounts in

---

[8] The basis for my coyness about this phrase should be evident from earlier remarks. The early Darwinians, I contend, were not *pre*-cognitive scientists; they were cognitive scientists in every interesting sense of the word.

particular has often tended to miss. Lamarckianism died slowly and painfully, and the reason for this is *not* (mainly) that no crucial deciding experiments were possible before the rise of genetics, nor that Lamarckianism gave greater comfort to those who read the first book of *Genesis* literally and clung to the immutability of species. Lamarck's thesis is, after all, like Darwin's, a mechanistic and evolutionary one.[9] Leaving aside Darwin's Christian fundamentalist opponents, whose anxieties had relatively little impact on debates among nineteenth-century biologists and psychologists, the chief difficulty faced by Darwinians in winning their triumph, as convincingly argued by Richards (1987), was the difficulty in unifying evolution by natural selection with the evident human (and animal) capacity for learning of (relatively) non-sphexish behavioral dispositions.[10] This problem was independently addressed by Lloyd Morgan (1896), Osborn (1896) and Baldwin (1896a, 1896b, 1896c); the latter posthumously won the name for their idea, which is thus now known in the literature as 'the Baldwin Effect'.

Which interpretation of the Baldwin Effect is of evolutionary importance, and which interpretation of it was intended by Baldwin, are matters of controversy. Simpson (1953), who was responsible for naming 'the' effect after Baldwin, understood it in the following way. Suppose that some individuals in a population cognitively discover a fitness-enhancing behavior (a kind of process Baldwin called 'organic selection'). This can release selection pressure in favor of conspecific lineages that develop an innate disposition to this same behavior, but who might not have survived long enough to evolve it in the absence of the clever pioneers they gradually displace. By this combination of events, what began as a consequence of plasticity can later be fixed in the genome as a sphexish property; Darwinian mechanisms can thus mimic Lamarckian ones. Simpson's interpretation indeed seems to be true to Baldwin's own (Godfrey-Smith 2003a). However, the victory Simpson accorded to Baldwin was intended to be pyrrhic, since although Simpson granted that Baldwin Effects could occur, he doubted that they were of evolutionary significance. More recently, Dennett (1991, 1995)

---

[9] Lamarck even had a mechanistic hypothesis of his own that was intended to underlie his evolutionary one. See Lamarck (1809, v. 1 and 1822, v. 2).

[10] As Richards (1987) shows, Darwin's *own* most pressing problem lay in accounting for altruism, both in people and in the social insects. He overcame this difficulty by appealing to community (group) selection, an idea that was discredited for several decades in the second part of the twentieth century, but has lately made a comeback under an interpretation more careful than Darwin's (Sober and Wilson 1998). I shall say more about this below.

and Deacon (1997) popularized what each referred to as the Baldwin Effect in providing their accounts of the evolution of (respectively) intelligence and language. In fact, both Dennett's and Deacon's proposals seem to be (somewhat different) versions of what Odling-Smee and colleagues (1996, 2003) have dubbed 'niche construction'.[11] For an account of the role of niche construction in the evolution of the human mind that generalizes over both Dennett's and Deacon's suggestions, see Sterelny (2003). Niche construction emphasizes the extent to which cognitive plasticity and its consequences, especially in social species, exerts influence on the direction and rate of evolutionary change: intelligent social animals profoundly transform their environments, and thereby create new configuration of selection pressures – including new pressures for cognitive plasticity itself. Note that while Baldwin's mechanism, insofar as it actually arises, *is* an instance of cognitive plasticity influencing evolution, it acts to *reduce* plasticity in the long run.

Godfrey-Smith (2003b) denies that Dennett's version of the Baldwin Effect is *either* Baldwin's version or an instance of niche construction. On Dennett's mechanism, cognitive pioneers increase selection pressure for plasticity in conspecifics that is *biased* toward rapid mastery of what the pioneers learn incompletely and with difficulty using general learning mechanisms. This is indeed not *quite* Baldwin's interpretation, because he did not seem to appreciate the importance of the way in which the original learning modifies the selection landscape – that is, he did not hit upon the dynamic of niche construction, just as Godfrey- Smith (along with Griffiths 2003) charges. Godfrey-Smith's reason for asserting that Dennett's mechanism is not really niche construction can be dismissed.[12] However, Dennett's mechanism is closer to Baldwin's than generic niche construction is, since Dennett, like Baldwin, emphasizes genetic adaptation in the later generations for mastery of *specific* tasks,

---

[11] In light of Godfrey-Smith's (2003b) skepticism that Dennett's version of the Baldwin Effect is an instance of niche construction, this claim needs argument. I will momentarily provide some.

[12] Godfrey-Smith objects that the selection pressures on Dennett's later-generation learners were always present but 'dormant', rendering the niche construction dynamic accidental rather than necessary. Dennett (2003) rightly responds that the idea of 'dormant' selection pressures is a generally unhappy one. But, in any case, there is no evident reason why, if Godfrey-Smith's objection applied to Dennett's mechanism, it would not apply equally to niche construction processes in general. Yet Godfrey-Smith explicitly denies that his objection applies to Deacon's mechanism.

rather than for enhanced individual and/or cultural learning capacities in general.

I think we must agree with Godfrey-Smith and Griffiths that the first two generations of Darwinians, because they missed niche construction dynamics, failed to find the general process by which the evolution of intelligence most powerfully feeds back on genetic evolution in general. Nevertheless, they were heavily preoccupied with *trying* to identify such a process; it was indeed concerns with the nature of *cognition* that dominated the serious scientific debates over Darwinism in the late nineteenth and early twentieth centuries. The capacity of natural selection to explain human cognitive capacities is thus not a mere by-product of Darwinian theory: that capacity is among its chief and outstanding triumphs, even if one that was incompletely realized until recently. As Richards (1987) documents, early Darwinians saw this aspect of the project as obligatory. Some who later lost heart, such as Romanes and Wallace, stressed failure to account for cognition as the basis for their apostasy. As the lively debates among Darwin's predecessors demonstrate, little barred the way to acceptance of evolutionary theories *sui generis* except religious dogmatism, of a kind which even serious theologians of Darwin's day only rarely embraced. Many pre-Darwinians, and later anti-Darwinians, accepted that species changed, to the point where they merited being regarded as new species, under the influence of environmental pressure. What was truly world-changing about Darwin's idea of natural selection was the way in which it reframed the question of the relationship between learning by lineages and learning by individuals – that is, the relationship between phylogeny and cognition.

In fact, I suggest that while acknowledging that the early Darwinians fell short of contemporary insights, their emphasis on *local reductions* of cognitive plasticity is something contemporary cognitive science would be unwise to entirely forget. However much natural selection might favor *general* increases in cognitive plasticity under some circumstances, it will support it only up to limits. All environments, after all, include some dimensions of medium and long-run stability. Indeed, in the absence of these, selection would find no constraints to give it purchase over random drift. What will thus often tend to carry the highest fitness coefficient is plasticity *within* particular task-domains whose governing parameters do not vary. Repeated learning of invariances from one generation to another, after all, is wasteful. Why would natural selection not instead enhance the likelihood that an organism will learn particular solutions to those tasks that are both invariant and of most pressing importance for survival and reproduction? In species capable of learning by imitation, the discovery of an effective task-solution by some individual organisms may spread by cultural transmission through a subset of the rest of the population. That subset is likely to consist, statistically, of precisely those individuals who are genetically endowed with the same, or similar, task-relative plasticity as the original discoverers. This is the *aspect* of niche construction given special emphasis by Dennett, and toward which Baldwin was clearly groping.

Since the speed at which natural selection operates is many orders of magnitude slower than the pace of cultural transmission in humans, it is unlikely that what we think of as our highest cognitive abilities – the sort on which much, if not most, work in AI has concentrated, and which theorists of niche construction likewise bring to center stage – are genetically programmed. However, subtle interrelationships between general plasticity and genetic limitations are more likely to be encountered with respect to some skills we take for granted, and whose physical complexity we overlook, precisely *because* they do not require much, if any, explicit training. In Ross (1994) I argue that it should, at least initially, strike us as surprising that people do not need to learn to use standard office staplers by laborious trial and error. Why surprising? Consider the complexity of the motions involved in stapling; to quote from Ross (1994, 262–263):

> The degree of force with which the head of the stapler must be struck and the angle at which one's hand must impact it have to be calibrated extremely precisely lest one crumple the bar of the staple and impale the sheets through only one prong. Furthermore, the motion involved in the blow is not uniform; one winds up to generate a high initial velocity of impact, but eases back just at the moment of striking in order to bring fine concentration of pressure to bear on the spring in the head.

The intended suggestion here is of course not that people are born with an innate 'stapling algorithm'. The point, rather, is to raise a question. There is nothing physically less complex about the motions involved in stapling than about those involved in swinging a golf club. Nor is it true that the success criteria on the former task are looser than on the latter; most ways one could hit a stapler with a human hand lead to unequivocal failure, just as do most ways of hitting a golf ball. Yet children master the stapling task with ease, while it requires a great deal of practice to develop a reliable golf swing, and famously, for most golfers their optimum level of achievable reliability remains frustratingly low all their lives. What explains this difference? Questions of this sort were prominent for Baldwin and his contemporaries.

A robot equipped with a GOFAI-style AI program would be very unlikely to be able to move smoothly from one design of stapler to another, or to play an actual game of golf if weather conditions and the host of other relevant variables were not strictly controlled. A PDP system, given a range of input features that did not make any dynamically relevant variables invisible, would learn both algorithms, but equally laboriously in each case. Reflection on evolution, however, yields a plausible speculative answer. Our near-relatives the chimpanzees, and therefore, presumably, our near-common ancestors, regularly hammer on things with rocks in order to break them. Both force and accuracy are important: if one is attempting to crack a nutshell with a stone, it will not do to smash both the shell and the nut into pulp, which is what will happen if one does not hit the shell in the right place and with the right degree of force. This is, in its rough essentials, the same problem as that faced by the user of a stapler. Here is a case where a cognitive skill *has* plausibly been in use by our ancestral line for a long enough period that something like what Baldwin hypothesized might have occurred; in his terms, natural selection may have taken over from 'organic selection'. By contrast, it is difficult to think of any primitive skill that resembles the biologically peculiar motions that one must learn in developing a good golf swing. Of course, our ancestors have been hitting things with clubs for a great while – but not while keeping one arm straight and looking at the target only after the swing is completed. Furthermore, the ability to make par, unlike the ability to accurately hammer, is entirely unrelated to reproductive fitness. In the case of golf skills, therefore, it is highly unlikely that natural selection has specifically equipped us well; the entire load must be borne by a combination of cultural and individual learning. That is, any person interested in playing golf must learn to do so entirely, as it were, from scratch, but for the fact that, thanks to cultural transmission, she can benefit from the acquired wisdom of others who have already mastered the game.

Where natural selection has supplanted aspects of cognitive learning, so that it is appropriate to speak of innate knowledge, evolution's lack of foresight will have tended to produce solutions that a clever engineer would regard as clumsy; in contemporary computer science, these are called kludges. This is a problem for both traditional and connectionist AI. It is *especially* so in the case of connectionism, since a PDP system's highly general learning rules and highly *particular* task environment interact unpredictably. They will thus tend to produce kludges for which there is no reason to expect biological parallels, but which, because of the problem of interpretation discussed above, can neither be readily identified, nor, where they generate sphexishness in the wrong places (from the biological point of view), repaired without tearing the whole system down and starting again. As Dennett (personal correspondence) points out, connectionist researchers generally are not concerned with whether a given process of self-redesign they are modeling is best conceived of as cultural learning, learning in the individual, or learning over evolutionary time by the genome – that is, they precisely bury the distinction between the true Baldwin Effect, on one hand, and niche construction and epigenetic processes, on the other (Griffiths 2003). While I agreed with Godfrey-Smith that Dennett, in his own way, also fudges the *historical* distinction by reading an element of niche construction into Baldwin that was not there, he at least does not lose the *causal* distinction.

It is possible to lean too far in the direction of Baldwin. This is the mistake of evolutionary psychologists such as Barkow, Cosmides, and Tooby (1992), and Pinker (1997), who promote the idea that natural selection has genetically locked in *most* of the learning our hominid ancestors acquired during the Pleistocene by equipping us with task-specific and largely automatic modules cued by environmental contingencies. As a result, according to them, modern humans are generally maladapted to their current environment. While some element of modularity is likely an important part of human cognitive architecture, as I have been emphasizing, evidence falls very far short of supporting the so-called 'massive modularity' hypothesis of the evolutionary psychologists. (See Karmiloff-Smith 1994 and Griffiths 1997 for criticisms.) Essentially, their problem is exactly Baldwin's: they simply ignore niche construction, imagining that the environment as it was when our ancestors' brains grew must be the environment to which our cognitive resources passively adapted.

The probability that natural selection has partly taken over from cognitive and cultural learning with respect to some tasks but not others – i.e., that Dennett's mechanism has played a role here and there, but by no means everywhere, in our cognitive evolution – raises a discovery problem for cognitive science. There may be no general principles, but only a rich vein of self-amplifying historical accidents, that distinguish tasks for which evolution has built modules or quasi-modules from tasks for which it has not. Here, one might suppose, is an ideal domain for investigation by means of the simulations of artificial life. Unfortunately, retracing evolution's steps, in the way that AL attempts, undermines the very methodological argument in its favor if it skips too far ahead and tries to simulate late steps in long chains of evolutionary development without working through the earlier phylogenetic process- es that formed their platforms. AL researchers have therefore tended to concentrate on modeling relatively simple organisms in simple envi- ronments. In this respect they have followed Darwin's empirical focus on (for example) snails. Since the cognitive plasticity of such organisms is severely limited, so, perforce, is the relevance of such epigenetic learn- ing as they do to cognitive science. Much research in AL has shied away from cognition and moved toward the study of subcortical and direct environmental control; there are more cross-references between the AL and robotics literatures than between the AL and AI literatures.

Though Darwin himself appreciated the importance of applying his theory across the phylogenetic scale, this research impasse also resem- bles the situation in which Darwin's successors found themselves. Most nineteenth-century students of Darwin found little difficulty in accept- ing natural selection as a better explanation than Lamarckianism for the acquisition of what they called 'instincts' – that is, in our terms, genetically heritable knowledge that does not require individual learn- ing. But it was clear to Darwin from the outset that his program would fail if it could not account for the development of salient capacities that appear to be uniquely human. Language-use, was, of course, rec- ognized as one such capacity, but not the most troubling. Since Chomskian linguistics, with its emphasis on the generative capacities that are often supposed to be a specifically human endowment, had not yet appeared on the scene, nineteenth-century thinkers were often wont to view human language-use as simply a refined form of the com- municative abilities observable in many other species.[13] Instead, as Richards (1987) shows, what struck them as most mysteriously and peculiarly human was the capacity to develop and refine *moral* dispo- sitions. Two aspects of these capacities must be distinguished: the dispo- sition for altruism, and what was widely taken – usually in a decidedly Eurocentric way – to be a self-evident capacity for moral *progress*. Darwin himself discussed the first aspect extensively in *The Descent of Man* (1871), and thought that he had found a satisfactory explanation. Though he understood the importance of reciprocity, which later

---

[13] If one is persuaded by the argument given in Churchland (1995, 257–264), they were correct in this view. Another non-Chomskian option is discussed by Tomasello (2005), who argues that humans' special linguistic behavior results from special human social properties rather than special wiring for language *per se*.

became central in evolutionary game-theoretic accounts, he placed major emphasis on group selection. He recognized, from reflection on social insects, that apparently altruistic behavior was not restricted to humans; this suggested to him that the thesis that an instinct for altruism could be produced by natural selection ought not to seem astonishing. Where individual organisms depend on reciprocal cooperation for survival, individuals who are members of groups where a disposition for altruism is widespread will be favored. An individual soldier ant is obviously not better off for sacrificing himself in defense of his colony; but neither he nor his colony would have been favored by selection in the first place had not some of his ancestors had the disposition to fight for their fellows, and passed on this disposition.

As noted earlier, the idea of group selection has only recently made a partial comeback following decades in disgrace. This is not the place to repeat its history, or to explore the relationship between group selection as Darwin understood it and the more refined concept of kin selection that had to await the synthesis of evolutionary theory and twentieth-century genetics. (It should be noted, however, that Darwin *did* anticipate the importance for altruism of sexual selection.) Here, I want only to point out that a major preoccupation of contemporary biologists and ethologists was also a prime concern of Darwin and his immediate critics. More interesting in the present context are the following facts: first, Darwin's hypothesis that morality could have an instinctual basis was *much* harder for his sophisticated contemporaries to swallow than the idea that *Homo sapiens* was descended from more primitive species. As reflected in the work of such immediate post-Darwinians as Spencer, Wallace, Huxley, Romanes, and others, the group selection hypothesis was viewed as troubling for two reasons: first, it seemed to explain *away* morality, in the Platonic or Kantian senses, altogether;[14] second, it left the second aspect of morality mentioned above, assumed moral *progress*, mysterious, since the sort of progress presupposed and emphasized by (e.g.) Spencer and Wallace had occurred much too swiftly to have been produced by any sort of natural selection, group or otherwise.

The controversy over the relationship between selection and morality has not abated since Darwin's time; if anything, it has grown more

---

[14] LaCasse and Ross (1997) and Joyce (2001) argue that this applies to any account of the natural evolution of morality, and that it should be viewed as an *accomplishment*, rather than a deficit. The view of moral dispositions advanced by Hume and Adam Smith is, it should be noted, broadly consistent with Darwinism, whereas that of Kant is not. See also Binmore (1994, 1998).

heated, thanks initially to the appropriation of the issue by eugenicists with political agendas (of both left and right), and, later, as a result of the emergence of sociobiology and its critics. Our interest for present purposes lies not in the history of the controversy itself, but in its relationship to current research in cognitive science. Moral psychology has been among the most recent areas of inquiry that have been integrated into mainstream cognitive science research. Empirical studies, of the sort seriously initiated by Piaget, have concentrated on two questions: the hypothesized existence of an innate moral *sense*, which emerges through distinct ontogenetic stages, and the extent to which such an emergent moral sense carries specific and universal moral *content*. Of course, Darwin and his near-contemporaries did not have available to them the means for performing the kind of systematic research on children which comprises a large bulk of the recent literature in moral psychology; they were generally limited to reflecting on anecdotal observation of the particular children with whom they were acquainted, usually their own. However, any hypothesis about the ontogeny of moral development derived from experiment must wrestle with the theoretical constraints imposed by evolutionary theory. The shelves are lately heavy of such theoretical exercises, many of them carefully informed both by biology and its intellectual history.[15] I will content myself here with the observation that, given the intensity attached to these issues by nineteenth-century psycho-biologists, wheels are bound to be laboriously reinvented by anyone who does not carefully study the vintage literature.

To urge, as I have done, that contemporary researchers in cognitive science are better off to the extent that they familiarize themselves with the work of Darwin and his immediate successors will hardly land as a bombshell; that evolutionary influences are becoming increasingly powerful in cognitive science is obvious to anyone who examines the relevant book catalogs; and the claim that researchers in any field ought, *ceteris paribus*, to know the history of their discipline is a truism. I have tried in this essay to say a bit more than that, however. First, the deep integration of psychology and biology that constitutes contemporary cognitive science was much tighter in Darwin's time than it was between the early part of the previous century, when the simultaneous rise of experimental psychology and classical genetics drove the disciplines apart for a time, and the very recent past. Second, the mere incorporation of biological plausibility constraints into cognitive science, as

---

[15] For one of the best, see Joyce (2006).

reflected in the growth of connectionist and AL research, does not necessarily, and often does not in fact, truly return us to the deep level of integration to which we should aspire. The extent to which we can come to understand human cognition is, I claim, almost equivalent to the extent to which we can come to understand its evolutionary etiology. I naturally regard it as a happy thing that this view seems to be spreading in the discipline, but I cannot agree with the opinion sometimes encountered that the most impressive advances in understanding the origins of our minds are a product of our own generation. Darwin was not the greatest evolutionary thinker because he was the first; after all, though he was the former he *was not* the latter. If I am right in maintaining that explaining cognition is virtually the same enterprise as understanding its etiology, then we should leave no scrap of Darwin's intellectual legacy unexamined, nor blush at the boldness of calling him the greatest of cognitive scientists.[16]

References

Baldwin, J.M. (1896a). Consciousness and evolution. *Psychological Review* 3: 300–308.
Baldwin, J.M. (1896b). On criticisms of organic selection. *Science* 4: 727.
Baldwin, J.M. (1896c). A new factor in evolution. *American Naturalist* 30: 441–451; 536–553.
Barkow, J., Cosmides, L., and Tooby, J. (eds) (1992). *The Adapted Mind.* New York: Oxford University Press.
Binmore, K. (1994). *Game Theory and the Social Contract Volume One: Playing Fair.* Cambridge, MA: MIT Press.
Binmore, K. (1998). *Game Theory and the Social Contract Volume Two: Just Playing.* Cambridge, MA: MIT Press.
Chomsky, N. (1959). Review of B.F. Skinner, *Verbal Behavior. Language* 35: 26–58.
Churchland, P.M. (1995). *The Engine of Reason, the Seat of the Soul.* Cambridge, MA: MIT Press/Bradford.
Clark, A. (1987). The kludge in the machine. *Mind and Language* 2: 277–299.
Darwin, C. (1871). *The Descent of Man, and Selection in Relation to Sex* (2 volumes). London: Murray.
Deacon, T. (1997). *The Symbolic Species.* New York: Norton.
Dennett, D. (1978). *Brainstorms.* Montgomery, VT: Bradford Books.
Dennett, D. (1984). Cognitive wheels: The frame problem of AI. In C. Hookway (ed.), *Minds, Machines and Evolution.*Cambridge, UK: Cambridge University Press, pp. 129–151.
Dennett, D. (1991). *Consciousness Explained.* Boston: Little Brown.

[16] I would like to thank Andy Brook, Dan Dennett, Malcolm Forster, and a seminar audience at the Université du Québec à Montréal for their comments on earlier drafts of this chapter.

156   *The Prehistory of Cognitive Science*

Dennett, D. (1995). *Darwin's Dangerous Idea*. New York: Simon and Schuster.
Dennett, D. (2003). The Baldwin Effect: A crane, not a skyhook. In B. Weber and D. Depew (eds), *Evolution and Learning*. Cambridge, MA: MIT Press, pp. 69–79.
Fodor, J. (1983). *The Modularity of Mind*. Cambridge, MA: MIT Press/Bradford.
Forster, M. and Sober, E. (1994). How to tell when simpler, more unified or less ad hoc theories will provide more accurate predictions. *British Journal for the Philosophy of Science* 45:1–35.
Godfrey-Smith, P. (2003a). Between Baldwin skepticism and Baldwin boosterism. In B. Weber and D. Depew (eds), *Evolution and Learning*. Cambridge, MA: MIT Press, pp. 53–67.
Godfrey-Smith (2003b). Postscript on the Baldwin Effect and niche construction. In B. Weber and D. Depew (eds), *Evolution and Learning*. Cambridge, MA: MIT Press, pp. 107–108.
Graubard, S. (ed.) (1988). *The Artificial Intelligence Debate*. Cambridge, MA: MIT Press.
Griffiths, P. (1997). *What Emotions Really Are*. Chicago: University of Chicago Press.
Griffiths, P. (2003). Beyond the Baldwin Effect: James Mark Baldwin's "social heredity", epigenetic inheritance, and niche construction. In B. Weber and D. Depew (eds), *Evolution and Learning*. Cambridge, MA: MIT Press, pp. 193–215.
Hanson, S., and Burr, D. (1990). What connectionist models learn: Learning and representation in connectionist networks. *Behavioral and Brain Sciences* 13:471–518.
Haugeland, J. (1985). *Artificial Intelligence: The Very Idea*. Cambridge, MA: MIT Press/Bradford.
Hofstadter, D. (1985). On the seeming paradox of mechanizing creativity. In Hofstadter, *Metamagical Themas*. New York: Basic Books, pp. 526–546.
Hume, D. (1748/1977). *An Enquiry Concerning Human Understanding*. Indianapolis: Hackett.
Johnson, D. and Erneling, C. (1996) (eds), *Reassessing the Cognitive Revolution*. Oxford: Oxford University Press.
Joyce, R. (2001). *The Myth of Morality*. Cambridge: Cambridge University Press.
Joyce, R. (2006). *The Evolution of Morality*. Cambridge, MA: MIT Press.
Karmiloff-Smith, A. (1994). *Beyond Modularity*. Cambridge, MA: MIT Press.
LaCasse, C. and Ross, D. (1997). Morality's last chance. In P. Danielson (ed.), *Modelling Rational and Moral Agents*. New York: Oxford University Press, pp. 340–375.
Lamarck, J-B. de (1809). *Philosophie zoologique* (2 volumes). Paris: Dentu.
Lamarck, J-B. de (1822). *Histoire des animaux sans vertèbres* (7 volumes). Paris: Verdiere.
Langton, C. (ed.) (1989). *Artificial Life*. Redwood City, CA: Addison-Wesley.
Langton, C., Taylor, C., Farmer, J.D. and Rasmussen, S. (eds) (1992). *Artificial Life II*. Redwood City, CA: Addison-Wesley.
Lenat, D. and Guha, R. (1990). *Building large knowledge-based systems: Representation and inference in the CYC project*. Reading, MA: Addison-Wesley.
Marr, D. (1982). *Vision*. San Francisco: Freemont.
McCulloch, W. and Pitts, W. (1943). A logical calculus of ideas immanent in nervous activity. *Bulletin of Mathematical Biophysics* 5: 115–123.
Morgan, C.L. (1896). *Habit and Instinct*. London: Arnold.

Odling-Smee, F.J., Laland, K. and Feldman, F. (1996). Niche construction. *American Naturalist* 147: 641–648.

Odling-Smee, F.J., Laland, K. and Feldman, F. (2003). *Niche Construction: The Neglected Process in Evolution*. Princeton: Princeton University Press.

Osborn, H. (1896). A mode of evolution requiring neither natural selection nor the inheritance of acquired characteristics. *Transactions of the New York Academy of Science* 15: 141–148.

Pinker, S. (1997). *How the Mind Works*. New York: Norton.

Richards, R. (1987). *Darwin and the Emergence of Evolutionary Theories of Mind and Behavior*. Chicago: Chicago University Press.

Ross, D. (1990). Against positing central systems in the mind. *Philosophy of Science* 57: 297–312.

Ross, D. (1994). Instrumental realism and the idea of embodied knowledge. *Research in Philosophy and Technology* 14: 251–269.

Ross, D. (1995). *I nuovi percorsi dell'inlligenza artificiale*. Naples: Edizione Scientifiche Italiane.

Rumelhart, D., McClelland, J. and the PDP Research Group (eds) (1986). *Parallel Distributed Processing: Explorations in the Microstructure of Cognition* (2 volumes). Cambridge, MA: MIT Press/Bradford.

Simpson, G. (1953). The Baldwin Effect. *Evolution* 7: 110–117.

Sober, E. and Wilson, D. (1998). *Unto Others*. Cambridge, MA: Harvard University Press.

Sterelny, K. (2003). *Thought in a Hostile World*. Oxford: Blackwell.

Tomasello, M. (2005). Beyond formalities: The case of language acquisition. *The Linguistic Review* 22: 183–197.

van Gelder, T. (1991). What is the "D" in "PDP"? A survey of the concept of distribution. In W. Ramsey, S. Stich and D. Rumelhart (eds), *Philosophy and Connectionist Theory*. Hillsdale, New Jersey: Lawrence Erlbaum.

7

Wundt's Theoretical Psychology: An Unknown Legacy from a Gilded Age

Arthur L. Blumenthal

Historical prologue

The end of the nineteenth century was a time of glittering cultural, industrial, educational, and scientific growth. An emerging Germany was aglow with its new political unity and was flushed with pride, wealth, and expansion after the victory in the Franco-Prussian war. It was also at its highest historical position of dominance in science and education. Scholars from around the world were flocking to German universities to become certified in their professions and to receive the best scientific and academic jobs when returning home. Industrialization had come late to Germany, but when it hit, it expanded with a speed unmatched elsewhere. It was an age of the machine and of new technologies which influenced many patterns of thought. It was also a high age of philosophy – after approximately two centuries of leading philosophical developments in German-dominated Continental philosophy, German philosophers seemed at a critical crossroad, approaching an explosion of long-smoldering conflicts.

This was the context in which a reputedly new academic discipline emerged – the so-called 'new' psychology which was associated with Wilhelm Wundt's opening of a Psychological Institute in the philosophy department at Leipzig University. That institute included the first formally recognized effort to establish experimental psychology, and it rode the crest of the wave of prosperity in Wundt's time and place to become for a while a dominant force in psychological work and thought worldwide. There were, of course, many antecedents to this development, including preceding trends in the German philosophical literature that pointed in this direction, and also some successful earlier efforts in experimental psychology such as Fechner's psychophysics, Donders's reaction-time research, and earlier experimental work on psychological processes by Wundt himself.

The tentative first edition of Wundt's *Grundzüge der physiologishe Psychologie* (*Principles of Physiological Psychology*) appeared in 1874–1875, generating immediate international interest and enthusiasm. His use of the term 'physiological' in that title was a local parochial usage that most textbook writers have lost sight of today. Here that word actually indicated 'experimental', for the new psychology was to be based on the model of the recently successful development of physiology as an experimental science. Thus the new psychology was adapting the instrumentation of the physiology laboratory for the study of mental processes. Wundt's psychological system was clearly not a system of physiological psychology in the modern American sense of that phrase.

Though he had a background of training in physiology from his years of work as an assistant in Hermann Helmholtz's laboratory in Heidelberg, Wundt's arrival at Leipzig in 1875 signaled his acceptance as a philosopher. Later American accounts of the history of modern psychology would describe it as a breaking away from philosophy. For Wundt, however, it was seen as a breaking away from physiology in the form of the discovery of a different level of natural phenomena. He was thoroughly rooted in classical German idealist philosophy, which was a strong influence in shaping these views and in shaping his general psychological theory. He soon applied that theory to his in-depth interdisciplinary involvements in several fields (linguistics, logic, cultural studies, ethics, and more). And he still retains the distinction of having written more than any other psychologist alive or dead.

The growth of Wundt's Psychology Institute reflected the prosperity of the city and state that supported it. Just after the turn of the century it grew into a multistoried affair with subdirectors in charge of separate divisions devoted to research in psychophysics, emotion, psycholinguistics, perception, development and pedagogics, and cultural studies. It was elaborately equipped with the best of the scientific instrumentation of that day. All of this, however, was brought to a sharp halt by two events. One was the onset of World War I, which depopulated the institute and crippled it economically. The other, which appeared at about the same time, was the rise of 'antipsychologism' in German universities, primarily in philosophy departments. It was associated with new positivistic and materialist trends, and it worked against the career advancement of Wundt's students. In the depths of Germany's economic collapse after the War, Wundt's large private library and paper collection were sold to a university in Japan, where they remain today.

The institutional and academic–political record of those events has been well documented in a doctoral dissertation by D.K. Robinson (1987). The controversies swirling around the issue of psychologism, with Wundt on center stage, has been documented in detail in a recent book by M. Kusch (1995).

Wundt's historically significant *Principles* in two volumes later expanded to three, which never appeared in English translation except for Edward Titchener's rendering of a short segment of the opening chapters that focused on subjects entirely preliminary to the core of Wundtian psychological theory. But those volumes and many more of Wundt's writings were translated into Italian, Spanish, and Russian. After the Bolshevik Revolution, the Russian translations were largely suppressed or ignored.

In the English-speaking world the seldom and poorly translated state of Wundt's many books and journal articles has often discouraged authors of modern textbooks, leading to a hasty dismissal of Wundt. With little analysis of his theoretical system nor of its historical and cultural context, this reputed founding father of modern psychology became the source of myths and antagonisms that served as the springboard for later justifications of other systems and schools of thought. That a pattern of myth-creation arises in this situation might be natural, especially for something that is little understood or little approved of in the context of other intellectual traditions that were opposed to or competing with the Wundtian academic empire.

In spite of its large mass and its many satellites, Wundtian psychology fell into a fatal eclipse soon after Wundt's death in 1920 at the end of his unusually long career (sixty years). The subsequent fadeout of his name from intellectual history occurred amidst the chaos, tragedies, and flames that spanned the outbreak of World War I to the end of World War II, which was also a period of radically shifting trends in intellectual history, especially in psychology.

Wundt's system of thought is understandable enough, whether one endorses it or not. When it is examined in a dispassionate way, in its original sources, with a serious effort at understanding, it remains fairly redundant across the many years and the many applications it served. All Wundt's works in psychology and in his psychologically oriented approach to linguistics, philosophy, ethics, and logic employed the same core psychological principles. Unfortunately, a number of powerful historical myths, resolutely kept alive by present-day textbook writers, still stand in the way of an accurate examination of Wundt's theory. In order to describe that theory properly, we need to face two of the most entrenched myths: (1) that Wundt was the father of an introspectionist school of psychology, and (2) that Wundt's psychology was atomistic, and by analogy to chemistry, that it compounded mental structures from sensory elements. Both of those statements are blatantly false, but they have formed exceptionally good stories for later textbook writers who have developed them as reasons for new turns in psychology that appeared in the early twentieth century.

Wundt's opposition to introspectionism

Wundt was likely history's most vocal campaigner against classical armchair introspection in psychology. In his earlier days that approach to psychology was referred to as 'reflection psychology', i.e., reflecting on one's private inner experience. For a few of the many examples of Wundt's refutations of introspectionism, see Wundt (1882, 1883, 1888, 1893, 1900a, and 1907a). In a reaction going against Titchener, who was an advocate of the use of introspection as a source of psychological data, Wundt directed the following sharp barb specifically at him in 1900a:

> Introspective method [*introspektive Methode*] relies either on arbitrary observations that go astray or on a withdrawal to a lonely sitting room where it becomes lost in self-absorption. The unreliability of this method is today rather universally recognized. (Wundt, 1900a, p. 180)

That comment appeared after approximately twenty years of Wundtian polemics and ridicule directed at introspectionism.

One source of the misinterpretation of Wundt as an introspectionist came from the flawed translation into English of his shorter and philosophical *Outlines of Psychology* in which the translator (C.H. Judd) used the word 'introspection' in a loose and contradictory way. See Danziger (1990) for the most complete analysis to date of the misinterpretation of Wundt as an introspectionist.

As must be emphasized, Wundt had initially offered his new psychology in opposition to the old reflection psychology, opposing the old introspection with a new method of scientific observations of humans (*Selbstbeobachtung*) which he considered to be scientific because it used objective procedures that were controllable and replicable. These were initially the methods of psychophysics and of reaction-time measurement that emerged in the 1860s. Other laboratory procedures appeared later, especially those involving the early polygraph-style apparatus for the study of emotional reactions. And Wundt's experiments always involved more than one individual – at least one for the manipulation of apparatus and the taking of measurements and another to respond to stimuli.

It is easy to translate *Selbstbeobachtung* simply as 'introspection', without studying how these terms were used or what their users said they meant by them in the late nineteenth century.

Wundt's opposition to classical elementistic psychology

In many modern introductory textbooks, Wundt's psychology is briefly dismissed as a system of mental elements based on an analogy with chemistry. In approximately the first half of Wundt's awkwardly translated *Outlines of Psychology*, we find his concern with the analysis of the qualia of immediate experience and with an effort to dimensionalize many of the qualitative variations of human experience. Upon closer reading of the original, however, we find that in Wundt's view any proposed elemental qualia are only theoretical abstractions and can never, he argued, be observed in isolation. Experience in his system is always a unified irreducible construct or configuration – a creative synthesis of emergent qualities. His first theoretical principle was this holistic creative synthesis (*schöpferische Synthese*) notion, which was at the center of his earliest efforts at psychological theory in 1862 and remained there until his death in 1920.

In a 1914 translation of a history of psychology text by Otto Klemm, one of Wundt's prominent students, we can find Wundt's expression of his more complex approach to notions of elemental experiential qualities: 'The psychological elementism concepts ought not to be compared with the analysis of matter into atoms, but rather with the analysis of a movement into components or into the momentary velocities of a moving point' (quoted in Klemm 1914). This more complex Wundtian view reflects a very motion-oriented process, or at least a motion model, which underlies his system. The motion that was involved was, of course, that of the stream of consciousness.

Any system can develop from an analysis of the simple to the complicated without being an elementistic theory. In overlooking that caution one could confuse method and phenomena. A superficial reading, or a reading of an isolated section of Wundt's works, could lead to that interpretation, as it apparently has. But whoever attributes that approach to Wundt as his basic orientation has not read him well. Wundt developed his scientific views of mental processes in reaction against the true elementistic psychology of his time and place, namely the system of Herbart that was dominant in Wundt's early days in Germany, and which Wundt argued against throughout his career. This argument accompanied moves into other disciplines in which he was operating as an anti-Herbartian. It can be seen especially well in his writings on psycholinguistics and on cultural studies.

The case of Wundtian psycholinguistics is most instructive. Late nineteenth century linguistics research was often dominated by the German linguist Hermann Paul who applied Herbartian elementistic models to the analysis of language structure. This was a highly taxonomic approach which emphasized the sequencing or chaining of the smaller phonemic or, sometimes, word units of language. Drawing on a distinctly different orientation from his background in idealist philosophy, particularly from some of the earlier speculations about language by Wilhelm von Humboldt, Wundt attempted to foment a revolution in linguistic thought to overthrow the entire Herbartian taxonomic orientation. To do that Wundt focused on the syntactic or grammatical level of language. He was once widely credited as being the first to use tree-diagrams for analyzing sentence structure. His point was that sentences, and the momentary holistic mental impressions that they represent, are the fundamental 'units' of language. And further, that sentences reflect creative syntheses that can vary infinitely in their form. Any smaller units, such as words, have meaning only to the degree that they are embedded in or related to some expressed or implied sentence. Even the meaning of the sentence may be determined by some greater psychological context in which it is embedded. Great debates raged in the turn-of-the-century linguistics literature between the linguists who followed Paul and those who followed Wundt. For a summary of that whole episode, including its major players and the more prominent research, see Blumenthal (1970). For a summary of similar theoretical developments in Wundt's later expansion into the broader area of cultural psychology (*Völkerpsychologie*) see C. Schneider (1990).

In English-speaking countries, the received literature of an elementistic associationism came from the British Empiricist philosophers. German adherents to that orientation, however, largely read and followed Herbart's highly mechanistic and atomistic version of associationism. Wundt steadfastly adopted the name of 'Voluntarism' for his school of thought to emphasize his concentration on central control processes that were not given as much depth in Herbart's system. Voluntarism or 'the psychology of the Will', was much alive at that time in certain wings of German philosophy, the writings of Schopenhauer being a prominent example. Though Wundt participated in the spirit of that trend, he found most of it, such as Schopenhauer's writings, to be entirely too mystical. Many modern American textbooks have erroneously referred to Wundt's system as being titled 'structuralism' which, on the contrary, is the name that the Englishman Titchener was using for his quite different school of British Empiricism at Cornell. Titchener, who was extremely influential in early American psychology, had spent two years in Leipzig to earn his doctorate in psychology because no such degree was offered at that time in his native England.

At an early date in his career Wundt had concluded that the prevalent mechanistic and associationist theories in psychology lacked an adequate conception of a central control process. And because of that they did not, he felt, distinguish between automatic and controlled behaviors – a critical distinction in Wundt's growing body of theory. It was a distinction that was beginning to show, he believed, in his earliest psychological data derived from reaction-time research. Volition in his system is synonymous with 'selective attention' for which he also used the old Leibnizian term 'apperception.' It referred to the attentional focus whether in memory, perception, thought, motor control, or any other psychological process. The creative synthesis phenomena were also found to be a capacity of central focal attention. This was all presented in refutation of Herbart's mental chemistry or elementism, which Wundt ridiculed as having no more theoretical sophistication for psychology than the model of a billiard table on which the balls (elements) are rolling around and colliding with one another.

The following statement is repeated in numerous forms throughout Wundt's works:

> There are absolutely no psychological structures that can be characterized in their meaning or in the value of their contents as the sum of their elemental factors or the mere mechanical results of their components. (*Logik* III, 1908, p. 276)

The leading Herbartian in experimental psychology, in Wundt's time, was G. E. Müller at Gottingen, who developed a high-precision style of laboratory psychology and who made the greater contributions to research procedure and apparatus design, but who had less enthusiasm for theory construction, at least the type of theory coming from Wundt's hands. Though inspired by Herbartian associationist theory, which was not based on experimentation, Müller definitely represented the experimentalist, *par excellence*, whereas Wundt was the theorist, *par excellence*. In contrast to Wundt, Müller was also an arch-materialist and in his hands psychology was often being folded back into physiology. Although he made significant methodological contributions to psychophysics, paired-associate learning, and sensory studies, Müller may have received less attention in history texts because he had far fewer students than Wundt had, the reason being that he subjected students to the same exacting standards that were applied to his careful design of apparatus. It was extremely difficult to meet Müller's very strict requirements when applying to study with him, and those who were accepted rarely produced work that he approved of. Wundt, however, admitted seemingly anyone who wanted to study at his institute regardless of their background. For a summary of Müller's life and works see E. Haupt (2000).

Wundt's science of consciousness

The source of the above myths about Wundt as introspectionist and elementalist can often be located in reactions against, and negative interpretations of, his commitment to constructing a science of consciousness, or at least to the particular shape that science took in his hands. His evolving theory was built around notions of purposivism, emotion qualities, and goal-oriented action, and it expressed his long-argued opposition to another trend of thought that grew dominant near the end of his life, helping to bring about the eclipse of his psychological system. That thoroughly anti-Wundtian trend was philosophical materialism.

Here is Wundt's statement on the matter, a statement that appears repeatedly in his works. It reflects a view that he seemed even more dedicated to upholding than the opposition to atomistic associationism:

Matter is a hypothetical conception which we ourselves, impelled by the relative constancy of some impressions and by logical forms of thought, have manufactured. To suppose that this hypothetical substrate which we have constructed among other of our ideas can exert any influence on those other ideas or on our thoughts in general ... is perfectly absurd. It is a supposition that could arise only as a result of first transforming a product of conceptual thought into a being independent of thought, and then, to complete the absurdity, to regard mental activity itself as a phenomenon similar to its own product. (1897, p. 46)

And again in another work we read as follows:

> Substance is a surplus metaphysical notion for which psychology has no use. And this accords with the fundamental character of mental life, which I would always have you keep in mind: It does not consist in the connection of unalterable objects and various states. In all its phases it is process and is active rather than a passive existence, a development [*Entwicklung*] rather than a fixed condition. The understanding of the basic laws of this process is the primary goal of psychology. (1892, p. 495)

If we accept psychology's traditional definition as the study of consciousness, as Wundt did, then how would the research psychologist proceed? Wundt began with his 'actuality principle' which is the statement that we take consciousness to be a natural process – a basic immediate reality and not some mystical or spiritual notion. Instead we have the simple natural observations of consciousness in the alternations between sleep and wakefulness, in measurable lapses of attention, or in other fluctuations that, as Wundt's laboratory was designed to show, could be manipulated and measured with some precision. His first psychological experiment in the 1860s concerned the measurable temporal alternations of consciousness when someone tries to attend to two stimuli at once. A long tradition of reaction-time research developed from those early tests. Indeed they have continued into the cognitive psychology of the present day as, for example, in the dichotic listening experiments or in the form of other Wundt-style research as found in M. Posner's *Chronometric Explorations of Mind* (1978).

To deny psychology its traditional subject matter, consciousness, would for Wundt be like denying other scientists their subject matters, such as denying the existence of stars and planets in astronomy. To say that there is no phenomenon to be studied here, or that what we call consciousness can be spoken of only in terms of the physics and chemistry of the brain, or of the behavioral actions among organisms and environmental objects, would, to Wundt, simply mean that there can be no psychology – because then there is only physics, chemistry, biology, and zoology. The scientific approach to Wundt's subject matter was, again, opened up by the discovery of reaction-time methodologies and also by psychophysics methodology in the form of quantitative analyses of systematic discriminative reactions to events and energies.

Views about the reality of consciousness close to Wundt's were expressed well by George Miller a century later in 1981 in his review of trends in American cognitive psychology. Miller and Wundt both argue that all moving living creatures must be conscious because their motility reveals it especially in their patterns of safe navigation. Any number of behavioral indications, in the view of these theorists, reflect the existence of consciousness. If all moving life forms are conscious, then automatized processes, or complex unconscious controls, are the result of a progressive development that occurs as organisms become more complex. That is, all mental/behavioral capacities in the Wundt–Miller view had originally required awareness. Through repeated use most behaviors become automatized.

What most characteristically distinguishes Wundt's theory, however, is its emphasis on one aspect that he held as the principle form and basis of consciousness – namely, impulse, desire, or urge. The German word was *Trieb*, a term that became synonymous with Wundtian psychology, at least among many Continental writers, if not among Anglo-American reviewers of the field. In Wundt's usage that term did not carry the connotation of instinct that is sometimes assigned to it. It had, in his usage, a more emotion-like and less mechanistic connotation.

Concerning Cartesian dualism

Wundt combated Cartesian mind-body dualism in several ways. Consciousness and the brain, as he always argued, must be viewed as being two sides of the same coin – parallel views of one unity. Descartes, he thought, had been seduced by mystical variations of materialism. These views are widely found in those chapters in the *Principles* or *Outlines*, or *Essays*, in which he summarizes intellectual history as it bears on forms of psychological theory. He also argues that consciousness can never be described as a stage upon which certain events play for a while and then retire to some place off-stage only to be called back for a later reappearance. The process of consciousness is an always evolving, never repeating, stream. Memory is only a new construction that is attributed to the past, but logically can never be a revival of a bit of the past which no longer exists. The rate and capacity of that flow can, however, be measured – which was the major direction of the early laboratory. The particular dimensions or qualia of the process up to and including the variations of emotion were studied, again, with techniques of psychophysics and early approximations to multidimensional scaling.

When something is left behind subsequent to an image, emotion, or thought, then the only thing that we can logically speak of as being left behind is some hypothetical change in our conceptualized nervous system. And, argues Wundt, although we may discuss those changes in the language of neurology or chemistry, we will never find consciousness in them through chemical or physiological observations. To say that we could eventually see the emotional quality of pain by looking through a microscope at a piece of nervous tissue was, for Wundt, a thing of nonsense that he apparently could not abide. It was also a violation of logic, for him, to speak of bits of consciousness floating around somewhere that are not within the set we define as immediate awareness.

In developing a description of the operating characteristics of immediate awareness from laboratory observations and measurements, Wundt adopted a field-theory language, which can be glimpsed in a rare English rendering in his one, and very brief, pop-psychology writing – *An Introduction to Psychology* (1911). The greater field of awareness was seen as holding within it a narrow bottleneck of a small field of focal attention. The greater outer field was the short-term memory periphery of awareness which has a very large, though brief, information-holding capacity thoroughly measured over the many years of activity in the Leipzig laboratory. It was found to be largely a passive temporal delay of the flux of impressions, memories, and feelings. The central focus, however, was found to be the seat of voluntary control and was describable as flexible in how it moves through the field and in how it can group small impressions into one larger unified object (or the act of chunking to use a contemporary term). The attentional focus can also narrow down on the smallest of impressions and move in various ways to capture parts of the greater flux of momentary impressions. All of that applies to the control of motor behavior just as to perceptual or memory impressions. It was the study of the time constraints on the movements and actions of selective attention that was the target of the long program of reaction-time research, largely the study of processes of voluntary and involuntary decision and choice. For further examples and references see Blumenthal (1977).

Wundt's 'actuality principle' also reflects his strong opposition to classical faculty psychology because he describes consciousness as one basic process. In that view our references to perception, recognition, memory, thinking, or daydreaming only refer to different slants on one and the same process. Its operating characteristics were found to be the same in all these actions. They all involve the same bottleneck of central selective attention. They are all limited by the same central reaction times. They all exhibit the same limitations in capacity (short-term memory spans/perceptual spans of six or seven chunks – Wundt 1910).

They are all equally under the same temporal constraints of short-term memory. They are all influenced in the same way by affective-motivational states. They all reflect the same emergent phenomena associated with the holistic nature of mental events in which the whole is always more than the sum of the parts. Associative phenomena (which Wundt saw as affecting only peripheral aspects of consciousness) behave the same way in all forms of consciousness. And in the study of development all forms of consciousness reflect the same patterns of growth.

An elaborate technical literature

Wundt's relatively shorter *Outlines of Psychology* does not give a good picture, or even much of a picture at all, of the experimental psychology of his time. For that you must dig rather deeply into his three-volume *Grundzüge*, massive in technical detail and also packed with philosophy and intellectual history. For a sample of Leipzig experimentalism, one would likely fair better by examining the volumes on experimental work written by those who remained close to Wundt as primary assistants in the Leipzig laboratory. Wilhelm Wirth was in that role longer than any other, being active in experimental work there at least for seventeen years. See Wirth's *Die Experimentelle Analyse der Bewusstseinsphänomene* (*Experimental Analysis of the Phenomena of Consciousness*), 1908; or see Lehmann's *Die körperlichen Äusserungen psychischer Zustände* (*The Bodily Expressions of Psychological States*), 1899, which concentrates on emotional phenomena.

Wundt's early 1860s studies of the timing of the fluctuations of consciousness when a person attempts to attend to two stimuli simultaneously had by the end of the century generated an elaborate production of laboratory apparatus for controlling all sorts of stimulus presentations and for measuring the time and intensity of the most delicate reactions. Many of those now strange-appearing devices, from the pre-electronic age, can still be found in exhibits of historical scientific instruments. They have become much sought-after collectors' items today among avid antiquarians. They were first displayed to the American public at the 1893 World's Fair in Chicago when Wundt's student Hugo Münsterberg brought them there in the form of a large exhibit. Included were all manner of tachistoscopes, voice keys, physiological reaction sensors, delicate mechanical devices for presenting all forms of stimulation, and all conceivable manner of time recording devices, which apparently recorded all sorts of reaction times in milliseconds as effectively as does our contemporary electronic instrumentation. But the early apparatus required that a mechanic, with the skill of a watchmaker, be on the premises constantly to keep the innumerable springs and gears oiled, adjusted, and running properly. They all contributed to the discoveries of temporal constants in the operation of focal attention, namely that in its integrative and dynamic actions it is limited to approximately 1/10th of a second reaction times, or that short-term sensory storage of large amounts of information in the periphery of consciousness has a brief duration around 3/4 to one second. Short-term memory, when properly controlled and measured, has an apparent decay rate of around 10 to 20 seconds.

A more accessible English-language view of these findings and the technology underlying them is available because of the American psychologist R.S. Woodworth. The story begins with the work of the American philosopher–psychologist G.T. Ladd who in 1887 attempted to imitate Wundt with the publication of his own *Elements of Physiological Psychology*. Ladd was not, however, sophisticated in the new experimentalism in this field. In 1911, Woodworth revised and updated Ladd's book and added to it better coverage of the now-large body of experimental findings in the field, still largely Wundtian. He continued to upgrade the coverage of the field in the form of large mimeographed manuscripts that were distributed to his students. These were finally published in 1938 as his famous *Experimental Psychology*, considered to be a classic in twentieth-century psychology. A close examination of the context of the book, even its reference list, shows it still to be heavily based on the outline of the Leipzig experimentalists, although by 1938 Wundt's prestige had lapsed and Woodworth apparently pulled away from any identification with Wundt. The book does, however, give some help in picturing the style of the Leipzig laboratory, even though much of the Wundtian theory is missing.

The central control process

To say in the simplest terms why Wundt pressed forward endlessly in his anti-mechanist campaign, we may explain in the fewest words that it was because psychological theories based on models from classical mechanics were not, for Wundt, at all sophisticated in their treatment of desire, feeling, urge, motivation, nor self-control. And those topics took a central place in his theoretical system.

As early as 1858 when the young Wundt was involved in medical and physiological research, he was arguing that there are phenomena in biology and psychology that require types of explanation which differ fundamentally from the pattern of explanation found in physics and chemistry – the former, he argued, had to involve notions of purposivism and goal-oriented actions. At the time when his history-making laboratory was just getting underway at Leipzig he wrote, 'The course of both general and individual development shows that desires or urges (*Triebe*) are the fundamental psychological phenomena from which all mental processes originate' (1880, II, p. 455).

Urge or desire is the primitive state of the volitional process in this system. The notion of 'volition' is not employed here in the sense of 'free will' but rather refers to actions that are under the control of a system of emotional tones, impulses, and automatizations that channel the flow of experience and behavior. When we talk about a central control process in human consciousness we cannot, argued Wundt, mean the same process that occurs in primitive animal life. It must be, rather, that elemental impulses and urges constitute the initial control. As the process evolves in higher life forms, it surely must expand and differentiate. More complex forms of urge, desire, and impulse must arise. It makes sense, Wundt argues, to conjecture that impulses and urges at least become more numerous as life evolves, with complex organisms having more to their central control process, which means that it may involve the simultaneous presence of several urges at once – and so the act of this inner emotional control of behavior must be considerably complicated by multiple and often competing drive states. With the appearance of more highly evolved nervous systems, says Wundt, we have conscious deliberation, decision, and choice influencing the predominance of one volitional urge over another, and that, again, was a primary focus of the reaction-time research. In Wundt's technical vocabulary, volitional states are seen as occurring in varied forms or levels from primitive 'impulses' (in which only one urge is present) to 'volitional acts' (in which more than one impulse is present but one predominates) to 'selective acts' (in which many impulses are present and a conscious choice is made among them). For more details of this analysis, see Danziger's summary (1980).

At this point, a principle of the greatest importance enters Wundt's theory. Innate reflexes, autonomic nervous system functions, automatic skills, and routine actions of all kinds are conceived as having all once been primitive voluntary activity under the direct and deliberate control of focal attention. Either through a prolonged process of biological evolution or through one of automatization by prolonged practice do these actions drop away from the focus of central control to be encapsulated in the nervous system as automatic control schemata. When conscious voluntary activities become routine through frequent rehearsal, they require less and less attentional control. This in turn frees the central attentional process to move in new directions. When an infant first begins to walk or talk, its whole attention is dominated by that activity. Later, when those behaviors have become highly automatic, they occur in a reflexive manner so that the child's attention is freer to focus on other goals or behaviors while the child is walking or talking.

The particular forms and qualities of consciousness in this theory are also the repositories of a long evolutionary history. Every mental event, each emergent form or quality, in this philosophy is ultimately to be explained as evolving from a volitional central control process. The syntheses of experience take their particular form because they have long had a particular value for the organism. But perceptual and other mental constructions are all originally motivated, only later becoming automatized or functionally autonomous. Reflexes too, in this theory, are explained as automatized volitions.

The emotion system

Emotion is crucial to Wundt's system because it is the root process of the volitional urges and impulses. The emotion theory was designed to depict the quality space that would represent the variations of emotional colorings of the fields or processes of consciousness. It did not appear, however, until the 1890s when it was developed as a tridimensional theory, and like previous work was experimentally based. One dimension was that of arousal, varying from extreme excitement to extreme quiescence. Another was that of pleasure/pain. The third was that of high attentional effort or tension versus the inattentive letting go of the attentional focus. Experimental studies of bodily reactions in emotional states that seemed to correlate with this system appeared in some quantity at Leipzig around the turn of the century. The whole effort was quite the opposite of the approach to emotion coming from William James and his American colleagues. The James–Lange theory viewed emotional experience as the result of antecedent peripheral bodily reactions. Wundt (1891) argued that he could not see the Jamesian view as anything but illogical. Data from his Leipzig laboratory workers seemed to him to indicate quite clearly that emotion must be experienced or conceived of first and only secondly (and not even always) expressed in peripheral bodily reactions. The Leipzig emotion

research program was ambitious for its time in view of what it demand-
ed in laboratory instrumentation, particularly in the measurement of
delicate autonomic system reactions.

Perhaps the most scientifically and experimentally based approach
to the study of human personality to the present time is that of the
investigations made by Hans Eysenck and his colleagues. (A detailed
summary is found in C. Monte, 1991.) Eysenck's work has effectively
related current knowledge about the brain's arousal system, pleas-
ure/pain centers, and other self-control systems to his rigorous quan-
tifications of behavioral dimensions of personality variation. Eysenck
is also unusual for his thorough and accurate knowledge of the history of psychology. As a result of that awareness, he acknowledges that
his work is an extension of the work and modeling of emotional
processes begun by Wundt. Though there was little discussion of personality theory in Wundt's day, he still exploited his efforts at dimen-
sionalizing emotion to account for personality variations in ways that
Eysenck has elaborated.

Further general characteristics of the stream of consciousness

In the concluding chapters of many of Wundt's works, one finds summaries of a number of further thematic principles that he had been
developing for describing the operating characteristics of consciousness.
Those summaries emerged as a set of principles which were offered as
further general principles of the stream of consciousness. They are six
related generalities about the characteristics of the flow of the stream of
consciousness that started with and evolved from his initial principle of
creative synthesis.

That first principle of *creative synthesis* would necessarily have to be
introduced early in any description of Wundt's thought. Again, it is
the postulation of a central construction of emergent qualities. By the
1890s it had been expanded by the elaboration of several more deriv-
ative or related principles totaling six in all. The first three concerned
the microgenetic processes of immediate consciousness. The parallel
second three principles concerned the longer developmental and historical processes.

The second of these principles is that of *psychological relativity*, which
describes mental processes as having their existence and identity only
as part of larger configurations of experience. Whereas the first principle has to do with emergent qualities in the synthesis of experience, the

second refers to the differentiations of experience through the analytical process of selective attention. It was to illustrate that any item of mental focusing has meaning or identity only as it is related to some context. In Wundt's elaborate writings on psycholinguistics, for instance, words can have meaning only as a function of their membership in some present or implied sentence, and the uttered sentence is itself meaningful only as it relates to some larger mental context (see Blumenthal's 1970 translations from Wundt's *Die Sprache*, 1900b).

The third principle is that of *psychological contrasts*, which is an elaboration of the second principle. Simply stated, antithetical experiences intensify each other. After a period of pain, a slight pleasure will loom large; similarly, a sweet substance tastes sweeter if eaten after a sour substance. Emotional elation may dispose one to a subsequent period of depression. The examples of such opponent processes were numerous in Wundt's discussions.

The fourth principle is the first of the three developmental principles that concern longer-term processes. It was called the principle of *the heterogeneity of ends*. A change produced by a purposive volitional action is often different from the change intended, and that discrepancy results in further action. The changes that result here are often emergent social, intellectual, and cultural forms.

Fifth is the principle of *mental growth*. As cultural or mental forms evolve and become progressively differentiated, older and simpler forms emerge into more elaborate forms that must be understood through their relation to the earlier parent forms. The evolution of the world's languages was a prominent example because Wundt had contributed heavily to the technical literature on linguistics. In the case of individual development, he cited at length the unfolding of language in the child. The child's language, from this view, begins with impulses, urges, or desires that are reflected in global emotional gestures. The language development then proceeds in accord with the unfolding and differentiation of those original germinal forms.

Sixth is the principle of *development toward opposites*, which is the long-term parallel of the principle of psychological contrasts. It is the statement that the development of attitudes and cultural forms fluctuates between opponent historical or developmental processes. A period of one type of activity or experience evokes a tendency to seek some opposite form of experience or action. These fluctuations, as Wundt observed, are found not only in the life and experience of the individual, but also in the cyclical patterns of history, economic cycles, and social customs.

Conclusion

Wundt's theoretical system reached maturity in the 1890s. Thereafter much of his work on the basic psychological system was embellishment. Perhaps the best source for tracking the development of his thought is through the theoretical essays and position papers that he published in the journal he edited, the *Philosophische Studien*. One of those important papers was the one concerning psychological causality published in 1894. In there he gives the following summary statement (my translation):

If I were asked what I thought the value for psychology of the experimental method was in the past and still is, I would answer that for me it created and continues to confirm a wholly new view of the nature and interrelations of mental processes. When I first approached psychological problems I shared the general prejudice natural to physiologists that the formation of perceptions is merely the work of the physiological properties of our sense organs. Then through the examination of visual phenomena I learned to conceive of perception as an act of creative synthesis. This gradually became my guide, at the hand of which I arrived at a psychological understanding of the development of the higher functions of imagination and intellect. The older psychology gave me no help in this. When I then proceeded to investigate the temporal relations in the flow of mental events, I gained a new insight into the development of volition ... an insight likewise into the similarity of mental functions which are artificially distinguished by abstractions and names – such as 'ideas', 'feelings', or 'will'. In a word, I glimpsed the indivisibility of mental life, and saw its similarity on all its levels. The chronometric investigation of associative processes showed me the relation of perceptual processes to memory images. It also taught me to recognize that the concept of 'reproduced' ideas is one of the many fictions that has become set in our language to create a picture of something that does not exist in reality. I learned to understand that 'mental representation' is a process which is no less changing and transient than a feeling or an act of will. As a consequence of all this I saw that the old theory of association is no longer tenable. It must be replaced by the notion of relational processes involving rudimentary feelings, a view that results in giving up the stable linkages and close connections of successive as well as simultaneous associations. (1894, pp. 122–123)

References

Blumenthal, A. (1970) Language and Psychology: Historical Aspects of Psycholinguistics. New York: John Wiley.

Blumenthal, A. (1977) The Process of Cognition. Englewood Cliffs, NJ: Prentice-Hall.

Danziger, K. (1980) Wundt's theory of behavior and volition. In R. Rieber (ed.) Wilhelm Wundt and the Making of a Scientific Psychology. New York: Plenum Press.

Danziger, K. (1990) Constructing the Subject: Historical Origins of Psychological Research. Cambridge: Cambridge University Press.

Haupt, E. J. "Georg Elias Müller." In Kazdin, A.E. (ed.) (2000). Encyclopedia of psychology, Vol. 5. (pp. 332–334). Washington, DC, US: American Psychological Association; New York, NY, US: Oxford University Press.

Klemm, O. (1914) A History of Psychology. New York: Scribner's.

Kusch, M. (1995) Psychologism: A Case Study in the Sociology of Philosophical Knowledge. London: Routledge.

Ladd, G. (1887) Elements of Physiological Psychology. New York: Scribner's.

Ladd, G. and Woodworth, R. (1911) Elements of Physiological Psychology. New York: Scribner's.

Lehmann, A. (1899) Die körperlichen Äusserungen psychischer Zustände. Leipzig: Engelmann.

Miller, G. (1981) Trends and debates in cognitive psychology. Cognition, 10, 215–225.

Monte, C. (1991) Beneath the Mask: An Introduction to Theories of Personality. Chicago: Holt, Rinehart, and Winston.

Paul, H. (1886) Prinzipien der Sprachgeschichte. Halle: Niemeyer.

Posner, M. (1978) Chronometric Explorations of Mind. Hillsdale, NJ: Erlbaum.

Robinson, D.K. (1987) Wilhelm Wundt and the Establishment of Experimental Psychology, 1875–1914: The Context of a New Field of Scientific Research. Doctoral Dissertation, University of California, Berkeley.

Schneider, C. (1990) Wilhelm Wundt's Völkerpsychologie. Bonn: Bouvier.

Wirth, W. (1908) Die experimentelle Analyse der Bewusstseinsphänomene. Braunschweig: Vieweg.

Woodworth, R. (1938) Experimental Psychology. New York: Henry Holt.

Wundt, W. (1862) Beiträge zur Theorie der Sinneswahrnehmung. Leipzig: Winter.

Wundt, W. (1880) Grundzüge der Physiologischen Psychologie (2nd edn). Leipzig: Englemann.

Wundt, W. (1882) Die Aufgaben der experimentellen Psychologie. Unsere Zeit. Reprinted in Wundt, W., Essays (2nd edn). Leipzig: Englemann, 1906.

Wundt, W. (1883) Über psychologische Methoden. Philosophische Studien, 1, 1–40.

Wundt, W. (1888) Selbstbeobachtung und innere Wahrnehmung. Philosophische Studien, 4, 292–309.

Wundt, W. (1891) Zur Lehre von den Gemüthsbewegen. Philosophische Studien, 6, 335–393.

Wundt, W. (1892) Vorlesungen über die Menschen und Thierseele (2nd edn). Leipzig: Voss.

Wundt, W. (1893) Logik. Stuttgart: Enke.

Wundt, W. (1894) Über psychische Causalität und das Prinzip des psycho-physis-chen Parallelismus. Philosophische Studien, 10, 1–124.

Wundt, W. (1896) Grundriss der Psychologie. (trans. C. H. Judd as Outlines of Psychology, 1897). Leipzig: Englemann.

Wundt, W. (1897) Ethics, II (2nd edn) (trans. by E. Titchener, J. Gulliver, and M. Washburn). New York: Macmillan.

Wundt, W. (1900a) Bemerkungen zur Theorie der Gefühle. Philosophische Studien, 15, 149–182.

Wundt, W. (1900b) Die Sprache. Leipzig: Englemann.

Wundt, W. (1906) Essays. (2nd edn) Leipzig: Englemann.

Wundt, W. (1907) Über Ausfrageexperimente und über die Methoden zur Psychologie des Denkens. Psychologische Studien, 2, 301–390.

Wundt, W. (1908) Logik (3rd edn) Stuttgart: Enke.

Wundt, W. (1910). Principles of Physiological Psychology (Volume 1, 2nd edn) (trans. by E. Titchener). London: Swan Sonnenschein.

Wundt, W. (1911) Einführung in die Psychologie. (trans. as Introduction to Psychology by R. Pinter). Leipzig: Voigtlander.

8

Frege: Furnishing Formal Foundations

Peter Simons

1. Introduction

If Gottlob Frege could have been told that one day his work would be seen as important to the prehistory of cognitive science, he would have been surprised and perhaps dismayed. For much of his career, Frege opposed 'the devastation ... brought about by the incursion of psychology into logic'[1] and while his opposition to psychologism was neither as systematically presented nor as influential as Husserl's, his criticisms of psychologism in logic were more incisive. Psychologism is the view that logical laws describe regularities in thought processes and that logic should consider what goes on when people actually think, judge, surmise, and infer. In Frege's formative years, logic was heavily affected by the prevalent empiricism in Germany, and his work in logic and its philosophy is a rationalist reaction to this. Paradoxically, the very tools Frege developed to demonstrate the correctness of his rationalistic and anti-psychologistic views have turned out to be indispensable to cognitive science: the formal analysis of language, the concept of a formal system, its rigorous syntax, proof theory and semantics, and the exact analysis of many forms of meaning, reference, and thought. Indeed, cognitive science may be seen in part as attempting to fill the gaps Frege left in his account of thought, which suffers from a simplistic view of the mental.

This paper aims to elucidate in what respects Frege's work was to provide formal foundations which were to become indispensable for the later development of cognitive science. First we outline Frege's many

---

[1] *Foundations of Arithmetic*, p. xiv.

achievements and occasional failures, setting them in the scientific context of his time. The next section details his genial and revolutionary advances in logic. His excursions into philosophy of language, described next, represent the place where Frege's views most closely impinge on cognitive concerns. Finally, we explore Frege's legacy for logic, language, and philosophy, showing how his innovations were carried forward.

2. Frege's work in its context

Gottlob Frege (1848–1925) was by training a mathematician, and his undistinguished university career was that of a conscientious but overworked, misunderstood, and under-recognized professor of Mathematics with what were regarded as odd interests. Though Frege's place in the history of mathematics and its philosophy is in retrospect a noble one, we here simply note that he crowns the tradition of those mathematicians, including Bolzano, Cauchy, Dedekind, and Weierstrass, who strove for greater formal rigor at the basis of pure mathematics. In a minor review, he bemoaned the sad state of explanation about the basic concepts and laws of arithmetic, unwittingly embarking on his life's work when he set out to give exact definitions of these concepts and rigorous derivations of those laws. This led him to consider how one arithmetical proposition follows from another, and thus to logic.

In those days in Germany, logic was considered the preserve of philosophers and the philosophy then prevalent was a form of scientific naturalism, reacting against the excesses of German idealism earlier in the century. Philosopher–scientists such as Helmholtz, Weber, Wundt, and Mach were encouraging the view that empirical and experimental methods could succeed where armchair philosophical speculation had failed. The British empiricists from Locke to Mill, and their use of scientific method in the examination of the mind, were regarded highly, experimental psychology was emerging, and it was widely assumed that a suitable psychological typology and method were indispensable to an accurate account of logic. Logic textbooks of the time contained detailed accounts of such mental concepts as thought, conception, sensation, association of ideas, judgment, and inference, as a prelude to their accounts of syllogistic deduction, induction, and scientific method. The mathematical analysis of logic initiated in 1847 by Boole and continued in England by Jevons, Venn, and others was known to very few, the main exception being the mathematician Ernst Schröder. When news of the English approach did cross to Germany, its extensional treatment of terms as standing for classes was widely rejected by German philosophical logicians, who, in the tradition of Leibniz and Kant, thought of terms as standing for concepts, classes being the mere extensions of these and a calculus of such extensions unworthy of the name of logic. Into this near-vacuum stepped Frege, and with the advantages of scant prejudicial foreknowledge and analytic genius he revolutionized logic forever.

Frege considered Kant's question about the epistemological status of the truths of arithmetic. Are they, as John Stuart Mill supposed, well-confirmed empirical generalizations, which might nevertheless conceivably be falsified? Against this it would seem that they could not be falsified by any experience whatever. Are they then as Kant supposed, *a priori* but synthetic? Frege agreed with Kant that this is the status of the truths of geometry, which in Frege's view require intuitive as well as purely conceptual or logical input for us to have knowledge of them. But Frege considered that Kant was wrong about arithmetic and analysis. The truths of these branches of mathematics are *a priori*, but Frege thought they might be not synthetic but analytic truths, like the truths of logic. In order to decide this, it is necessary to know which truths are logical and which are not. *Logicism*, the view that the truths of arithmetic are logical and analytic, had been held by Leibniz. Frege's career turns around his attempt, heroic but unsuccessful, to demonstrate the truth of logicism.

Of the ways in which one arithmetical proposition may follow from others, one seems not to be purely logical, namely the principle of mathematical induction. In its simplest form this says that if the first natural number has a certain property, and the successor of any number (that number plus 1) having that property itself has the property, then all numbers have that property. Certainly this is an inference form not found in standard logic textbooks up to the nineteenth century, and it seemed to be distinctive of mathematical rather than purely logical reasoning. If Frege could show that mathematical induction was a logical principle, then a serious obstacle to logicism would be removed. Frege recognized that mathematical induction is a particular case of a more general form of reasoning about a sequence of objects standing one to another in any relation. What Frege did, which bears the stamp of genius, was to *define* the general notion of *following after* in any sequence, known as the *ancestral* of a relation, in purely logical terms. Thus the logically inexact notion 'and so on' or 'etc.' and the corresponding notational device of three dots can be eliminated. The definition is purely general since no particular objects, properties, or relations are mentioned. With the definition in hand, and defining a number as anything which follows after zero in the sequence of successorships, the principle of mathematical induction becomes a simple special case. The terms used in the definition go far beyond anything with which traditional logic could cope: terms like *relation, every property, every object to which a given object stands in a certain relation,* and others. Frege tried at first to analyze these notions and make them precise using ordinary German, but quickly became dissatisfied with the vagaries and ambiguities of vernacular forms of expression. In particular he rejected the traditional analysis of propositions into subject and predicate. Relational propositions abound in mathematics and are needed to define the ancestral. In relational propositions, which name is subject and which is predicate is a superficial matter: the propositions *oxygen is heavier than hydrogen* and *hydrogen is lighter than oxygen* say the same thing as far as logic is concerned, so the division into subject and predicate is of no logical significance, and Frege rejected it. In its place he put a much more flexible and more widely ranging distinction between a function and its argument or arguments. As a mathematician, Frege was familiar with this idea and he was the first to analyze the notion in depth and extend its scope beyond its original home in mathematics. Frege introduced astonishingly many further innovations in logic, which we shall consider in the next section.

Frege's first book *Begriffsschrift* (1879) set out the logical language he intended to replace ordinary language for the purpose of establishing logicism, and showed how to define the ancestral, but it does not broach the question of logicism. The appearance and content of the book were forbidding, probably because Frege was little aware just how revolutionary his new ideas were, and to the extent that the book was noticed, it was not well received. One of his reviewers, Schröder, accused him (justly) of ignorance of Boole's earlier introduction of algebraic methods into logic. Frege quickly researched Boole's work and decided (justly) that his own work was better, but his forceful and illuminating replies to the Boolean logicians could not find a publisher.

Chastened by the poor reception of *Begriffsschrift*, now recognized as a supreme masterpiece, Frege wrote his next work, *Die Grundlagen der Arithmetik* (*The Foundations of Arithmetic* 1884), in lucid German prose without intrusion of logical notation, and took due account of what previous authors had said before proceeding to outline his logicist program for arithmetic. The first part of the book ably demolishes existing empiricist and formalist theories of arithmetic, while the second part explains Frege's own view, that numbers are abstract objects, the extensions of certain concepts. *Grundlagen* is without doubt the finest single work in the history of the philosophy of mathematics, but again it was miserably received, even by those, such as Georg Cantor, who should have gained most from it.

Undaunted, Frege pressed ahead with demonstrating logicism by showing how to derive the basic laws of arithmetic from those of logic. In the course of doing so he made several changes to the elements of his logical system, which forced him to rewrite his derivation. In particular he clarified his notion of a function, and generalized the idea of the extension of a concept to that of the value-range of any function, concepts being seen as a certain kind of function. These changes were first presented in an essay 'On function and concept' (1891), which introduces all the primitives of Frege's mature logical system except his definite description operator. The most important general change, however, was Frege's distinguishing, within what he had previously called the *content* of a judgment or meaning of a sentence between *sense* and *reference*. Logic and mathematics deal with the items of reference, objects, and functions, but these items may be referred to in different ways, by expressions differing in sense. This changed how Frege viewed identity, and he presented the distinction and argued for it in a separate essay, 'On sense and reference' (1892), which encapsulates in miniature a whole philosophy of language. With these alterations presented in essays, and his logicist program already sketched in prose, Frege could concentrate on publishing his proof of logicism. The first part of this was published as Volume I of *Grundgesetze der Arithmetik* (*Basic Laws of Arithmetic*) in 1893. It presents the logically primitive concepts, their syntax and meaning, gives the axioms ('basic laws') and rules of inference, derives a number of logical theorems and principles about the numbers zero and one. Frege clearly intended to follow up quickly with a second volume, but the usual dismal reception delayed publishing, and when Frege eventually published the second volume ten years later it was at his own expense.

In the meantime Frege sallied forth into controversy with leading mathematicians and philosophers of his time. The only philosopher who had seriously taken notice of his work was Edmund Husserl, whose *Philosophie der Arithmetik* appeared in 1891 and contained a criticism of Frege's definition of number. Frege wrote a scorching review in which he decried what he saw as the debilitating psychologism of Husserl's approach. Husserl's next book, the *Logical Investigations* of 1900–1901, starts with its own detailed and influential critique of psychologism, and it is hard not to believe that Frege's criticism influenced Husserl's new views, though Husserl was niggardly in his acknowledgement to Frege. Giuseppe Peano wrote to Frege criticizing what he saw as the wastefully large number of primitive concepts in *Grundgesetze*. Frege replied by showing that Peano's own logical notation was in fact the less economical. Peano published the exchange, and his later system contains improvements due to Frege's criticism. When David Hilbert's *Axiome der Geometrie* appeared in 1899, Frege wrote to Hilbert criticizing the approach, which takes the primitive terms such as *point* and *line* as uninterpreted and provides axioms affording what Hilbert termed an 'implicit definition' for them. For Frege a definition had to be explicit and the primitive terms of an axiomatic theory had to be fully interpreted. The exchange of letters was again published, but this time Frege did not have the better of the argument: Hilbert's view of axiomatic systems has become orthodoxy, while Frege's insistence on a single determinate meaning seems outmoded.

Frege's rival Schröder started publishing his monumental *Vorlesungen zur Algebra der Logik* in 1891. It is the largest and most definitive work of the Boolean algebraic tradition. Frege intended to write a review of the whole work when it was complete, but a review of the first volume by Husserl prompted him to publish some briefer 'Critical elucidations' in 1895. Like other Booleans, Schröder was an extensionalist: his basic calculus applied to classes. Husserl showed that an intensional interpretation of the calculus as concerning concepts would also work. Frege accepts that intension (roughly, sense) and extension (roughly, reference) should be distinguished, but agrees with Schröder that logic deals with reference. He differs from both Husserl and Schröder in taking general terms (monadic predicates) to have concepts as their references: classes are the value-ranges of concepts and are signified by singular terms, not general terms. Like Husserl, Frege criticized Schröder's lack of distinction between element and unit subclass. The lack of this distinction embroiled Schröder in a paradox from which he extricated himself only by distinguishing different types of classes: classes of individuals, classes of classes of individuals, and so on, and not allowing the types to mix as values of a single variable. Frege was scathing of the move: 'This contradiction comes like a thunderbolt from a clear sky. How could we be prepared for anything like this in exact logic! Who can go surety for it that we shall not again suddenly encounter a contradiction as we go on? The possibility of such a thing points to a mistake in the original design. Mr. Schröder ['s ...] expedient, as it were, belatedly gets the ship off the sandbank; but if she had been properly steered, she could have kept off it altogether.' (*A Critical Elucidation*, 91)

Later, as he was preparing Volume II of *Grundgesetze* for publication, Frege was himself struck by a bolt out of the blue. A letter from Bertrand Russell arrived in which for the first time Frege found himself praised in the highest terms, but the same letter disclosed that a contradiction could be derived from Frege's logical principles. This was Russell's Paradox. Various similar contradictions follow from Frege's axioms: the simplest formulation is that the class of all classes that are not elements of themselves both is and is not an element of itself. Stunned, Frege replied to Russell and in their correspondence they tried different ways to avoid the paradox. By the time Volume II appeared in 1903, Frege had patched up a repair, restricting and weakening the offending logical principle ('Basic Law V'). Soon, however, Frege realized that the repair blocked his proof that every number has a successor, and he had not the heart or energy to pursue a new course, such as the elaborate type theory that Russell proposed, or the axiomatic set theory of Zermelo. He later wrote that the paradoxes had shown set theory to be impossible, and the very end of his life sees him abandoning logicism and experimenting with a geometrical foundation for all numbers.

The contradiction overshadowed the rest of the second volume of *Grundgesetze*, which contains the beginnings of an interesting and distinctive logicist account of the real numbers, preceded by a prose survey and criticism of extant theories paralleling that for natural numbers in the *Grundlagen*, but by now marred by tedious criticism of minor figures and uncharitable carping at major ones such as Dedekind and Cantor. There was evidently more planned, but Frege never published the rest.

Frege's last years were marked by disappointment, unhappiness, and bitterness. He still kept occasional contact with younger men. Rudolf Carnap attended his logic lectures in Jena before the First World War, but no personal relationship developed. Frege's (lost) correspondence with Schröder's adherent Leopold Löwenheim apparently convinced him that a Hilbertian formal arithmetic was possible. Like others, he placed high hopes in the young Ludwig Wittgenstein, but was deeply dismayed by Wittgenstein's unscientific, aphoristic approach to logical questions in the *Tractatus Logico-Philosophicus*, which Frege was one of the first to see in typescript. His remaining essays leave logicism unmentioned and deal with logic and semantics, with the Platonic senses of sentences and with the logical constants. This series of essays, called *Logical Investigations*, remained incomplete at his death, which passed largely unremarked in 1925. Frege died believing his life's work to have failed.

Frege was unjustly undervalued for most of his lifetime, though his correspondence shows he was in contact with many of the foremost minds of his age. The discovery of the contradiction which undermined his work also ushered in his wider recognition, praised by Russell and Whitehead, Wittgenstein and the Polish logicians, but their advances tended to mask his work. Frege's *Nachlass*, collected by Heinrich Scholz in the 1930s, was only partly copied when it was destroyed in a 1944 air raid. Since 1945 Frege's reputation has grown steadily: his works, *Nachlass* and correspondence have been published and widely translated, and there is a large secondary literature on his work. Such fine logicians as Church and Carnap have acknowledged their indebtedness and incorporated many of his ideas into their own work. He is now widely recognized as the greatest logician since Aristotle, an unmatched philosopher of mathematics, a fine philosopher of language, and one of the first and most astute practitioners of what is now called analytic philosophy.

3. A logical revolution

Since its inception logic had seen sporadic novelties and reforms. The person who most promised to transform logic after Aristotle and the Stoics was Leibniz, and Leibniz anticipated two centuries of development in logic, in particular the developments in the term logic that are associated with the name of George Boole. Leibniz had savage ambitions for logic. In his view, an exact analysis of concepts would lead to a universal alphabet of thought, enabling every expressible proposition to be analyzed in terms of its ultimate conceptual components. These elements of thought would then be combined in a fixed number of ways, enabling every thinkable thought to be uniquely represented in terms of its logical atoms, and all logical relations between thoughts to be calculated mechanically. Calculation would replace and resolve disputation. There would be a universal language directly representing concepts and thoughts. The graphic representation of concepts, a *Begriffs-Schrift*, would give this language perceptible form. This term *Begriffs-Schrift*, conceived by Adolf Trendelenburg, became Frege's name for his logical language, and Frege examined Leibniz's writings at a time when no one else of significance in Germany did so. Frege accepted Leibniz's idea that a logical calculus would enable one to test mechanically the logical relations among different propositions. He drew back from Leibniz's universalist optimism by suggesting that such calculi should be conceived and constructed for special purposes, rather than trying to embrace a universal medium. Structural formulae in chemistry (as practiced by Frege's chemistry professor Geuthner and carried further by Kekulé) allowed signs for atoms to combine perspicuously into signs for molecules. Symbolic formulae would likewise enable one to exhibit perspicuously the logical relations among propositions.

But Leibniz did not afford relations their rightful place: there are no relational variables or logical constants connecting relations as are envisaged and outlined by Boole's contemporary Augustus De Morgan. Frege accepted relational propositions as having a distinct form from non-relational ones: in *Caesar is human* there is only one singular term, whereas in *Caesar loves Brutus* there are two. In Frege this emerges as the distinction between one-place and two-place functions: $f(a)$ versus $g(a,b)$. Frege was not the only logician in the nineteenth century expanding logic to cope with relations. His particular innovations lie elsewhere, and they are legion.

Frege separated the content of judgments from their assertoric force. An assertoric sentence, like *gold is heavier than silver*, expresses a judgment. Its content is capturable by a noun phrase, *that gold is heavier than silver* or *gold's being heavier than silver*. In Frege's logical script a judgment or assertion is written |—A, where the vertical stroke | marks the act of judging or asserting. In 1879 the horizontal or content stroke — merely showed that what follows signifies a judgeable content, but from 1891 it signified a certain function. In 1879 Frege explicitly distinguished judgeable contents from nonjudgeable ones. One can judge *that gold is heavier than water*, but not *that 2* or *that house*. From 1891, the content of judgments was distinguished into the thought (sense) expressed and the truth-value (reference) signified. The reference of names expressing thoughts is one of the two truth-values, the True and the False. By the later interpretation of the horizontal stroke as signifying a function, so that — x may be read as *x's being the True*, Frege made it unnecessary in his logic to distinguish judgeable from unjudgeable contents, since he prefaced all contents judged or asserted by the horizontal symbol. Hence even the sign —2 has sense and reference: it refers to the False, since 2 is not the True. Who asserts |—2 asserts falsely, whereas in the logic of 1879 this sign was meaningless.

Frege introduced signs for negation and the material conditional, and gave them their truth-functional meanings. He knew that other propositional connectives like conjunction and disjunction are definable in terms of these two. Frege's notorious two-dimensional graphical notation, employing a branching tree of horizontal and vertical strokes, allowed complex propositions using only these connectives to be notated without parentheses, with a complex of strokes standing to the left of a vertical array of variables.

The axioms that Frege gives for formulas containing just these signs, the inference rule of *modus ponens* that he gives and the rule of uniform substitution which he implicitly assumes suffice to axiomatize classical propositional calculus. Frege was not interested in such a partial system, and pressed on, without marking the step, to other logical constants. He introduced the universal quantifier, notated by a concavity in the horizontal, a graphical device automatically delimiting a quantifier's scope. He is aware that an existential quantifier is definable using the universal and negation, but he never introduces such a definition. The axioms he gives and the rules he implicitly supposes for dealing with the quantifier, including substitution of higher-order functions, sufficed in 1879 to axiomatize what we now call second-order predicate calculus. By 1891 he was distinguishing different levels of function syntactically and so introduced different axioms and rules for universal quantifiers binding variables of different levels. Frege's conception of and notation for quantification make it effortless to construct and interpret multiply quantified sentences, enabling one to distinguish, for example, *every event is caused by some event* from *some event causes every event*, and constituted the most significant single advance in logic since the Greeks. Before Frege, multiply quantified sentences were hard to understand, construct, and disambiguate. Thereafter, they were within everyone's grasp. The difference is comparable to that brought to arithmetic by decimal notation.

In the later logic Frege introduced two extra notions. In *Grundlagen* he had argued that the cardinal numbers zero, one, two, ... are extensions of certain concepts. Until then he had no logical notation or axioms for extensions. Characteristically, Frege introduced a more general notion and notation making extensions a special case. Every function was associated with a unique object, its *Wertverlauf* or *value-range*. For the function $f(x)$ the range is an object written $\varepsilon f(\varepsilon)$. Where f is a concept, the value-range is an extension. Between value-ranges and objects a relation $\cap$ is defined, so that $a \cap \varepsilon\, f(\varepsilon) = f(a)$. Where f is a concept this relation corresponds to set membership. Value-ranges are taken to be identical precisely when their functions take the same values for the same arguments. This axiom (Basic Law V) was to prove Frege's undoing.

The second notion introduced is a definite description operator. Frege describes it as a 'substitute for the definite article' in his logical script. Its sole logical use in Frege's system is in conjunction with ranges to define the relation $\cap$, which thereafter does all the work.

These seven functions -- the horizontal, conditional, negation, quantifier, identity, value-range, and description functions – are the primitives on which Frege in 1893 hoped to build all of arithmetic and analysis, with the help of axioms, rules, and definitions.

In introducing his primitives Frege takes great pains to elucidate their meaning in terms of the notions, assumed understood, of the True, the False, and the application of a function to an argument or arguments to yield a value. His semantic stipulations fail to determine an expression's reference in one case only: value-ranges. Compatibly with Frege's axioms, the value-range for a given function might be any one of many objects. Frege thought he could stipulate the value-ranges as new functions were introduced, but he badly misunderstood the effect of the axioms he had already accepted. By defining a concept H so that for all objects a, $H(a)$ is the True if and only if a is the value-range of some concept f such that $f(a)$ is the False, it can be shown according to Frege's logic that $H(\varepsilon -H(\varepsilon))$ is both the True and the False. This is one form of Russell's Paradox.

The reasons for this disaster and the ill fate of Frege's subsequent attempted repair to the system are too involved and peripheral to our purpose to pursue here. The short version is that Frege was too liberal in allowing there to be value-ranges for arbitrary functions. In his earlier 1879 logic, the problem did not arise because there are no value-ranges: the earlier logic is consistent. Likewise, once Frege had worked out that he had no well-motivated yet consistent way to repair his system, he dropped value-ranges and confined his logic to the second-order predicate system he had originally propounded. Lacking, as he saw it, the means to define numbers as logical objects, he abandoned logicism, and he seems not to have had the will to explore the idea of numbers as quantifiers or other higher-order functions such as we find in Russell and Whitehead's *Principia Mathematica*. The type theory of that work went against the grain for Frege: he had already rejected such a theory in Schröder. In any case, as the experience of Russell and Whitehead and the later results of Gödel were to make clear, the logicist thesis that the truths of arithmetic and analysis are logical could not be upheld.

Frege's logical practice was almost as revolutionary as his logical ideas. He carefully distinguished expressions in the system from talk about them, gave his rules with precision, formulated conditions as to what may count as a definition, explained his proofs with care and constructed them elegantly. It was a generation before such care and exactness were found again among logicians. The expressions of his logical system were built up in a syntactically unambiguous way with the intention that the sense and reference of every complex expression should be uniquely determined by the sense and reference of its constituents and the way in which they were combined. This is what we now call semantic compositionality: in Frege's hands it sprang into existence fully formed. Every proof could be checked against Frege's axioms and rules as to whether it really was a correct derivation or not. As he envisaged, all proofs were executed without gaps in the reasoning, and all assumptions made plain to see as the antecedents of conditionals. Frege's lectures and some small papers show that he was able to use his script to formulate with precision the involved concepts and reasonings of mathematicians. Thus Frege came nearer than anyone before him to realizing the Leibnizian ideal for logic.

In one respect Frege's views remain remote from current understanding and practice. Since he envisaged the signs of his script as endowed with sense from the elucidations given them, his axioms are meant to be self-evidently true, and his rules to be truth-preserving. So his idea of an axiomatic system is traditional, whereas the views of Schröder and other Booleans that a calculus may admit of different, equally good interpretations, or of Hilbert that a set of axioms be uninterpreted, are alien to him. For this reason Frege never envisaged the possibility of an investigation of the semantic properties of a formal system, such as consistency, completeness, and independence, or the difference between proof-theoretic and semantic properties.

4. Foundations of a theory of language

Frege's abortive attempt to use ordinary language for the purposes of logical formalization appears to have permanently marked his attitude to the vernacular. For scientific purposes everyday language is too imprecise and multifarious. Frege compared it to the general-purpose eye, whereas he wanted a precision tool like the telescope.

Frege's artificial language, unlike the vernacular, was to express conceptual content as directly as possible. Its signs and distinctions record only what is significant for inference. Like many nineteenth-century logicians following Kant, Frege takes the judgment to be the prime unit of thought, concepts being obtained by analysis from judgments rather than judgments from the synthesis of concepts. But whereas for others this priority thesis remained an empty formula, in Frege's hands it woke to life. Most specifically, Frege uses it in his *Grundlagen der Arithmetik* to define the concept *natural number* using words that taken at face value seem to presuppose this concept. In particular, the following concepts occur in the chain of definitions leading to the definition of *natural number: being in one-to-one correspondence; being a concept under which as many objects fall as fall another concept; being the number belonging to a concept; being numbers of concepts such that one more object falls under one than the other; succeeding; succeeding zero.* Simply looking at the words we use to render these concepts in ordinary language would lead us to suppose that Frege's definition of number is circular. Frege insisted that we must consider declarative vernacular sentences as a whole and not automatically suppose they build up their meanings from their constituent words. This preserves his chain of definitions from real circularity, as their translation into his symbols makes plain.

Frege's functional analysis of complex contents initially took functions to be expression-patterns, but he later gave up this linguistic view in favor of an ontological conception of functions as objective entities of their own peculiar kind, 'unsaturated', 'incomplete', or 'in need of supplementation' by comparison with the complete or 'saturated' objects, designated by expressions he called 'proper names'. This shift from a linguistic to an ontological conception gave him a clearer semantic picture of the distinction between functions and objects, and induced him to make distinctions of kind and level among functions: functions are distinguished according to the number of their arguments and their level. First-order functions have objects as arguments, second-level functions have first-level functions as their arguments and we can define third-level and mixed-level functions if we wish. In his later logic, Frege made an extensive use of the value-ranges of functions in place of the functions themselves. Since value-ranges are objects, this effects a reduction in the level of functions he needs to consider for particular purposes, and several of the definitions proposed for higher-level functions in *Begriffsschrift* are replaced by ones using functions defined for value-ranges in *Grundgesetze*. With the benefit of hindsight, it is obvious to us now that this reduction had to fail. Cantor had proved that there must be more functions over any domain of objects than objects in the domain, yet Frege's assumption of a distinct value-range for each function negates this inequality. Russell was led to discover the inconsistency of Frege's system by considering Cantor's result.

The principle of semantic compositionality is only clearly statable once the analysis of the structure of expressions has reached the level of exactness that Frege provides. Thus the fact that '2' signifies the number 2 and that '3' signifies the number 3 and the pattern '$x + y$' signifies the function of numerical addition of any two arguments x and y

Peter Simons 191

together conspire to make it inevitable that the expression '2 + 3' should signify the number 5. The compositionality principle is employed by Frege to indicate how the semantic value or reference of a function is determined by its yielding the values it does for all its arguments. Frege insists, as a condition of adequacy of a scientific language, that every functional expression be definable for all potential arguments. There are two reasons for this.

The first is that if a concept (a special type of function) is not defined for certain objects, then this means the corresponding sentential content is without truth-value, and the principle of bivalence, that every judgment be true or false, is violated. The second reason is that Frege was critical of the mathematical practice of piecemeal definition, whereby a sign such as '+' defined in one context, e.g., among whole numbers, is extended in its use to a wider class, e.g., all rational numbers. Frege criticizes this because it may lead to contradictions if the new usage turns out to be incompatible with the old. Frege critcized mathematicians for being reluctant to introduce new symbols for new concepts, preferring to soldier on with old ones. Frege's strictures against piecemeal definition are too extreme: the practice, although sloppily applied then, can be safely employed provided one always takes the trouble to show new definitions do not contradict the old. Frege's insistence leads to him having to specify, often by arbitrary stipulation, values of functions like addition for objects way outside the domain of numbers, such as heavenly bodies. It is part and parcel of his seeing the objects of the world (the items signifiable by proper names) as forming a single, logically undifferentiated domain, and is another reason for his logical downfall.

Since '2 + 3' signifies 5, we are entitled to say that the equation '2 + 3 = 5' signifies the True, and assert it by saying '2 + 3 equals 5', which assertion Frege writes not as the equation but as $\mid$— 2 + 3 = 5, expressing the *judgment* that the equation is the True. Though both sides of the equation signify 5, they do so in different ways, the one simply as that number, the other as the sum of 2 with 3. The way in which we arrive at the recognition that the equation is true is by evaluating the sum function for these two arguments and noting that its value is 5. Thus we arrive at the number 5 as what the left-hand side of the equation designates by a different, more circuitous route, from the way we do on the right-hand side, where the numeral requires no evaluation at all but simply signifies the number by standard convention. As a result of such a difference in the way we arrive at the expression's reference, it is possible to be unaware initially that the equation is true. In this case this is hard to see, but a more elaborate numerical equality like

$$[A] \qquad 6589 \cdot 2104 = (27 \cdot 504233) + 248965$$

makes the point more clearly. When we perform the calculation for each side and find that the result is the same in both cases, we discover the truth of the equality. In the *Begriffsschrift*, Frege had ascribed the ability to make such a discovery to the fact that the expressions on both sides are distinct in appearance, but this explanation will not do, because if we allow ourselves to use different naming conventions, for example, using Roman numerals, we can form true equalities like 'V = 5' where the two sides have different symbols, but it is evident to anyone merely knowing the convention that the equality is true. The difference between the two numerical expressions on either side of the equation [A] is due to something less superficial than mere difference of sign; it would show up in any naming convention having the same power as ours. On this basis, Frege claims that a sign is regularly associated not only with the item it refers to, its reference (*Bedeutung*), but also the way this is given, the sense (*Sinn*). To understand an expression is to grasp its senses, but expressions with different sense can have the same reference. To make the point, Frege chose the Babylonians' empirical discovery that the Morning Star is the same heavenly body as the Evening Star: if the equality had been a mere tautology, as we might think considering its reference alone, they could not have enlarged their knowledge by this discovery. By this distinction, Frege is thus able to account for our ability to *discover* the truth of identity statements, including equations like [A].

The distinction between sense and reference was not a new distinction. It, or something close to it, was behind similar oppositions: lekton and object in the Stoics, significatum and appellatum (nominatum) in some medievals, extension and comprehension in the Port-Royal Logic, denotation and connotation in Mill. But Frege characteristically extended the distinction beyond other accounts, which mainly confined their attention to nominal terms, and made it a cornerstone of a systematic semantic theory. The first extension of the distinction was to full clauses. Whereas for Frege the *Bedeutung* of a clause was its truth-value, its *Sinn* was the proposition expressed, which Frege unhelpfully called a 'thought' (*Gedanke*). A thought in this sense is not mental but the common abstract content of many acts of thought. Frege's choice of truth-values as the *Bedeutungen* of sentences or clauses was and remains controversial. Frege may have been partly playing on the connotations of the term *Bedeutung*, which in everyday German, apart from meaning 'meaning' or 'significa- tion', can also mean 'significance' or 'importance'. The truth-value of a clause is what is of paramount importance about it from a logical perspective. But a more systematic reason for taking clauses to refer to truth-values seems appropriate. Frege lays great stress on an object's being associated with conditions for recognizing it as the same, identity condi- tions. It is crucial for something *a* to count as a fully fledged object that it has determinate identity conditions, that is, for sentences of the form $a = b$ to have a determinate truth-value for all objects *b*. The lack of such identity conditions is precisely what prevents Frege from accepting the idea that numbers can be properly introduced and legitimated as refer- ences of expressions like *the number of Xs* by means of the equivalence

the number of Xs = the number of Ys, if and only if there are as many Xs as there are Ys

because this equivalence alone is impotent to prescribe on the truth- value of propositions such as,

the number of Xs = q

where 'q' need not take the form of 'the number of Ys'. Hence, for Frege, to be an object and to have determinate identity conditions are one and the same. The elucidation of identity that Frege adopts is one he ascribes to Leibniz, that expressions signify the same thing when one expression may always be replaced by the other in a sentence *salva veritate*, i.e., without changing the truth-value of the sentence. Hence the *Bedeutung* of an expression is whatever it is that, by being the same, guarantees that different expressions standing for it are substi- tutable for one another *salva veritate*. In the case of a name it is what the name signifies. In the case of sentences, since any true sentence may be replaced by another true sentence *salva veritate*, and likewise any false sentence by any other false sentence, the only thing that remains which can be the same under all substitutions *salva veritate* is the truth-value: any more specific item associated with the sentence, for example, the proposition it expresses or the fact that makes it true, is insufficiently general.

It was typical of Frege that he should be alive to possible counterex- amples to this principle. Here are two possible counterexamples. When expressions are used to name themselves, in *suppositio materialis*, they signify not their usual references but expressions of the type they them- selves are. Hence it is unsurprising that while '2 + 2 = 4' is true, ' "2 + 2" = "4" ' is false. I have indicated the fact that we are using the expres- sions to name expressions by the standard device of quotation marks, but

quotation marks are only one device among many. The second possible
counterexample considers expressions not quoted but used in indirect
speech, as when one reports on the content of what someone says or
believes. For example one may believe that Mark Twain wrote *Tom
Sawyer* but not believe that Samuel Clemens wrote *Tom Sawyer*, because
one is ignorant that Mark Twain is Samuel Clemens. But if 'Mark Twain'
and 'Samuel Clemens' both name the same man, how can 'John
believes that Mark Twain wrote *Tom Sawyer*' be true and yet 'John
believes that Samuel Clemens wrote *Tom Sawyer*' be false? Frege's solution is to deny that *in such a context* the terms 'Mark Twain' and 'Samuel
Clemens' are naming the man. Rather, he says, they are naming the
sense which those expressions standardly have when naming the man.
This appears odd and arbitrary at first blush, but it is perfectly analogous
with saying that when used in *suppositio materialis*, the expressions
name not the man but the expressions, as when we state, perfectly correctly, 'The name Mark Twain is a pseudonym but the name Samuel
Clemens is not a pseudonym'. In the context 'the name ...' a name
names itself, not its usual reference; in the context 'John believes that
... wrote *Tom Sawyer*' it names a sense.

As a result, Frege not only turns aside a possible counterexample to
his principle that the reference of an expression is that whose identity
guarantees substitution *salva veritate*, but he uses his newly developed
theory of sense to do so. Frege's account of such contexts of indirect
quotation and the description of what people think and believe,
descriptions of so-called propositional attitudes, has met with criticism.
It seems to commit him to a hierarchy of indirect senses and references,
since indirect contexts may be embedded to any depth, as in 'John
thinks that Maisie doubts whether Mary believes that he will marry
Cynthia'. Frege could reply that if the facts of tortuous usages require
such complexity, his theory can provide it. Then again it is said that in
'Mary believes that Samuel Clemens did not write *Tom Sawyer*' the name
'Samuel Clemens' must name the man, because we can cross-refer using
pronouns: 'Mary believes that Samuel Clemens did not write *Tom
Sawyer*, but she is wrong, because he did.' Clearly the pronoun 'he' refers
to Clemens/Twain, and surely it picks up the reference of the name in
the first occurrence, which must therefore name the man. This case is
harder, but pronouns are slippery, and one might claim the 'he' is what
Peter Geach has called a 'pronoun of laziness',[2] simply avoiding a

[2] P. T. Geach (1962) *Reference and Generality*. Ithaca: Cornell University Press.

tedious repetition of the name. Since the same name can be used in a sentence now directly, now indirectly, this is no longer a counter-example to Frege's theory. Again there are cases where a name used in a report of an attitude or saying is clearly used directly, and not in the sense meant by the bearer of the attitude, as in 'Oedipus believed that his father was an obnoxious roadhog', when we know that Oedipus's father was not known to him as his father. But such cases simply show that belief contexts are complex and varied, not that they automatically require a change of reference. Frege's theory can be challenged, but it is still a strong contender.

The other dimension in respect to which Frege's theory is systematic is when considering the senses of functional expressions, including predicates and quantifiers. Just as functional expressions combine with other expressions to produce saturated or complete expressions, and the functions which are their references are saturated by other things to give objects as their values, so the senses of functional expressions are themselves functions which combine with other senses to produce complete or saturated senses. The parallelism between saturated (complete) and unsaturated (incomplete) runs across signs, senses, and references in close harmony. Frege denies that in a predication such as 'Brownie is a horse' there is need of a logical copula to glue the names 'Brownie' and 'horse' together into a predication: rather the concept-word itself is unsaturated: the true logical unit is not the noun 'horse' but the verb phrase 'is a horse', and there is no logical category of names which includes both singular names and common names. In this, Frege opposed tradition. Whereas most logicians would have said that a concept is the sense of a predicate expression or a common noun, and a class (the extension) is the reference of such an expression, Frege regarded concepts as incomplete references, with other functions being the senses determining them. The class corresponding to a concept-word, e.g., the class of horses corresponding to the concept-word or predicate '(is a) horse', was not the reference of a concept-word, since concepts and concepts words are unsaturated; rather it is an object referred to by a saturated expression, 'the class of things which are *F*'. This parallelism compelled Frege to deny, in his essay 'On Concept and Object', that an expression like 'the concept *horse*' names a concept: concepts, being unsaturated, can only be named by an unsaturated expression like '... is a horse'. He is forced to claim, counterintuitively, that the concept *horse* is not a concept but an object.

The sense of a clause or sentence is a proposition, or as Frege called it, a *thought*. It is such propositions, for whose timeless existence Frege argued eloquently in his late essay 'The Thought',[3] that are the primary bearers of truth and falsity, and they are referred to indirectly in reporting propositional attitudes. Propositions form the common content of beliefs, opinions, and surmises, shared by all who think the same thing. They are what we understand when we understand a sentence, and they are what we understand in common when we successfully communicate using sentences. They are neither physical nor mental, but inhabit a 'third realm' of abstract, objective but acausal things, along with the objects of mathematics. This Platonistic view became stronger in Frege's philosophy as it developed: earlier statements about numbers and contents can be interpreted in a more Kantian or conceptualist vein. And although Frege lived to see his conviction in the objective existence of logical objects such as numbers and classes shaken by the inconsistency in his logical system, his faith in the objectivity of propositions and other senses remained undiminished.

Natural language does not obviously present us with timeless propositions as the contents of its sentences. For most of the history of Western philosophy it was assumed that propositions, being expressible in tensed sentences, like 'Brownie is galloping', would change their truth-value over time, for example, this proposition would be true at times when Brownie is galloping and false at others. Frege needed to explain how the context-dependent or variable element in sentences and other expressions is compatible with their senses being timeless or invariant. We now know this as the question of the semantics of indexical expressions. Tenses form just one case: the same goes for demonstratives, personal pronouns and in general any expressions whose references vary systematically according to the context in which sentences containing them are uttered. One might suppose that the linguistic meaning of an expression is its sense, but this can apply only to those expressions quite void of any indexical element, since the truth-value of 'It's raining' varies with the place and time of utterance, whereas the linguistic meaning does not. Conversely, Frege holds that the sense of an expression determines its reference, so if the sense of 'It's raining' were fixed across all occasions of use, it could not vary in reference, its truth-value. Hence the linguistic meaning cannot be the sense.

Frege's solution to this is discussed only briefly but it is ingenious. It is to take the *expression* to include more than just the words spoken. Alongside the words will be some appropriate aspects of the context or

---

[3] First of a series of articles posthumously published together as *Logical Investigations*.

situation of utterance, such as the speaker, time, place, addressee. Frege claimed in 'The Thought' that in this case the time of utterance is part of the expression of the thought. The complete expression is then a hybrid made up partly of words and partly of real context, and this hybrid determines a sense uniquely. However, Frege does not go on to elaborate how the linguistic meaning and the context cooperate to determine a sense. In this as in many other respects, we may be disappointed about the sketchiness of Frege's views, but since he was a mathematician pursuing logic, and not a philosopher of language, the brevity is understandable.

The sense of an expression (whether purely verbal or hybrid) is what we understand when we know 'what it means': it is what we fail to understand when someone speaks a language that is unintelligible to us. Frege calls the relation that human speakers have to the senses of expressions which they understand 'grasping' (*erfassen*) the sense. To grasp a sense is to be put thereby into indirect cognitive relation to the expression's reference. If I grasp the sense of the expression 'the fourth US President to be assassinated' I am by that very fact thinking about John F. Kennedy, whether or not I know that Kennedy was this fourth assassinated President. As we use language in everyday situations, however, the strict relationship between an expression, its sense and its reference is not always obeyed. Some expressions, such as 'Odysseus' or 'the greatest prime number' or 'Odysseus returned to his homeland from Troy' may wholly fail to have a reference, even though they have a clear enough sense. A name of a person, such as 'Dr. Gustav Lauben', may awake different associations in different people and they may thereby associate different senses with it. One person may think of Dr. Lauben as the only doctor living in such and such a house, while another may think of him as the only person born in a certain town on September 13, 1875. For normal communication it does not matter if these senses do not exactly match, as long as we are clear that they have the same reference.

Likewise in his logical reconstruction of mathematics, Frege recognizes that there may be some looseness of fit between expressions we understood previously, such as '2', and how they are to be understood upon logical reconstruction, such as 'the value-range of the concept of being equinumerous with the concept of being identical with 0 or identical with 1'. Indeed it is not even obvious that in such cases the *reference* of the reconstructed logical item is the same as that of its intuitive predecessor. Such readiness to allow a measure of stipulation to enter his system is seen in Frege's conventional stipulation that the truth-values are to be identified

with their own unit value-ranges.[4] However, Frege did not intend his logi-
co-mathematical system to faithfully capture *all* the nuances of previous
intuitive mathematics, since he regarded this as defective. For scientific
purposes, Frege would not tolerate truth-value gaps or referenceless names,
whereas these abound in unreconstructed discourse.

5. After Frege

Frege's efforts in logic and the foundations of mathematics revolutionized both areas, but his achievements were slow to gain recognition. The
first person fully to appreciate Frege's greatness, Bertrand Russell, ironically also informed Frege of the contradiction in his system which put
paid to Frege's logicist efforts. After the discovery of this contradiction,
Frege's efforts were bypassed by those of others – Russell and Whitehead,
Hilbert, and Zermelo – who were intent on providing their own solutions to the problems Frege's work had raised. Russell and Whitehead
attempted to carry the logicist project forward under the weight of complications incurred by adopting ramified type theory as a way of avoiding paradox, but their need to assume the dubious axioms of infinity and
reduction cast doubt on the success of their attempt to derive mathematical theories from pure logic alone. Hilbert concentrated on the need
to provide finitary proofs of the consistency of mathematical theories.

Both Hilbert's program and the logicism of Russell and Whitehead
were dealt a severe blow by Gödel's discovery of the incompleteness of
the formal arithmetic of natural numbers with addition and multiplica-
tion. This incompleteness applied to any system powerful enough to
formulate such arithmetic, such as higher-order logic and type theory.
Gödel's second incompleteness proof showed that the consistency of
such systems could only be proved in more powerful and hence theoretically less secure systems. Gentzen and others succeeded, using kinds
of transfinite induction, in providing consistency proofs for increasingly comprehensive parts of pure mathematics. In time the threat of radical inconsistency requiring a complete rethinking of logic receded.
Such inconsistencies as appeared in powerful systems of logic were cor-
rigible by minor repairs. Mathematicians, to the extent that they took
an interest in such foundational matters, 'voted with their feet' for set
theory as a foundational medium; they remain confident of its consistency, but no one pretends that it is a pure logic.

----

[4] In *Grundgesetze*, Section 10.

By contrast, the system of pure logic that Frege established, namely higher-order predicate logic, has proved to be adequate to *formulate* (but not prove) the principles of the mathematical theories, arithmetic and analysis, that interested Frege. In the period between 1915 and 1968 attention was concentrated almost exclusively on the first-order fragment of this logic, that part where only singular nominal variables are quantified, for which Gödel showed completeness in 1930, and for which most results of model theory were proved. Despite its completeness, however, the expressive limitations of this system mean that it is unable to characterize interesting theories categorically, that is, so that all models are isomorphic and have the same cardinality. It is not possible to define in first-order logic what it means to be finite, or to confine models of the Peano axioms to the obvious intended ones. By contrast, all models of second-order Peano arithmetic are isomorphic. Frege never considered confining attention to only the first-order part of his logic.

In the 1930s, it was shown by Alonzo Church that even the first-order part of predicate logic is not decidable, that is, there is no mechanical procedure which sorts the theorems (valid formulas) from the non-theorems (invalid formulas): if a formula is valid, this can be shown mechanically, but if it is invalid, no single mechanical test suffices. The question of decidability, the decision problem, was investigated for many theories. When investigating such problems, it was crucial to fix what is meant by a mechanical procedure. Of the several mutually equivalent definitions which emerged, the most striking was that of a Turing machine, due to Alan Turing. Turing's machines were theoretical in nature, but they were described in a way which invited physical realization. Nearly all modern digital computers conform to the principles governing Turing's machines, though their use of stored programs is closer to equivalent ideas of the American logician Emil Post. Church himself developed a different but theoretically equivalent account of computability, based on his lambda calculus. The lambda calculus, like Frege's logic, is based on the concept of a function, and embodies a notation and principles for both abstracting functions from contexts and applying the functions so abstracted to new arguments. Frege's account of the ancestral in the *Begriffsschrift* contains a powerful and rarely mentioned notation in which one can abstract and apply functions in much the same way as the lambda calculus, but the notation was not carried forward into the later logic, where value-ranges take over equivalent roles.

Frege was the first logician to specify in detail and with precision the principles governing a logical system: he laid down clear canons of definition, upon which modern treatments offer only incidental improvements, and was the first to formulate clear rules of inference, including substitution. His proofs remain to this day a model of clear exposition, elegant derivation and flawless procedure. He was also scrupulous in differentiating between the symbols and formulas within his formal language and the expressions used to talk about them. So precise was Frege's work that it was a quarter of a century before such precision was attained again, in the work of Łukasiewicz and Leśniewski.

Frege's view of the axioms of his system was old-fashioned by contrast with the ideas of Hilbert and other mathematicians of the time. Frege retained the view that axioms should have a determinate sense and should be self-evidently true, this truth being preserved by the inference rules. However, the shaky nature of self-evidence was exposed cruelly by the inconsistency of his own system. Frege was also reluctant to admit that his formulas might be given a different sense, or might not be determinate in sense. Having taken pains to make clear to the reader exactly what the primitives of his system meant, he saw no need for a distinction between proof-theoretic and semantic considerations. Those logicians who had been accustomed to the Boolean idea of logic as a calculus, such as Schröder, allowed that the proof procedure of a system might be characterized in abstraction from its interpretations, of which there could be many.

Frege, by contrast, regarded manipulations of signs without determinate meaning as a mere game. This was formalism, a view he had been combatting in the philosophy of mathematics for decades. What he did not realize was that the crude formalisms he had successfully ridiculed were giving way to a more sophisticated position using the very tools he was introducing, of formal systems with a precise proof procedure. Frege's insistence on the universality of his system, its application to all things in all circumstances, made it very difficult for him to consider alternative interpretations or interpretations which would fit only some models and not others. Hence Frege was unable to appreciate the need for a division between proof-theoretic and semantic studies, and the considerations of soundness, completeness, and other model-theoretic notions which such a division bring in their train. The breakthrough in this area was Alfred Tarski's definition of truth for formalized languages.

Tarski's semantics followed in the tradition established by Frege, Russell, and other Poles in considering only the extensional side of meaning: truth-values, individual references, functions, classes, and relations in extension. Russell had talked about intensional matters, but apart from the ramification in ramified type theory, which it was agreed the axiom of reducibility undid again, did not thematize them. Frege, however, had introduced sense alongside reference, although he too had agreed with the extensionalists that logic and mathematics is *about* extensions, even if we only gain access to them via intensions. As soon as one considers thematizing intensions, however, as when reasoning about the content of propositional attitudes, or considering the identity conditions of propositions and other senses, the question arises as to how to introduce intensional elements into logic. Two of Frege's greatest admirers among logicians, Church and Carnap, undertook the task of formulating a logic of intension as well as extension. In Carnap's case, an additional motivation was to provide a semantics for modal logic. Frege, like other extensionalists, took a deflationary view of modality. For him, to call a proposition necessary was merely to say one had some law in mind from which it followed. Carnap's logic of intension and extension, and his investigations of modal logic, marked the beginning of a much wider study, pushed forward intensively by Richard Montague, of logical systems apt for the expression of formal principles governing features found in natural languages but not in the logic of the extensionalists, such as modality, tense, indexicality, and intentionality. While Frege would have had little sympathy with the motivation for such studies, his work had provided the means by which it could be pursued.

In the years following 1950, Frege's works were increasingly widely translated and discussed, those unpublished works which survived bombing were published, and due principally to the tireless advocacy and commentary of Michael Dummett, Frege somewhat belatedly took his deserved place in the pantheon of great philosophers. He also came to be regarded as the father of analytic philosophy, and indeed there is no doubt that his concerns have been echoed through much analytic philosophy, and that those influenced deeply by him – Russell, Wittgenstein, the Poles, Carnap, Quine – are the foremost analytic philosophers. The reception of his work was, however, ironically reversed from his own estimate of what is important: he was at first appreciated primarily as a philosopher of language and philosophical logician, his philosophy of mathematics gaining appreciation much later, and his logic and mathematics themselves remaining underexposed. Frege said that he fought against language, and was forced to occupy himself with language despite its not being his proper concern.

Frege spent much of 'The Thought' considering the distinction between ideas and thoughts (propositions). Ideas are private, subjective, and mental; they are dependent upon their bearers or subjects and inaccessible to others. They contrast with physical bodies and other objective things which are part of the objective causal order, but they also contrast with propositions, which are likewise objective but not part of the causal order. How then do we come into cognitive access with propositions, or, as Frege says, *grasp* them? Frege admits that he cannot supply an account, he merely says that just as our awareness of physical things is based on some mental aspect going beyond mere sense-impressions, so the mental can enable us to grasp propositions. In this way propositions, which are in themselves causally inert, may indirectly exert a causal influence, via thinkers who grasp them. Frege's account of the mental is not clearly mistaken – his solid common sense realism sees to that – but it is by the standards of its day undifferentiated and commonplace. It is hardly surprising that a mathematician should not be concerned to elaborate a phenomenology, not least as a result of his aversion to the intrusion of psychology into logic. So we can find little that Frege has contributed directly to the philosophy of mind beyond his insistence on the objectivity of the content of thinking.

This makes all the more imperative a resolution of the initial paradox, that while he would have been surprised to have been told so, no one did more than Frege to furnish formal foundations for cognitive science. The paradox dissolves on consideration of the adjective 'formal'. While Frege did not contribute to the philosophy of mind, he made incomparable advances in formal logic, and contributed influentially to the philosophy of language, in particular to the theory of meaning. To the extent that cognition requires thinking, and thinking is expressible in language, and to the extent that the formal manipulation of information follows algorithmic patterns akin to those of formal inference, Frege's contribution to the foundations of cognitive science is essential and inescapable.

Literature

Frege wrote in German, and a scholarly approach to his work requires one to consult it in the original. However, he wrote in a particularly clear and unphilosophical German which has been generally well translated,[5] so it is possible to get a good understanding from the translations. In the list

---

[5] The only serious dispute has been over how to translate the semantic terms *bedeuten* and *Bedeutung*. For the latter, all the following have been suggested: indication, denotation, nominatum, reference, meaning. We have used 'signify' or 'refer to' for *bedeuten*, and 'reference' for *Bedeutung*. The forthcoming translation of *Grundgesetze* will leave the latter term untranslated.

below are the main works, listed chronologically in the first German edition with English translations, major secondary literature, and important works directly influenced by Frege.

Primary works

A Critical Elucidation of Some Points in E. Schröder, Lectures on the Algebra of Logic' *(1895) (trans. by P. Geach). In P. Geach and M. Black, Translations from the Philosophical Writings of Gottlob Frege.* Oxford: Blackwell, 1980, pp. 86–106.
Begriffsschrift, eine der arithmetischen nachgebildete Formelsprache des reinen Denkens. Halle: Nebert, 1879. English translations: (1) Begriffsschrift. S. Bauer-Mengelberg (trans.). In: J. van Heijenoort (ed.), *From Frege to Gödel. A Source Book in Mathematical Logic*, 1879–1931. Cambridge, MA: Harvard University Press, 1967, pp. 5–82. (2) Conceptual Notation. T.W. Bynum (Trans.), in G. Frege, *Conceptual Notation and Related Articles*, T. W. Bynum (ed.). Oxford: Clarendon Press, 1972, pp. 101–203.
Die Grundlagen der Arithmetik. Breslau: Koebner, 1884. Translation: *The Foundations of Arithmetic*, J.L. Austin (Trans.). Oxford: Blackwell, 1950.
Grundgesetze der Arithmetik, begriffsschriftlich abgeleitet. Jena: Pohle. Vol I 1893; Vol. II 1903. Partial translation *Basic Laws of Arithmetic. Exposition of the System*, M. Furth (ed. & trans.). Berkeley: University of California Press, 1964. A complete English translation is in preparation.

Posthumous collections

Kleine Schriften, I. Angelelli (ed.). Darmstadt: Wissenschaftliche Buchgesellschaft, 1967. Translation: *Collected Papers on Mathematics, Logic, and Philosophy.* Oxford: Blackwell, 1984.
Logische Untersuchungen. G. Patzig (ed.). Göttingen: Vandenhoeck & Ruprecht, 1966. Translation: *Logical Investigations,* P. Geach and R.H. Stoothoff (trans.). Oxford: Blackwell, 1977.
Nachgelassene Schriften. Hamburg: Meiner, 1969. Translation: *Posthumous Writings.* Oxford: Blackwell, 1979.
On the Foundations of Geometry and Formal Theories of Arithmetic, Eike-Henner W. Kluge (trans.). New Haven: Yale University Press, 1971.
The Frege Reader, M. Beaney (ed.). Oxford: Blackwell, 1997.
Translations from the Philosophical Writings of Gottlob Frege, P. Geach and M. Black (trans. and ed.). Oxford: Blackwell, 1980.
Wissenschaftlicher Briefwechsel. Hamburg: Meiner, 1976. Translation: *Philosophical and Mathematical Correspondence.* Oxford: Blackwell, 1980.

Selected secondary literature

Burge, T. (2005). *Truth, Thought, Reason. Essays on Frege.* Oxford: Clarendon.
Dummett, M. (1973). *Frege. Philosophy of Language.* London: Duckworth.
Dummett, M.(1991). *Frege. Philosophy of Mathematics.* London: Duckworth.

Selected works influenced by Frege

Carnap, R. (1947). *Meaning and Necessity. A Study in Semantics and Modal Logic.* Chicago: University of Chicago Press.
Church, A. (1941). *The Calculi of Lambda-Conversion.* Princeton: Princeton University Press.

Husserl, E. (1891). *Philosophie der Arithmetik*. Halle/S: Pfeffer. Translation: *Philosophy of Arithmetic*, D. Willard (trans.). Dordrecht: Kluwer, 2003.

Russell, B. (1903). *The Principles of Mathematics*. London: Allen & Unwin.

Whitehead, A.N. and Russell, B. (1910–1913). *Principia Mathematica* (3 vols). Cambridge; Cambridge University Press.

Wright, C. (1983). *Frege's Conception of Numbers as Objects*. Aberdeen: Aberdeen University Press.

9
Remembering William James

Tracy B. Henley

It is hard to imagine that anyone attracted to this book – those that bought it for themselves, or even the student flipping through it in the library stacks – would not have some sense of William James as a figure in the history of cognitive science. After all, James is commonly held to be the patriarch of American psychology; if you know anything about him it is likely to be that he wrote on 'the stream of thought'. And what is cognitive psychology anyway, once we delete the jargon and strip away the finery, but still further analysis of thought?

I mention this for two reasons. First, it is my goal in this chapter to tell you a few interesting tidbits about William James and his ideas concerning what we today would call the province of cognitive psychology that you might not have already known. Second, it serves as a nice setup for the major task of this chapter – seriously addressing the connection James has to modern cognitive science. Some historians (e.g., Robinson, 1993) have argued that James has no real influence on contemporary psychology – including cognitive psychology. To facilitate a critical examination of such a claim, I will begin with a brief biographical sketch of William James, then present a selective overview of some of James's ideas on cognitive processes. With that as foundation, we can investigate James's legacy for, and connection to, the modern era.

William James: A biographical sketch

We are fortunate to have many different accounts of William James from a diversity of sources. Literally dozens of academics have written about him and his influence on their lives and careers (e.g., Angell 1911; see also the *Psychological Review*, 50 (2), 1943 for a series of essays by notables such as Allport, Dewey, and Thorndike in honor of William

James). Varied others such as W.E.B. DuBois (the founder of the NAACP), Winifred Smith Rieber (the famed portrait artist), and Helen Keller (the blind and deaf writer) also recorded their experiences with the man. The composite picture is of a short, wiry, and fragile man, yet energetic and masculine. His alert blue eyes were charming, but betrayed the wisdom of a sage as well as the intensity of raw genius. As Rieber quipped, 'his mind seemed to have blown in on a storm' (see Joralemon 1980).

He is universally remembered as a gentleman in the finest sense of that word, and altruistic kindness seems to be the trait that everyone he encountered was impressed by. Sober, serious, and tranquil, there was also that boyish grin that evidenced William had a fun-loving, indeed impish side as well. You can virtually select any page of his many published volumes at random and find that imp's sense of humor leaking through. Last, his knowledge-base and interests were painfully broad in scope, spanning not only the troublesome topics of philosophy and psychology but unabashedly reaching into the unknown – into such areas as religion, mysticism, spiritualism, even psychic phenomena.

For the reader interested in 'James the man', let me recommend two relatively recent biographies: Townsend's (1996) *Manhood at Harvard: William James and Others*, and Simon's (1998) *Genuine Reality: A Life of William James*. Although neither offers anything particularly new about James as he relates to cognitive science, they both provide a rich exploration of how James came to 'be', and of his personal life.[1]

Early years

William James was born on January 11th, 1842, in New York City. His grandfather – also William James – was an Irish immigrant who by the time of our William's birth was among the wealthiest men in New York State. James's brother, Henry, is the noted Henry James of American literature. His father, Henry James, Sr., was a self-styled iconoclastic theologian, strongly influenced by the philosophy of the mystic Emanuel Swedenborg. Lears (1987) suggested that, based in part on Henry Sr.'s

---

[1] We do not have room to offer a complete biography of William James. The reader is directed to Evans (1990) for a chapter-length treatment with attention to his intellectual development culminating with the publication of the *Principles*, and to Myers (1986) for a relatively contemporary and thorough consideration. Perry (1935) is something of classic on the subject, Allen (1967) provides a book-length coverage, and Lewis (1991) offers a somewhat more global look at the entire James family. A surprisingly large number of others, going back over sixty years, also exist.

interpretation of Swedenborg's ideas, the James children were taught a value system that made self-assertions in defiance of God's will and defined morality in terms of submission of one's own will to God. Even if true, this surely sounds worse than it was. By all accounts (e.g., Myers 1986) the James household was filled not only with love, but also with freedom of expression and intellectual stimulation designed to prepare the children to be self-sufficient. Both travel and educational opportunities for the children were especially valued, and while still a young boy William probably encountered Emerson, Thoreau, Tennyson, and John Stuart Mill – not just in books, but in person.

Young William then grew up with much privilege – his father was a noted intellectual who had connections with many of the era's leading figures, as well as being independently wealthy from his own inheritance. This is evidenced from William's own formal education, which began with a series of governesses. From age nine until about thirteen he was rooted in New York, but over the next five years William's education included periods in England, France, Italy, Germany, and Switzerland. As a result, he was widely read, passable in several languages, but had no clearly focused interests.

With respect to 'higher' education, William began with a foray into art (including study with William Morris Hunt in Rhode Island) before entering the Lawrence Scientific School at Harvard when just nineteen. Virtually every biographer of James includes the fact that William labored over 'what to be when he grew up' to the point of pathology. Some (e.g., Lewis 1991) have suggested that his father's influence prodded him away from art and into science. One of the James's Boston neighbors, Charles Eliot, served as his chemistry teacher before rising to become Harvard's president.

It took William until age twenty-seven to complete his M.D. at Harvard, and the interim had its twists and turns. For example, there was an interest in biology, culminating with a trip alongside Louis Agassiz to Brazil in 1865. There were also trips to Europe, in part to battle the 'insomnia, digestive disorders, eye-troubles, weakness of the back, and sometimes deep depression' (James 1920, Vol. I, p. 84) that vexed William as he struggled to find himself and a vocation. It was on such a therapeutic trek that William developed an interest in psychology – making time to hear Emil du Bois-Reymond and Hermann von Helmholtz – in Germany and becoming familiar with Claude Bernard's work in France (Taylor 1990) before returning to Harvard.

For the next few years William lived at home, continued reading voraciously in areas of interest to him, saw a series of modest works accepted for publication (mostly reviews), and struggled with illnesses usually seen as resulting from depression or some related psychological cause. It was near the end of this period that William had his infamous encounter with the writings of French philosopher Charles Renouvier, from which he embraced free will and was somewhat liberated from his psychosomatic ailments. Although many writers suggest that reading Renouvier 'cured' William of his depression, that is not the case. Myers (1986) credited any meaningful improvement in his condition to his 1878 marriage to Alice Howe Gibbens, and an analysis of his letters clearly shows that even then the symptoms never fully disappeared. As an aside, although all five of the James children were accomplished in their own way, each suffered from what we *post hoc* might identify as psychological problems. For example, even his loving family was frequently worried that Henry spent too much time in his own little world, and Lewis (1991) chronicled Robertson's alcoholism and hospitalizations, called Alice a neurotic invalid, and suggested that Wilkinson never fully recovered from his service in the Civil War.

William felt his reading of Renouvier was a 'crisis' and wrote 'my first act of free will shall be to believe in free will' (James 1920, Vol. I, p. 147). If one accepts Lear's thesis, then we might take these words literally to be William's act of defiance against his father and Henry Sr.'s theology. Other, more definitive biographies (e.g., Myers 1986), suggest less Freudian interpretations. At any rate, it was no doubt a turning point, and soon William started work teaching physiology at Harvard.

William found 'the work very interesting and stimulating' (James 1920, Vol. I, p. 168), and by all accounts was an excellent teacher. Eliot was impressed enough to offer him a permanent appointment, and in 1875 William taught his first course in psychology. Although one might rightly think of William James more as a psychological philosopher than as a psychologist proper, his first teaching in philosophy actually did not occur until 1879.

As philosopher and psychologist

William's 'relationship' to the whole field of psychology – not just his legacy for modern cognitive psychology – is complex and subject to interpretation. On the one hand he was a founding member of the American Psychological Association (APA) and twice served as its president (only G. Stanley Hall was similarly honored). He authored perhaps the greatest work ever written for the discipline, *The Principles of Psychology* (1890), and the book even meant enough to him that he worked on it during his honeymoon. This effort, as well as his impact on Harvard students such as Thorndike and Hall, mark him as *the* father of American psychology as a science.

On the other hand, we know that William came to find psychology – or more precisely the German style of experimental psychology ('brass-instrument' and 'algebraic-formula filled psychology') tedious. His career can be reasonably seen as a movement away from (at least physiological or experimental) psychology into philosophy (see Starbuck 1943). Impish barbs about both Wundt and Fechner can be found in the *Principles*, two men he saw as establishing scientific psychology. Allen (1967) argued that near the end of his life he even *feared* that he would be known and remembered as a psychologist.

The standard story then is that soon after William James introduced this new German style psychology to America, he likewise brought in a bona fide German psychologist – Hugo Münsterberg – to take control of it at Harvard (as early as 1892). Taylor (1992a) has tried to provide something of an alternative by actually reviewing James's empirical efforts and suggesting that James was looking toward a French, not German, model for American psychology (Taylor 1990). Several recent scholars (e.g., Howard 1992) have similarly suggested that James himself was always more interested in the softer side of psychology – its philosophical issues, perhaps even 'clinical' psychology.

Although I cannot imagine anyone who would object to merely asserting William's importance to psychology, given that this is an essay about his impact on one subfield of modern psychology at least some 'pointing to' evidence seems in order. For the purpose of this chapter, it still should suffice to say that William James's contributions to American psychology in general can speak for themselves – that is, he remains a key figure in our discipline's history as taught through textbooks and as created by scholarly historians. Moreover, celebrations of him and his *Principles* were ubiquitous in the early 1990s, as both his magnum opus and the APA were honored with regal centennials. William James was 'in the air', and several anthologies (e.g., Donnelly 1992; Johnson & Henley 1990) as well as special issues of leading journals provided *prima facie* testimony to his enduring importance. And, as a final example, prior to the widespread rediscovery of William in the 1990s, Malone (1990) noted that although dead for over seventy-five years, William James was still cited 255 times in 1987 according to the Social Sciences Citation Index. You can safely assume that there were not 255 articles published by historians of psychology that year, so his influence must extend beyond that small circle.

Final years

William's contributions did not stop with the *Principles* or with Münsterberg's arrival. In 1892 he completed his *Psychology* (the *Jimmy*, or *Briefer Course*), largely an abridgment of the *Principles*. Later books, such as *Talks to Teachers* (1899) and *The Varieties of Religious Experience* (1902), are replete with information for psychology. Even his philosophical system – pragmatism – is closely related. Thorndike urged James as late as 1905 to revise the *Briefer Course*, but not the *Principles*, on grounds that it was already a classic (Joncich 1968; King 1992). Although James seems to have considered the idea, it did not happen.

Ever the traveler, William attended the 1905 Psychological Congress in Rome and of course helped introduce Freud to America at Clark University in 1909. Although his formal connection to psychology at Harvard waned from 1897 onward, he remained an active member of the philosophy department until 1907.

In 1898, William likely suffered a heart attack, but that did little to slow him down. He spent much of the next ten years in Europe, and lecturing away from Harvard had all but become his day job. A prolific writer until the end, William became increasingly ill with heart problems during the summer of 1910. William James died on August 26th, 1910. He passed way resting peacefully in his wife's arms at about 2:30 a.m., while at his summer home in Chocorua, New Hampshire.

Cognition in *The Principles of Psychology*

In this section, my goal is to provide another brief sketch, this time about James's actual thoughts on cognitive processes. I want to start with a consideration of the *Principles*, including its organization. That organization I feel betrays a crucial theme in Jamesian psychology – the interplay between physiology and experience. In turn, that theme makes consciousness the central phenomenon for psychology (and so James's *Principles*). With consciousness seen as the central element of James's psychology, we can better appreciate what he did and did not elect to say about other facets of cognition.

The Principles of Psychology: An overview

As a writer William James had a true talent for being personal without being intrusive, and nowhere is this more evident than in his psychology. E.B. Holt (1942) explained,

James admits the reader to his workshop; where he, the whole man and untrammeled by academic mannerisms, is examining the facts, all the facts and all the appearances that present themselves as facts, and trying to find for them some intelligible arrangement. There is no window dressing. Inconvenient items are not banished into corners to get them out of sight. And where outstanding contradictions exist, there they are, exposed to view. (p. 34)

I am going to deliberately focus on William James's *Principles*, and to a far lesser degree the *Psychology* (the 1892 *Briefer Course*). Although he had many relevant published books and articles, and while there exists many correspondences that historians today enjoy sifting through that do contain tantalizing insights, if a Jamesian legacy for cognitive science endures, it surely is to be found in his most widely read and cited works.

In the mid-1870s Henry Holt wanted to publish a psychology textbook. Something like the 1870 edition of Herbert Spencer's *Principles of Psychology* seemed to be what was needed. Holt contracted John Fiske, a disciple of Spencer working at Harvard, but he was unable to complete the project (Evans 1990). Fiske, a member of the Metaphysical Club – which also included C.S. Pierce, Oliver Wendell Holmes, and William James – recommended James. Holt offered, and in early June of 1878 James accepted the task, negotiating with Holt a two-and-a-half-year time frame. Holt had wanted it by June of 1880, if at all possible; he got it in May of 1890!

There was of course some criticism (see Thorne & Henley 1997, for a short summary of both initial and much more recent criticisms), but on balance William James's *The Principles of Psychology* was very well received. The major objection was to the book's apparent lack of organization. It was true that many of the chapters represented articles that James had written (and published) in the twelve years and as such did not fit together seamlessly, but James himself (1892/1948) defended the book's organization as something he had planned.

The first ten chapters cover the basics: scope, method, current theory, the brain, conscious experience, and the self. Miller (1942) argued that within these early chapters James changes the face of psychology for evermore. Miller cited some thirteen points in which the psychology of his day was indebted to James for having freed the discipline of old and unproductive ways of thinking. Most of Miller's points – such as the distinction between consciousness and the content of consciousness, a philosophically plausible account of the unconscious, the phenomenological fact that one material object has many aspects, the recognition that consciousness is not an object, and the understanding of thought as our internal, mental representations (as they relate both to brain and behavior) – many in modern cognitive psychology take for granted as givens. But of course they are not, and seldom is James credited with the introduction of such issues.

The first ten chapters can be seen as providing groundwork for the later, more topical chapters. That topical material includes units on attention, conception, discrimination, association, perception, memory, imagination, and reasoning – all clearly of importance to cognitive psychology. But, a casual scan of the table of contents will not find a chapter on cognition *per se*. Why not, and what significance does that have for James as a figure in the history of cognitive science?

Explanation in psychology

There are at least three reasons why James did not have a chapter on cognition. The first ought to be obvious even from that casual scan of the table of contents – he divides the relevant material into several different chapters. This is clearly true, but why he does this deserves some explanation (and follows below). A second simple reason for why there is no chapter on 'cognition' is language. Although the term is in standard usage today, it was not during James's time. Similar arguments have been made in detail about the evolution of how psychologists use the term 'behavior' (see Angell 1913; Hibbard & Henley 1994; Leahey 1993). There is still a deeper and more interesting explanation.

Most textbooks in psychology today provide not one, but *three* explanations for psychological phenomena. Typically, one explanation will reflect that for many phenomena psychologists seek to provide a physiological explanation (say as in how testosterone can facilitate aggression). A second account will focus on how behavioral phenomena can be caused by the environment (such as how being rewarded for modeling aggression can lead to further aggression). The third is usually less specified, and serves to explain mental events or to make mental events causal in directing actions (e.g., defining depression as aggression turned inward). For example, in James McConnell's classic introductory text, *Understanding Human Behavior* (1986), we find the 'Intra-Psychic', the 'Social-Behavioral', and the 'Biological' modes of explanation being used throughout.

Adopting McConnell's terms, when James writes about the stream of thought he is thus providing an intra-psychic perspective. Walter B. Cannon's location of emotion in specific brain structures is an example of the biological perspective, and at times James' own account of both memory and discrimination are similar. The social-behavioral perspective is often still introduced with Thorndike's cats (and of course no introductory text bothers to note that his original research animals, chickens, were housed in James's basement). In places, James's account of habit, even of the self, follows this pattern of explanation.

My assertion is that each of the standard types of explanation found within contemporary psychology texts are also found, and used advantageously, in James's *Principles*. James was clearly an intra-psychic functionalist, indeed remarking to Ernest Jones and Sigmund Freud that 'the future of psychology belongs to your work' (Jones 1955, p. 57). However, James was also committed to the belief that thoughts correspond to brain activity and should ultimately have brains as the point of their causal departure. For topics that had a plausible biological explanation, James gave one. For matters more removed from biology, James provided a functional, sometimes social-behavioral, but often intra-psychic account.

If my little exercise works for you, then several things emerge as possibilities. First, and most trivially, we can argue for James's impact on subsequent textbooks in psychology. Second, and more importantly, it can also tell us why the material on 'cognition' is not grouped together like it is in a contemporary text. James subdivided the material because parts of it he wanted to explain one way, and other parts he was obligated to explain differently. *Within* chapters, James is usually offering a coherent narrative (remember that they were often previously published as freestanding essays) leading to a singular sort of explanation. What form that explanation takes – 'intra-psychic', 'social-behavioral', or 'biological' – varies greatly *between* chapters. I submit that a careful reading of James will support this claim, and that what his earliest critics flagged as disorganization and inconsistency was in part his attempt to group material by how he could best explain it. Although James might have talked about a certain aspect of memory as a 'Brain-Fact', he also understood that any discussion of the stream of thought is at best moments away from lapsing into mere metaphysical speculation. Because not all aspects of cognition could be explained in one way, James never imagined grouping them together as a 'unit'.

Phenomenology and physiology

I have suggested that James recognized more-or-less the same three modes of explanation that we use today in psychology. Some others surely tacitly agree with at least part of this when they explore James's connection to American behaviorism or to learning theory (McConnell's social-behavioral – e.g., Malone 1990; Robinson 1993). Likewise, most every commentator has seen in James's writing a tension between the remaining two of these modes of explanation; more commonly called the phenomenological (a subset of McConnell's intra-psychic) and the physiological (McConnell's biological). Indeed, the 'standard' way of interpreting the *Principles* is *as* a treatise exploring the tension between psychology as physiology (the stuff of Helmholtz and Fechner) and psychology as about the phenomena of everyday experience (to some degree, the stuff of Brentano and Stumpf).

Sometimes for James this tension takes the form of explicitly contrasting associative (empiricist) and faculty or 'mind-stuff' (rationalistic) theories, where at other times James exquisitely uses his own phenomenological experiences to argue for a physiological point (or vice versa, with some physiological fact setting a context for an experiential observation). The tension is there, although the relationship between these two perspectives is more complex than 'either-or'.

For Giorgi (1990), the *Principles* presented a continual paradox between a highly objective scientific realism and a highly subjective experiential realism. It seems clear that this tension was not one generated by confusion or misunderstanding on James's part, but by an attempt to have a science that used as its bedrock the data of experience. In his own introduction James wrote,

> I have kept close to the point of view of natural science throughout the book. Every natural science assumes certain data uncritically, and declines to challenge the elements between which its own 'laws' obtain, and from which its own deductions are carried on. Psychology, the science of finite individual minds, assumes as its data (1) *thoughts and feelings*, and (2) *a physical world* in time and space with which they coexist and which (3) *they know*. Of course these data themselves are discussible; but the discussion of them (as of other elements) is called metaphysics and falls outside the province of this book. This book, assuming that thoughts and feelings exist and are vehicles of knowledge, thereupon contends that psychology when she has ascertained the empirical correlation of the various sorts of thought or feeling with the definite conditions of the brain, can go no farther – can go no farther, that is, as a natural science. (1890, pp. v–vi)

Attempts to have a science with a primacy upon subjective experience characterize later works such as Köhler's *Gestalt Psychology* (1947), and Merleau-Ponty's *Phenomenology of Perception* (1945/1962). Of course, such traditions have historically remained in the wings in American psychology.[2] The tension between phenomenology and physiology was productive for James; he was not seeking to resolve it, but to exploit it.

Consciousness

Consciousness is made central in James's *Principles*, at least in part then, because of his understanding of what scientific psychology should be. The stream of thought metaphor arises *because* James had a view that psychology should be a natural science with its own independent subject matter (Giorgi 1990; Pollio 1990). For James, we must understand the structure of this most subjective experience if we ever hope to ascertain the 'empirical correlation of the various sorts of thought or feeling with the definite conditions of the brain'.

Kantor (1942) provided a nice analysis of the evolution of James's thinking about consciousness, noting that after much wrestling James allowed for non-conscious mental states, even experiences, but for reasons both metaphysical and pragmatic focused his efforts on conscious experience. James argued that no empirical evidence existed to give a materialistic explanation to conscious experience, and the scientist in him was eventually moved to ask 'Does "consciousness" exist?' (James 1904). His resolution to his own question was to dispel any temptations he may have had, or notions held by others, that consciousness was 'thing-like' and to postulate that consciousness existed as a functional process.

As Hilgard (1969) discussed, for James psychology should then concern what we are aware of (conscious experience), what brain states accompany such awareness, and whatever processes mediate the two. However, like most 'functionalists' in the philosophy of mind today (e.g., Block 1980), James recognized that saying how brains and experiences are interrelated, was risky business (the last chapter of his *Psychology* [1892/1948] presents his clearest thoughts on this matter). James was also painfully aware of how little was known about brains at that time and what aspects of brains correlated with what aspects of experience. James was committed to this project of functionalism and perhaps even to a reductive material realism that might lie beyond it,

---

[2] Not surprisingly, there is a strong interest in William James among contemporary phenomenologists. The interested reader is directed to Edie (1970, or for more detail 1987); Linschoten (1968); Stevens (1974); and Wilshire (1968).

but was left only with the level of experience to report upon in detail (including social-behavioral observations).

A terse charting of James's stream

Given all this, it is not surprising that James's first pass at explaining cognition was very experience-near. James noted that '*The first fact for us, then, as psychologists, is that thinking of some sort goes on*' (p. 224) and proceeded from there to argue that thought is sensibly continuous, and the best metaphor to describe it is that of a stream. James wanted in this preliminary exposure to both make and muddle some distinctions.

Among the distinctions he wanted to make is that thought is composed of two types: substantive and transitive. The substantive thoughts are those that we can report on, whereas the transitive thoughts are those that link the substantive thoughts. Transitive thoughts, or 'relations' as he typically refers to them, are not experienced in the same way as substantive thoughts. Substantive thoughts are thoughts, such as of 'that bird', 'last night', etc., but transitive thoughts are merely feelings, such as of 'but' and 'leads to'.

Among the distinctions he wanted to muddle is that of perceiving and thinking. James astutely noted that awareness is for the largest part of the day just an awareness of what we are perceiving, and is not 'thought', in some more formal sense, at all. James did not elect to pursue the full implication of this, but rather was content to conclude that thinking and perceiving are of a kind with respect to the flow of conscious experience.

Whether they are percepts or thoughts, they are 'stable images', and as such substantive parts of the stream of consciousness. The movement between them, from one to another, is ephemeral in nature, however. Thus James is dubious about both introspecting, and a psychology of, the transitive relations. Although he considered these transitive parts over and over, it was primarily the substantive parts that were to be accounted for (see Henley 1989, for a modern-day cognitive-science analysis of the transitive parts).

James frequently wrote of the substantive parts as if they were schema-like (in the tradition of Bartlett, Piaget, Neisser, etc.). That is, as if they were structured, and also stored away for future use. These schematic thoughts are always in flux; each instantiation leaving an effect on the schema itself. Thus, James echoes the Heraclitian point that no thought can be thought twice. Each thinking comes with a unique context, at least in its history, one that will change the schema in some (although perhaps insignificant) way. These substantive parts can also be of variable size. That is, we can be aware of a pack of dogs, one dog in the pack, or of the color of the fur about the one dog's face. As such, thoughts can vary in complexity from simple sensations to complex ideas. As an aside, I would claim that much of what Wittgenstein (a reader and fan of James) or Rosch (neither a reader nor a fan)[3] says about categorization is also anticipated in the discussion here.

James held that every thought has a 'fringe', that as described is very much like the Gestalt concept of figure/ground.[4] The point that James wanted to underscore is that we have no isolated or disconnected thoughts. Each thought occurs in the stream, happening at that time because of the relations that obtain between it and the previous thought, and contains about it a fringe of relational possibilities, one of which in conjunction with external events will direct us to the next thought, and so on, *ad infinitum*. A related argument of how the stream 'works' as – as well as the type of mental representations that would be needed to populate it – is found in Husserl and other 'phenomenological' contemporaries of Wundt. The implications of such a theory for modern cognitive science, indeed even the claim that you could not have modern cognitive science without such an understanding has been developed by Dreyfus (1982).

James seemed to suggest that the 'flow' or energy in this stream is the process of discrimination; of noticing change between one thought and the next. Change in the world is mirrored by change in thought. Recognize that this picture of mental events is mentalistic, physiological, and behavioral, all concurrently. It is change in the world, a behaviorist point, that serves as the impetus for flow of thought. James asserted, although did not belabor, that the brain itself must constrain thought, as it is somehow the fundament of all these activities. Still, he made all these claims in the language and spirit of a mentalistic, phenomenological, psychology.

---

[3] This is not intended as an *ad hominem*, but merely a report on several conversations I had with Rosch in 1987. Rosch asserted that she derived none of her ideas about categorization from James, and that she was very disappointed when she read the *Principles* with his views as they related to current issues in cognitive psychology.
[4] Connections between James and Gestalt psychology abound, and may be of special interest to readers of this book. An excellent starting point is Henle (1990).

The varieties of cognitive experience

The Principles of Psychology is a book of many things: the structure of mind, the nature of human freedom, and the status of this new science itself. The text is composed of twenty-eight chapters in which these issues, and a variety of others, are intertwined to form a psychology. At least seven chapters consider the nature of thought in a more-or-less direct fashion. In order, these chapters are: Stream of Thought, Conception, Discrimination and Comparison, Association, Memory, Imagination, and Reasoning. Having just sketched the stream of thought, I will briefly review those subsequent chapters with regard to James's ideas about cognition.

In his chapter on 'Conception', James ostensibly contradicts most of what he previously had to say about the substantive parts of thought. Herein we are told that thoughts are not individuated schematic structures, but rather 'states of mind'. Once unpacked, the contradictions for the most part melt away, and we find that his analysis seems remarkably compatible with current connectionist conceptions. As an example Rumelhart, Smolensky, McClelland, and Hinton (1986) wrote,

> Schemata are not 'things'. There is no representational object which is a schema. Rather, schema emerge at the moment they are needed from the interaction of large numbers of much simpler elements all working in concert with one another. Schemata are not explicit entities, but rather are implicit in our knowledge and are created by the very environment they are trying to interpret – as it is interpreting them. (p. 20)

James further suggested that although states of mind are in flux, ever changing with each experience of them, concepts do not change. 'Concept' is clearly a technical term for James, unlike our casual use of the term in cognitive texts today. For James, a concept is more of a philosophical entity of the sort Peter Abelard and William of Ockham labored over than a psychological phenomenon. James concluded this section with a discussion of the central act(s) of conception: (1) a concept is the same concept if it has the same set of connective relations to other concepts, (2) concepts can be discriminated between each other, (3) categories (my use of the term) of concepts are formed when either they have similar connective relations, 'a sense of sameness', or when we cannot meaningfully discriminate between them except in trivial ways (numeric distinctiveness, etc.). Each of these particulars hinges around the phenomenological 'sense of sameness', and are just somewhat different facets of viewing that phenomenon. James (1890) wrote,

Some conceptions are of things, some of events, some of qualities. Any fact, be it thing, event, or quality, may be conceived sufficiently for purposes of identification, if only it be singled out and marked so as to separate it from other things. Simply calling it 'this' or 'that' will suffice. To speak in technical language, a subject may be conceived by its *denotation*, with no *connotation*, or a very minimum of connotation attached. The essential point is that it should be reidentified by us as that which we talk about; and no full representation of it is necessary for this, even when it is a fully representable thing. (pp. 462–463)

In this chapter we find James stressing the distinction between 'states of mind' – what contemporary psychology might mean by 'current cognitions' – and concepts. For James, states of mind are closely related to the underlying brain states. Concepts are both the same as those mind/brain states and not the same. They are the same in that they refer to the same mental event, but concepts exist (in a metaphysical sense) at the level of experience, and as such have properties unique to them as entities of experience. James wrote 'amid the flux of opinions and of physical things, the world of conceptions, or things intended to be thought about, stands stiff and immutable, like Plato's Realm of Ideas' (p. 462).

The chapter on 'Discrimination and Comparison' contains very little that develops James's actual account of thought, but instead describes in detail the specific processes of discrimination and comparison. However, James did argue here that discrimination and those transitive relations form the foundation of our stream of thought. Indeed, in this chapter James intertwined what he said previously about the transitive parts of thought with the process of discrimination. Discrimination is tied to relations in the sense that we experience one object as *on* another object, we experience one object as *bigger than* another object, we experience one object as *moving from* its present surroundings, and so forth.

In this chapter James also made it clear that discriminations are 'natural' occurrences following from change in the world and change in brain states. However, James does hold that experience can improve our powers of discrimination, noting in detail that the more interest we have in something the more discriminating we can be. Similarities between Gibson's metaphor of 'tuning', Neisser's 'perceptual cycle', and a wealth of literature on expertise abounds.

Long before James, a well-articulated account of the associative nature of thought was provided. James was well versed on the details from Aristotle to Mill, as well as in the criticism that it had elicited. James supported the basic associationistic model, noting that it is a compelling account of many phenomena concerning our mental events. James argued in his chapter on 'Association' that associationism was a good account in part because he believed that it was neurologically plausible, indeed suggested, by what was then known about the brain. This of course is still basically true, as the current resurgence of associationism as modern connectionism attests (see Crovitz 1990; or Thompson 1990, for more on James and connectionism).

James also noted that associationism was appealing owing to the fact that objects in the world are in fact associated. In all this, he seems every bit the empiricist, arguing that the structure of the associations in the world was realized as the structure of associations in the brain. Subsequently, James spent most of this chapter addressing the standard criticisms and concerns; chiefly, how many laws of association are needed. He concluded after lengthy consideration that contiguity and similarity are the most basic and productive associative laws.

James's chapter on 'Memory' is one in which a modern day connectionist might revel (again, see Thompson 1990, for more details on this similarity). It is basically physiologically reductive in nature, although James did not forsake the value of reporting on, or providing explanations from, experience. James believed that memories, one of those substantive parts of thought, are both psychological and physiological. In some ways repeating his chapter on 'Conception', the essential philosophical distinction between brain states and concepts is made again. For James, two stories could be told about memory: one about the underlying physiology and another more interesting one about the experience of memory.

I will skip the details of the physiological story, which are not very useful for us here. However, caught in their midst is one important suggestion, namely that the transitive parts of thought, the relations, are merely physiological in nature and have no other reality. They may be experienced, but they are experienced as bodily sensations, feelings, and urges. They have no 'psychological' component at all since they do not correspond to any stored image. This too is very much in the spirit of connectionism.

Trying to put James's ideas into connectionist terms, one might say that substantive thoughts are stored in the sense that they can be recreated from their relational network. The relational network, however, is ontologically different from what it is storing (Smolensky 1988). James's view is that concepts are psychological entities – meaning here that they can be reflected upon – and are stored in virtue of their relations to neighbors, but the relations themselves are not material for thought.

For James, a memory, like a concept, was both a brain state and something more: something that we can reflect on, can hold before ourselves. Memories for James are never isolated entities but always bring with them their neighbors (that 'fringe' in the stream of thought). Because a concept at one level is just some relational network, it is not surprising that concepts remembered tend to activate the neighbors they are related to.

James's chapter on 'Reasoning' opens with the statement that concepts are imaginal in nature. Previously, James had noted that perception and thinking were basically the same, and here he underscored this belief. What this leads to is the idea that percepts, particularly visual images, are what is associated, owing from their 'worldly connections'. This has a host of implications for contemporary cognitive science, as has been noted by Park & Kosslyn (1990; see also Nickerson 1990). Indeed, James was basically arguing that perception, like conception, is both a brain state and a psychological state. At the level of a brain state it is 'raw data' that are associated. At the psychological level, these percepts are categorized and discriminated.

It is when James starts to cash out the nature of discrimination as a psychological process (recall it was previously discussed in more 'basic' terms) that he begins to sound most like a modern cognitive psychologist with interest in categorization.[5] For James, discrimination as a psychological process involves conscious analysis, but also (more automatedly) abstraction from the specific to the general. Both of these processes are afforded in virtue of the transitive relations that obtain for – indeed create and structure – our substantive thoughts. This explanation clarifies his previous linkage between discrimination and the transitive relations. This whole process of categorization, hinging as it does on discrimination and relations, when discussed at the 'psychological level' is called reasoning.

Frequently in this chapter James really does seems to mean by reasoning what modern cognitive psychologists would call categorization. James defined reasoning as the combination of memory and association, and so the model for category formation becomes one in which we structure categories based upon objects having common patterns of associations (relations). We reason by making discriminations between current percepts or thoughts and the memory of existing categories. Or

---

[5] The connections between James's thoughts about reasoning and modern efforts on categorization remain striking to me. While this essay did not seem the proper vehicle to explore my observations in full detail, I invite those interested to look at Chapters IX and XXII of the *Principles*.

as James puts it, 'knowledge about a thing is knowledge of its relations' (1890, p. 259).

James further illustrated his view of reasoning by discussing what he calls 'modes of conceiving'. These modes of conceiving are our current salient 'interests' that structure what we attend to, discriminate along, organize by, etc., with respect to incoming information. Such modes of conceiving are in some ways like Husserl's notions of noesis and noema, perhaps even episodic memory (Neisser 1981), or *ad hoc* goal-driven categories that filter our seeing and thinking (Barsalou 1983). As an example of the latter, we might, if bored, see all objects through the 'can it be played with' mode of conceiving. Or in contemporary terms, reasoning in this situation is the process of asking for each new bit of information, does it fit into the 'can it be played with' category.

William James and cognitive science

The opening paragraph of this chapter outlined what one might call the vulgar or common view. That is, James was a major early American theorist who wrote about lots of topics of interest to cognitive psychologists. Ergo, James is clearly an important player in the history of cognitive science. I attempted throughout the previous section to make explicit connections between James and topics dear to present-day cognitive scientists (e.g., schema, neural networks, categorization), and even to some cognitive psychologists (e.g., Neisser). Moreover, I noted several other writers (e.g., Thompson 1990) who have also tried to forge such links between William James's ideas and modern cognitive psychology.

Although I wholly endorse it, I call the idea that James is *obviously* a forefather of cognitive psychology, the vulgar view because it is one that has been challenged recently by some modern scholarship. At times this challenge has come from individuals who have studied James and found him lacking (e.g., Kimble 1990; see also footnote 3). Others (e.g., Myers 1992) seem to admonish us to look deeply at James and not be attracted by mere surface features of similarity. Alternatively, there are those who understand and appreciate James 'deeply', who still question his legacy (e.g., Robinson 1993).

Kimble is somewhat ambivalent about James's place in the age of cognition, and Myers seemed cautiously interested in developing the same sort of arguments that I have assembled here, but Robinson was forthright in his rejection of any Jamesian tradition. Robinson (1993) sketched James's mentalism, his pragmatism, and his pluralism in thoughtful detail. At each juncture he concluded that contemporary positions often linked to James (e.g., cognitive neuroscience) bear no meaningful connection to a Jamesian tradition.

Robinson (1993) characterizes James's pragmatism as an understanding that,

> The facts we single out for our own special attention are those that seem to be consequential to the choice of actions we must draw from the range of possibilities. We know in advance, however, that each choice will create yet other needs and challenges and that the selection of certain facts and the neglect of others will itself alter the range of possibilities. (p. 641)

As Robinson noted, many historians have wanted to connect behaviorism to James's pragmatism, but Robinson cautioned that 'Pragmatism of the Jamesian variety is found nowhere ... and, in a non-Jamesian variety, has been confined to behavioristic programs otherwise hostile to the Jamesian sense of the term' (p. 642). One might argue this point by appeal to the work of 'behaviorists' such as Edward Thorndike, J.R. Kantor, Roger Barker, or E.B. Holt. Although each of these four psychologists may be questionable as a solid representative of behaviorism, their debt to James and the influence of his thought on their careers is easy to document. If you understand behaviorism as a more monolithic enterprise characterized by someone like Skinner, then surely Robinson's conclusions are true. However, as you broaden what counts as behaviorism they become more tenuous. Still, our interest here is not with James's legacy for behaviorism.

Robinson (1993) astutely captures James's pluralism in his observation that

> James's pluralism recognizes that every entity has its environment and enters into unavoidable commerce with it. So, too, does each person. Pluralism, then, leads to an individualistic (ideographic) psychology that heaps suspicion if not scorn on every form of statistical lumping and clumping. (p. 642)

He goes on to note similarities between James and both Wittgenstein and Vygotsky – even Jerome Bruner – but cautions against comparisons to modern relativism or constructionism, both of which are popular in current social psychology. Extending beyond comparisons with these movements, Robinson (1993) also seems to have no confidence in the post-modern as he argued, 'Psychology now seems more intolerant than ever toward modes of inquiry and analysis that are not experimental, not grounded in so-called observables, not reducible to quantities, and not assessable statistically' (p. 642).

Not surprisingly, Robinson concluded that if James launched a tradition it was one that focused on a psychology of individual experience, and he asserted that from the students of Wundt onward such a tradition has been drowned out by opposition. Taylor (1992b), in discussing Gordon Allport as a Jamesian makes a similar argument about James's pluralistic legacy. If you believe that Allport and other self-described Jamesians in social psychology (e.g., Gardner Murphy) were not drowned out but have shaped the face of modern social psychology, then you are forced to admit a direct connection to William James. But again, our interest here is not with James's legacy for social psychology.

Robinson (1993) correctly described William James's mentalism as 'the recognition of mental life as personal, owned, and teleological, in addition to its being contextual, socially implicated, and ever passing' (p. 640). Robinson provided several admonitions against viewing today's cognitive science as a true descendent of James's mentalism that for the most part again (as with behaviorism and social psychology above) rest on his characterization of the field. Indeed, Robinson's whole argument really builds from the assertion that 'for all the various and often strident critiques, [mainstream psychology] remains confidently positivistic' (p. 638).

Let me hasten to add that at one level I am sympathetic to Robinson's point in all this that James's sense of psychology as a science differs significantly from that of most contemporary practitioners. Indeed, it may well be true that many modern researchers in areas such as cognitive neuroscience and computer modeling lack the philosophical background (dare I say sophistication) and the scope of vision (as they are typically working with local and circumscribed phenomena) to appreciate, or even be interested in James's mentalism, pluralism, or pragmatism. To the degree that one sees specific research programs – such as a cognitive neuroscience investigation of the physiology of some memory process, or constructing neural networks that understand spoken metaphors – as *defining* cognitive psychology, then questions about James's relationship to the discipline seem valid. Given that most people working and publishing in these areas do not know James or endorse his philosophy of psychology, where then is the connection, the legacy?

That having been noted, Robinson's characterization of the field remains off the mark. Robinson (1993) contends that 'cognitive psychology ... has essentially nothing of a Jamesian character at all. The removal of research from contexts of a plausibly realistic nature dooms it from the outset' (p. 642). There are still cognitive psychologists who are both philosophically sophisticated and after an integrative 'big-picture' concerning the place of cognition in human existence. Philip Johnson-Laird (1987) criticized Myers (1986) explicitly for not drawing such connections between modern cognitive science and psychology in the tradition of William James (see Myers 1992). Ulric Neisser's (Gibsonian) approach to an ecologically oriented cognitive psychology seems the perfect counter-example to Robinson's depiction of our field (e.g., Neisser, 1991).

In his 1987 Presidential Address to the Southeastern Psychological Association, Howard Pollio, founding editor of *Metaphor and Symbolic Activity*, described his psychology as mentalistic, pragmatic, and pluralistic in close to verbatim accord with Robinson's own summary of those elements. This was not coincidental, as Pollio explicitly labeled his phenomenological approach to psychology as a conscious continuation of William James' tradition (see also Pollio 1982, 1990). Here then is one established cognitive psychologist who is not 'experimental' in a positivistic sense, not grounded in observables, and largely opposed to quantities and statistics. Can we dispute his own claim that he and his students are carrying on the Jamesian tradition of an experientially based psychology of the individual?

As I have noted previously, Myers (1992) explicitly tackled the relationship between the current practice of cognitive psychology and William James. His analysis is fair, thought provoking, and one I readily recommend. At times he reasons like Robinson, noting 'beyond cognitive psychology's look, how would James have felt about its substance? He would have found it bewildering ...' (p. 52). But frequently his intuitions parallel my own. Indeed, his observation, 'one's attitude toward science and psychology largely determines one's attitude toward the *Principles* and the intellectual career of James' (p. 55), serves as a nice summary for my assessment of Robinson's analysis.

Conclusions

I have endeavored to weave an interesting story that concludes by suggesting that yes, William James was and still remains an important figure for cognitive science. I endorse that 'vulgar' view in part because: (1) Each time I read William James I am personally stimulated to explore some new facet of cognitive psychology. My dissertation in cognitive psychology arose directly out of reading James. (2) It seems that Robinson's (1993) essay on the topic begs the very question. No one bothers to write about the lack of a meaningful connection between Helmholtz or Hall and modern cognitive science, because no one ever imagined there was such a connection. (3) Most basically however, William James clearly wrote interesting stuff on the topics of cognition, and essays by contemporary cognitive notables contain statements such as

James's approach to the study of imagery is surprisingly contemporary.

Stephen Kosslyn (Park & Kosslyn 1990, p. 183)

The current science of the mind is addressing exactly those problems that James raised.

Philip Johnson-Laird (Johnson-Laird 1987, p. 13)

James set the stage for the much later flourishing of cognitive psychology and cognitive science.

W.K. Estes (Estes 1990, p. 149)

William James ... expressed ideas about brain localization and plasticity in neural networks that foreshadowed many aspects of current neurobiology of learning and even connectionist theory.

Richard F. Thompson (Thompson 1990, p. 172)

Such arguments on my part lack elegance, subtlety, even proper logical form (but, James hated formal logic). Nevertheless the four quotes do provide *prima facie* evidence not only for a connection, but also some sense of where that connection is being played out. Likewise, I have littered this essay with many *en passant* observations about James and various elements of current cognitive science. In most cases, references have been provided and stand as an invitation for interested readers to explore for themselves what, if any, substantive connection exists between William James and their own interests in cognitive science.

Acknowledgments

This essay began with a very different intentionality almost a decade ago. Both Mike Johnson and Steve Hibbard greatly influenced the content and further development of this material over the years as we continued to be impressed by, and discuss, the relevance of William

James to our efforts as cognitive psychologists. Most recently, Mike Thorne has helped to facilitate my many disparate ideas about James into this present form.

Bibliography

Allen, G.W. (1967). *William James*. New York: Viking.
Angell, J.R. (1911). Editorial: William James. *Psychological Review*, 18, 78–82.
Angell, J.R. (1913). Behavior as a category of psychology. *Psychological Review*, 20, 255–270.
Barsalou, L.W. (1983). *Ad hoc* categories. *Memory and Cognition*, 11, 211–227.
Block, N. (1980). *Readings in the Philosophy of Psychology* (Vols. 1–2). Cambridge, MA: Harvard University Press.
Crovitz, H.F. (1990). Association, cognition, and neural networks. In M. Johnson & T. Henley (eds) *Reflections on* The Principles of Psychology: *William James after a Century*. Hillsdale, NJ: Lawrence Erlbaum Associates.
Donnelly, M.E. (1992). *Reinterpreting the Legacy of William James*. Washington: APA.
Dreyfus, H.L. (1982). *Husserl, Intentionality, and Cognitive Science*. Cambridge, MA: MIT Press.
Edie, J.M. (1970). William James and phenomenology. *Review of Metaphysics*, 23, 481–526.
Edie, J.M. (1987). *William James and Phenomenology*. Bloomington, IN: University of Indiana Press.
Estes, W.K. (1990). Introduction: *Principles of Psychology*: 1890–1990. *Psychological Science*, 1, 149–150.
Evans, R.B. (1990). William James and his *Principles*. In M. Johnson & T. Henley (eds) *Reflections on* The Principles of Psychology: *William James after a Century*. Hillsdale, NJ: Lawrence Erlbaum Associates.
Giorgi, A. (1990). The implication of James's plea for psychology as a natural science. In M. Johnson & T. Henley (eds) *Reflections on* The Principles of Psychology: *William James after a Century*. Hillsdale, NJ: Lawrence Erlbaum Associates.
Henle, M. (1990). William James and Gestalt psychology. In M. Johnson & T. Henley (eds) *Reflections on* The Principles of Psychology: *William James after a Century*. Hillsdale, NJ: Lawrence Erlbaum Associates.
Henley, T.B. (1989). *The Primacy of Relations*. Unpublished Doctoral Dissertation, University of Tennessee, Knoxville.
Hibbard, S. & Henley, T.B. (1994). Is psychology really 'The study of behavior?'. *Theory & Psychology*, 4, 549–569.
Hilgard, E.R. (1969). Levels of awareness: Second thoughts on some of William James's ideas. In R. MacLeod (ed.) *William James: Unfinished Business*. Washington: APA.
Holt, E.B. (1942). William James as psychologist. In B. Blanshard & W. Schneider (eds) *In Commemoration of William James*. New York: Columbia University Press.
Howard, G.S. (1992). William James: Closet clinician. In M. Donnelly (ed.) *Reinterpreting the Legacy of William James*. Washington: APA.

James, H. (1920). *The Letters of William James* (Vols 1–2). Boston: The Atlantic Monthly Press.

James, W. (1890). *The Principles of Psychology* (Vols 1–2). New York: Henry Holt.

James, W. (1892). *Psychology: The Briefer Course*. Cambridge, Massachusetts: Harvard University Press, 1984.

James, W. (1904). Does 'consciousness' exist? *Journal of Philosophy, Psychology, and Scientific Methods*, 1, 477–491.

Johnson, M.G. & Henley, T.B. (1990). *Reflections on* The Principles of Psychology: *William James after a Century*. Hillsdale, NJ: Lawrence Erlbaum Associates.

Johnson-Laird, P.N. (1987, March 3). Introspection and the body: Critical review of G. E. Myers. *William James*. London Review of Books, p. 13–14.

Joncich, G. (1968). *The Sane positivist: A Biography of Edward L. Thorndike*. Middletown, CT: Wesleyan University Press.

Jones, E. (1955). *The Life and Work of Sigmund Freud*. New York: Basic Books.

Joralemon, D.R. (1980). Too many philosophers. *American Heritage*, 31, 17.

Kantor, J.R. (1942). Jamesian psychology and the stream of psychological thought.In B. Blanshard & W. Schneider (eds) *In commemoration of William James*. New York: Columbia University Press.

Kimble, G.A. (1990). A search for principles in *Principles of Psychology*. *Psychological Science*, 1, 151–155.

King, D.B. (1992). Evolution and revision of the *Principles*. In M. Donnelly (ed.) *Reinterpreting the Legacy of William James*. Washington: APA.

Köhler, W. (1947). *Gestalt Psychology* (rev. edn). New York: Liveright.

Leahey, T.H. (1993). A history of behavior. *The Journal of Mind and Behavior*, 14, 345–354.

Lears, T. (1987). William James. *The Wilson Quarterly*, XI, 84–95.

Lewis, R.W.B. (1991). *The Jameses*. New York: Farrar, Straus, and Giroux.

Linschoten, J. (1968). *On the Way towards a Phenomenological Psychology*, A. Giorgi (trans.). Pittsburgh: Duquesne University Press.

Malone, J.C. (1990). William James and habit: A century later. In M. Johnson & T. Henley (eds) *Reflections on* The Principles of Psychology: *William James after a Century*. Hillsdale, NJ: Lawrence Erlbaum Associates.

McConnell, J.V. (1986). *Understanding Human Behavior* (5th edn). New York: Holt, Rinehart, Winston.

Merleau-Ponty, M. (1945/1962). *Phenomenology of Perception*, C. Smith (trans.). London: Routledge & Kegan Paul.

Miller, D. (1942). William James: Man and philosopher. In B. Blanshard & W. Schneider (eds) *In Commemoration of William James*. New York: Columbia University Press.

Myers, G.E. (1986). *William James: His Life and Thought*. New Haven, CT: Yale University Press.

Myers, G.E. (1992). William James and contemporary psychology. In M. Donnelly (ed.) *Reinterpreting the Legacy of William James*. Washington: APA.

Neisser, U. (1981). John Dean's memory: A case study. *Cognition*, 9, 1–22.

Neisser, U. (1991). A case of misplaced nostalgia. *American Psychologist*, 46, 34–36.

Nickerson, R.S. (1990). William James on reasoning. *Psychological Science*, 1, 167–171.

Park, S. & Kosslyn, S.M. (1990). Imagination. In M. Johnson & T. Henley (eds) *Reflections on* The Principles of Psychology: *William James after a Century*. Hillsdale, NJ: Lawrence Erlbaum Associates.

Perry, R. B. (1935). *The Thought and Character of William James* (Vols. 1–2). Boston: Little, Brown.

Pollio, H.R. (1982). *Behavior and Existence*. Monterey, CA: Brooks/Cole Publishing Company.

Pollio, H.R. (1990). The stream of consciousness since James. In M. Johnson & T. Henley (eds) *Reflections on* The Principles of Psychology: *William James after a Century*. Hillsdale, NJ: Lawrence Erlbaum Associates.

Robinson, D.N. (1993). Is there a Jamesian tradition in psychology? *American Psychologist*, 48, 639–643.

Rumelhart, D.E., Smolensky, P., McClelland, J.L., & Hinton, G.E. (1986). Schemata and sequential thought processes in PDP models. In D. Rumelhart, J. McClelland, & The PDP Research Group (eds) *Parallel Distributed Processing. Volume 2: Psychological and Biological Models*. Boston: MIT Press.

Simon, L. (1998). *Genuine Reality: A Life of William James*. New York: Harcourt Brace and Company.

Smolensky, P. (1988). On the proper treatment of connectionism. *Behavioral and Brain Sciences*, 11, 1–74.

Starbuck, E.D. (1943). A student's impressions of James in the middle '90's. *Psychological Review*, 50, 128–131.

Stevens, R. (1974). *James and Husserl: The Foundation of Meaning*. The Hague: Nijhoff.

Taylor, E. (1990). New light on the origin of William James's experimental psychology. In M. Johnson & T. Henley (eds) *Reflections on* The Principles of Psychology: *William James after a Century*. Hillsdale, NJ: Lawrence Erlbaum Associates.

Taylor, E. (1992a). William James's contributions to experimental psychology. *History of Psychology Newsletter*, XXIV, 3–6.

Taylor, E. (1992b). The case for a uniquely American Jamesian tradition in psychology. In M. Donnelly (ed.) *Reinterpreting the Legacy of William James*. Washington: APA.

Thompson, R.F. (1990). The neurobiology of learning and memory: William James in retrospect. *Psychological Science*, 1, 172–173.

Thorne, B.M. & Henley, T.B. (1997). *Connections in the History and Systems of Psychology*. Boston: Houghton Mifflin.

Townsend, K. (1996). *Manhood at Harvard: William James and Others*. New York: Norton.

Wilshire, B. (1968). *William James and Phenomenology*. Bloomington, IN: Indiana University Press.

10
Freud's Interdisciplinary Fiasco

Patricia Kitcher

1. Introduction

My topic is, I fear, slightly undiplomatic for this interdisciplinary collection. I will try to show that, despite its many advantages, an interdisciplinary approach to cognitive science runs significant risks. Even worse, perhaps, I will try to defend one of the least popular intellectual figures among contemporary scientists, Sigmund Freud. The connection between the two projects is that, as I understand the development of psychoanalysis, it was an interdisciplinary theory and its interdisciplinary character was one of the main reasons for its unparalleled success. If my interpretive claim is correct, then it is simply inconsistent to believe both that interdisciplinary theory construction is the best way to go for psychology and that Freud was an intellectual charlatan because his theory was too ambitious.

Let me first situate Freud quickly. He was born in 1856 and died in 1939 at the age of eighty-three. He lived most of his life in Vienna but was forced into exile in London by the Nazis in 1938. (A number of his sisters and other family members were murdered in the Holocaust.) He wanted to be a theoretical biologist and planned at one point to do a doctorate under the philosopher Franz Brentano among others. Financial exigency drove him to medical school and neurology. At about the age of forty, he turned to psychology, attempting to build the first complete, interdisciplinary model of the mind ever. By the time of his death, the psychoanalytic movement that he founded reached around the world.

I have two goals for this chapter. First, I will briefly explain how Freud created psychoanalysis, by synthesizing a large number of diverse, but fundamentally compatible theories from different biological and social sciences in a simple, coherent, and comprehensive account of mental life. Ironically, the great attraction of psychoanalysis was its seemingly impeccable scientific credentials. Unlike dualistic and introspective approaches to psychology, psychoanalysis held out the promise of a unified theory of mentality, one that ranged from the highest intellectual attainments, including art, social organization, and morality, to the most bizarre phenomena of dreaming and madness, all grounded in an apparently firm biological foundation.

In the second part of the chapter, I will take up three of Freud's more instructive and costly errors. In each case I will also present examples where contemporary theorists appear to be following in Freud's missteps. Not to show any favoritism, my first two examples will be chosen from opposing schools within cognitive science and the last example of faulty interdisciplinary reasoning will, I suspect, include the vast majority of the cognitive science community. I will also include a fourth interdisciplinary error that Freud avoided, but that some of our contemporaries seem surprisingly willing to countenance.

2.   The integration of the disciplines in psychoanalysis

Freud developed the major hypotheses of psychoanalysis by integrating the results and approaches of at least eight different fields:

1. Neurophysiology (the field of his initial training)
2. Psychology
3. Psychiatry
4. Sexology
5. Philology
6. Anthropology
7. Sociology
8. Evolutionary biology

I will present just a few of the relevant results from some of these fields to illustrate how Freud incorporated and related the work of various disciplines in a general theory of the development and functioning of mental life.

From neuroanatomy and neurophysiology, he borrowed two discoveries. During the 1890's, it became apparent that the nervous system was made up of discrete neurons, which passed some form of electrical or chemical energy among them. Second, neural matter was widely believed to be reflexive: energy that came in from external or internal stimulation would flow around the system and then exit in a motor discharge.

Freud also adopted two leading methodological assumptions from psychology. The first was associationism, the view that many mental phenomena could be explained by appeal to associations formed between ideas when they were experienced together. A second and quite different approach was to try to understand how the mental apparatus was put together by decomposing it into functional units. These units probably had no precise or permanent spatial locations in the brain. They were not anatomical divisions, but divisions based on contribution to mental functioning – exactly the status that Freud attributed to his own mental divisions.

Psychiatry contributed three crucial hypotheses, most importantly, the view that neurotic behavior could be the product of ideas of which the subject was unaware. Besides making a connection between neuroses and unconscious ideas, many psychiatrists believed that disorders such as hysteria had a sexual origin. Finally, work on aphasia – some done by Freud himself – implied that ideas were represented in the brain in a complex way. The idea [cat], for example, would be represented by two different, but connected, clusters of ideas. One would include images of the cat's shape, fur, distinctive pattern of locomotion, and so forth; the other visual, sound, and motor images of the word 'cat'. Aphasia studies suggested that patients could lose, or lose the use of, one of these clusters without losing the other. They might retain the word, but lose its sense, or vice versa.

Let me now turn to a less familiar science, sexology. At the end of the nineteenth century and the beginning of the twentieth, a number of gifted naturalists and theoreticians tried to fathom the varieties and foundations of sexual behavior. Freud borrowed an enormous amount from men like Richard Krafft-Ebing, Havelock Ellis, and Albert Moll – with precious little acknowledgement of his sources. I will mention just three central contributions: the discovery of infantile sexuality, the notion of stages of sexual development, and the hypothesis that there was no one sexual instinct, but a collection of 'component' instincts, inherited from early humans and even 'lower' animals. So, for example, some unusual sexual practices might be explained by noting that in lower animals, sex can be linked to cannibalism. The idea was that, normally, these component instincts were suppressed by social forces and then integrated to produce adult heterosexual behavior.

Anthropology's contribution to psychoanalysis was not particular results, but a research program. Nineteenth-century anthropologists assumed that the human mind could be adequately understood only by going back to the minds of primitive ancestors and tracing lines of development. Access to primitive minds was to be achieved by studying artifacts of ancient cultures, contemporary 'savages' (i.e., groups outside of Western culture), and children. The rationale for studying peoples outside the loop of Western cultural transmission was that they would be very like the first humans. Beyond cultural transmission, it was widely believed that adaptations developed during the lifetimes of primitive peoples were repeated in childhood, because ontogeny was the rapid recapitulation of phylogeny and acquired traits could be inherited. Hence, children were another source of information about primitive human mentality.

The final major contributor to psychoanalytic theory that I will discuss is evolutionary biology. Evolutionary theory had a profound effect on the shape of psychoanalysis, in part, because it influenced all the other sciences on which Freud drew. Evolutionary thinking led psychology to look for mental systems that performed different functions – and evolved at different times. It inspired sexologists to consider stages of sexual development and their possible relation to 'lower' forms of life. Because of its insistence on the importance of origins to understanding mentality and civilization, nineteenth-century anthropology was later called 'evolutionary anthropology'. Sociology also adopted the evolutionary model of explanation: to account for a higher social achievement, such as religion or morality, it was necessary to trace its development back to earlier practices and, eventually, to conditions shared with animals.

The theory of evolution also entered psychoanalysis directly. Freud believed that although other theorists might posit instincts at will, only self-preservative and sexual instincts had been elevated to a scientific status by biology. He was also a recapitulationist and a committed Lamarckian, who stubbornly clung to the inheritance of acquired characteristics to the end of his life.

Let me now try to illustrate how Freud constructed his theories by incorporating and drawing connections among these various results and approaches. One of the most attractive features of psychoanalysis was its seemingly firm biological foundation. Freud assumed that neural matter functioned as a reflex. But on this model, the system would require energy from external stimulation or internal sources to propel it. His second biological assumption was that the basic endogenous sources were self-preservative and sexual instincts. Hence libido theory: the neural system was partly driven and largely influenced by instinctual sexual drives.

Notice that libido theory did not merely borrow results from neurophysiology and evolutionary biology. It showed how seemingly distinct and well-established facts could be related in an elegant and simple story. A reflexive nervous system needed sources of energy; sexual selection was a critical force in evolution; all psychological forces had to have a physiological basis. So Freud reasoned that gonads and other internal organs released a substance into the nervous system – libido – that both provided it with needed energy and constituted the physiological mechanism by which sexuality influenced behavior and so ultimately evolution.

Consider now Freud's central 'clinical' hypothesis: neurotic behavior was caused by unconscious ideas with sexual content. As noted, earlier work in psychiatry had suggested both halves of this claim, by linking neuroses both to unconscious ideas and to sex. Freud was able to increase their plausibility, however, by drawing on results from other fields to suggest social and psychological mechanisms for sexual ideas becoming unconscious and psychological and physiological mechanisms for them nonetheless influencing behavior.

To explain how ideas could become unconscious, Freud appealed to results in aphasia and to a fairly standard view of conscious thought. Like many before and since, he assumed that thoughts became conscious by being associated with speech and so with words. Work in aphasia had shown that ideas could be cut off from their word-representations. If conscious thought required the medium of words, then such ideas would be unconscious. Freud combined these considerations with the prevailing wisdom from sexology: aphasia studies demonstrated the possibility of unconscious ideas and partially explained the psychological mechanism by which they became unconscious; sexology documented the suppression of sexuality in thought and word, as well as deed, and so implied that ideas with sexual content were more likely than others to be unconscious. Hence these two apparently independent research traditions provided important confirmation for the psychiatric hypothesis that at least some minds were burdened by unconscious sexual ideas.

Psychology and neurophysiology provided a hypothesis about how these ideas might nevertheless affect behavior and, in particular, account for neurotic symptoms. Suppose that the nervous system were constructed as a reflex, with energy able to exit only through some type of motor discharge. Since speech itself was a motor activity, it provided an outlet for the energy acquired by conscious, but not unconscious ideas. Now assume that associationism is true: ideas that are frequently or dramatically experienced together tend to become associated. In his early *Project for a Scientific Psychology* (1895), Freud had appealed to recent work in neurophysiology to support psychology's long-standing commitment to association. If neural matter was discrete, with some kind of barrier between individual neurons, then there were at least two possible mechanisms for association. Energy running between two clusters of neurons that represented two ideas might break down the barriers and so facilitate later flows of energy from one cluster to the next; having two clusters of neurons simultaneously filled with energy might weaken the barriers between them, producing the same result.

By putting these theories together, Freud found a possible link between unconscious ideas and neurotic symptoms. When libido came into the system, it excited or filled sexual ideas. These ideas were cut off from motor neurons that could produce speech or action, however, so the energy pouring into the system flowed into ideas that had been accidentally associated with sexual ideas, which made the link to neurotic symptoms. For example, in one case history, Freud argued that his patient, Fräulein Elizabeth von R., suffered from severe neurotic pains while walking, because she was unconsciously in love with her brother-in-law and had had an intimate conversation with him during a long walk. When libido reactivated her unconscious sexual ideas, the energy passed to them was funneled off to the associated idea of pain in walking, which actually produced a motor reaction, severe leg pains and limping, and so finally rid the system of excess libidinal energy.

Thus, as he did with sexology and aphasia studies, Freud integrated the theory of association from psychology with the reflex model from neurology to produce an account that greatly enhanced psychiatry's claim that the neuroses could be explained by reference to unconscious ideas. The view that neurotic behavior was the result of unconscious sexual ideas may have entered psychiatry as a humble clinical hypothesis. But in Freud's hands, it became an elaborate, highly theoretical claim that incorporated results from neurophysiology, psychology, sexology, anthropology, and evolutionary biology. Further, as we have seen, Freud did not simply tie psychiatric claims to received views or recent results in each field; he tried to relate theories and results in the various fields to each other and so produce a comprehensive account of the mechanical and historical causes of abnormal – and normal – mental processes. To give some sense of what his global account looked like, I will briefly consider the oldest question about psychoanalysis: Why was he so fascinated by sex?

We have already considered a major reason: the elegant fit between the needs of a reflexive nervous system and the apparent endorsement of sexual instincts by evolutionary biology. Beyond psychiatry and evolutionary biology, anthropology and sociology testified to the centrality of sex in human life. Both assumed that marriage was a pivotal institution in civilization. But, as the well-known sociologist Edward Westermarck put it, marriage itself was 'rooted in the family [or dropping the euphemism, in sex]'. Further, sexual factors convincingly met the methodological standard that explanations of higher human accomplishments trace their lineage to conditions shared with lower animals.

Finally, Freud was led to see the advantages of sexual theories by work in sexology itself. Like many nineteenth-century theorists, sexologists debated whether sexual behavior was a matter of heredity or environment. Freud did not choose sides, but synthesized the best work in both traditions. As a result, he accumulated a large body of material relating sex to an impressive variety of human conditions. When he considered this material in light of the ideas of evolutionary biology, psychiatry, sociology, and anthropology just canvassed, he reached his grand, unifying theory of human mentality: all mental phenomena, from madness and dreams, to religion, art, and social mores could be understood as the expression of sexual instincts as modified by familial and social influences during the long course of human history on the one hand, and individual heredity and experience on the other.

Freud did not extrapolate from his patients' sexual difficulties to a pervasive role for sexuality in human life; he focused on the sexual aspects of his patients' lives and dreams, because many different sciences had stressed the importance of sex. Sex became the keystone of psychoanalysis, because it was the most promising bridge among neurophysiology, evolutionary biology, psychology, and human culture, and Freud yearned for what he called 'metaphysical' knowledge – for as complete theoretical understanding as possible of mental life.

Hence, in Freud's view of the relation of psychoanalysis to other sciences, sexology and psychiatry are at the center with psychoanalysis, which then formed a link between the biological and the higher mental sciences. Besides illustrating the interdisciplinary character of psychoanalysis, I hope that the preceding discussion provides some sense of why Freud believed that he was on the threshold of a major advance. By forging connections among recent discoveries in various relevant sciences, psychoanalysis opened up the possibility of a systematic theory of mentality that did away with scientifically dubious distinctions between mind and body, humans and other animals.

So far, I have described the positive role of interdisciplinary theorizing in psychoanalysis. I will now take up the darker side of the story, the difficulties that have contributed psychoanalysis' unenviable role as the textbook example of pseudo-science. I start with the biological foundations.

Error 1: Having more faith in a related discipline than the experts

As we have seen, Freud's two fundamental biological assumptions, the reflex character of the nervous system and libido doctrine, were both plausible nineteenth-century hypotheses and they comported extremely well with each other. Soon, however, both were in trouble. The very short and very sorry history of libido is that as endocrinologists learned more about the actions of the sex hormones, it became apparent that they did not act as Freud claimed. In particular, they did not supply energy to the rest of the body, including nervous system. Yet Freud ignored these developments, seemingly so convinced by the perfect fit between libido and the reflex model that he continued to believe that, eventually, libido would be found. The error I wish to highlight, however, concerns his other crucial biological claim.

The reflex doctrine entered psychoanalysis in the form of Freud's 'principle of inertia'. In the *Project for a Scientific Psychology* (written in 1895 but not published until 1950), he formulated that principle as follows: '[N]eurones tend to divest themselves of Q [i.e., nervous energy] ... or at least to keep [it] ... as low as possible ... to keep it constant' (S.E. 1, pp. 296–297). Contemporary analysts try to maintain the viability of psychoanalysis by claiming that Freud abandoned neurophysiological speculation in the 1890's and became a pure psychologist. This dodge is, however, textually indefensible. Freud tried to protect his theories from changes in the neurophysiological details by making a tactical retreat and not talking in terms of neurones and Q in his published works; he also changed the name to the more familiar 'pleasure principle'. Despite the more generic formulations, however, the principle of inertia is completely recognizable in his later works. So in 'Formulations on the two principles of mental functioning' (1911), he explained that motor discharge, under the sway of the pleasure principle, 'served as a means of unburdening the mental apparatus of accretions of stimuli' (S.E. 12, p. 221). In 1915, he presented a fundamental biological postulate: 'the nervous system is an apparatus which has the function of getting rid of the stimuli that reach it, or of reducing them to the lowest possible level' ('Instincts and their vicissitudes', S.E. 14, p. 120); in 1920, he cast the point in psychological terms: 'the mental apparatus endeavours to keep the quantity of excitation present in it as low as possible or at least to keep it constant' (*Beyond the Pleasure*

Principle, S.E. 18, p. 9). And in *The Interpretation of Dreams* (written in 1900 and revised eight times up through 1929), he stated bluntly that '[r]eflex processes remain the model of every psychical function' (S.E. 5, p. 538). Putting the point slightly differently, even though Freud ceased talking about neural reflexes, his presentations of the pleasure principle all presupposed that his readers accepted the reflex character of the nervous system. For if they did not, they would have no reason to find this principle true or even plausible.

There is no mystery about why contemporary Freudians try to distance psychoanalysis from the pleasure principle. Subsequent discoveries have revealed that it rested on a mistaken picture of neural action. Freud assumed that the neural system was quiescent, and that when invaded by stimuli, it reacted by discharging it. However, as Hebb (1982) has observed, by 1930, 'it began to be evident that the nerve cell is not physiologically inert, does not have to be excited from the outside in order to discharge'. It is important to realize how badly this change in the conception of neural action undermined Freud's position. If the nervous system is not driven by energy supplied from sources outside itself, then there would be no particular reason to believe that it tried to discharge this foreign energy or that it was burdened by excessive amounts of external energy. However, both the dream theory and the theory of the neuroses assumed the presence of energy needing discharge. This energy was supposed to be the instigator of dreams and the explanation for the tics, paralyses, and other bodily symptoms of neuroses. If the nervous system did not strive to discharge energy, then psychoanalysis had no explanation for these phenomena – and they were supposed to be its core *explananda*.

In 1930, Freud was seventy-four years old and in no position to rebuild psychoanalysis from the ground up, as this development required. He should have been aware of potential problems as early as 1906, however, when Sherrington published *The Integrative Action of the Nervous System*. Sherrington's central brief was that it was not enough to understand nerve cells, their modes of conduction, and simple reflexes. As the title implied, the key to future research lay in figuring out how neural reactions, including reflexes, were integrated to produce the smooth performance exemplified in physical activity.

Sherrington's book should have given Freud pause. The pleasure principle took the individual neuron as a model for the whole; since each neuron seemed to pass off energy imparted to it, so did the system as a whole. But here was an undisputed expert maintaining that it was no simple matter to extrapolate from individual neural reactions to the actions of the whole system. On the contrary, this was the great challenge facing neurophysiology.

Yet Freud continued to believe that his incorporation of ideas from neurophysiology into psychoanalysis was completely sound. Whether he simply did not bother to keep up or dismissed emerging difficulties as technical, he erred in having more faith in the smooth progress of this discipline than the experts. Even though the basic concepts of neuron and reflex endured, they needed to be supplemented by higher-level concepts in order to explain the possibility of complex, coordinated action. These complications had the potential to change the simple picture of neural action that Freud had captured in the pleasure principle. This was exactly what the experts were telling him, but he was not listening.

Although it led to a very costly mistake, Freud's attitude towards neurophysiology should not be seen as a blunder. From a distance, it is easy to regard problems in a neighboring discipline as relating only to details and so to have more faith in the resources of its basic concepts than the experts. This is, I believe, an endemic problem for interdisciplinary theory construction. It is also a perfect example of an interdisciplinary error that seems glaring in Freud, but that can pass unnoticed in contemporary discussions in cognitive science. Consider, for example, an exchange between philosopher Stephen Stich and computer scientist Paul Smolensky. In a wide-ranging paper, Smolensky tried to chart the implications of recent work in connectionism for issues in cognitive science. He began by listing several *caveats* about possible limitations of connectionism. I cite portions of three of these:

> It is far from clear whether connectionist models have adequate computational power to perform high-level cognitive tasks: *There are serious obstacles that must be overcome ...*

> It is far from clear that connectionist models, *in something like their present forms*, can offer a sound basis for modeling neural computation ...

> Even under the most successful scenario for connectionist cognitive science, many of the [other] currently practiced research strategies in cognitive science would remain viable and productive. (Smolensky 1988, p. 2, emphasis added)

In his comments on Smolensky's paper, Stich proposes to trace the implications for cognitive science 'if the project he describes can be carried off'. His argument is that the success of connectionism would go a long way towards establishing two philosophical theses that he has long supported, the elimination of 'folk psychology' and the demise of the symbolic paradigm in psychology.

My objection is not that Stich ignores Smolensky's warnings about limitations that may make connectionist success less likely. His ruminations are meant to be hypothetical: if connectionism is successful, then what follows? As Freud's example makes clear, the danger lies in the nature of the warning. Once Sherrington had pointed out that neurophysiology had to expand its horizons beyond individual neurons and reflexes, the fact that Freud's psychological theories were consonant with the simple neuron-reflex picture no longer implied that they were well grounded in physiology. Similarly, Smolensky offers reasons to believe that the current resources of connectionism are inadequate. It faces serious obstacles that may require important additions, either in the form of new computational breakthroughs or borrowings from other, more traditional approaches. Under these circumstances, showing that a particular philosophical theory comports well with the basic – but admittedly inadequate – explanatory constructs of connectionism does not provide evidence in its favor. For Smolensky's point is that complex mental processes probably cannot be modeled by the kinds of connectionist networks now available.

Error 2: Reversing epistemic dependencies

Freud's faith in the smooth progress of nineteenth-century sciences was not limited to neurophysiology; he also continued to believe in Lamarckianism, recapitulationism, and in the project of evolutionary anthropology. In decline during the teens, Lamarckianism and recapitulationism were firmly rejected by the scientific establishment during the 1920s. Nineteenth-century anthropology had assumed that it could make a major contribution to the understanding of human mentality and civilization by reconstructing the characteristics of primitive human minds and tracing their development. The comparative method that was supposed to provide enlightenment about primitive minds was severely criticized, however, and no interesting results had ever been produced. So by the early teens, this style of doing anthropology was also rapidly becoming out-of-date.

Freud clearly knew about these developments, but his reaction was one of stubborn defiance. In *Moses and Monotheism* (1939), for example, he noted that he had been placed in a 'difficult position' by 'the present attitude of biological science, which refuses to hear of the inheritance of acquired characters. ... [He] must, however, in all modesty confess that nevertheless [he] cannot do without this factor in biological evolution' (S.E. 23, p. 100). That is, since, as he constructed it, psychoanalysis required Lamarckianism, he was in all immodesty going to go on believing in it, whatever the experts said!

Lamarckianism, recapitulationism, and evolutionary anthropology were crucial to psychoanalysis, because it was primarily a genetic psychology. It explained current conditions by tracing them back to earlier events in the life of the individual – or in the history of the race. Over time, as Freud came to believe in the increasing complexity of mental dynamics, he felt that psychoanalysis had to rely more and more on explanations that appealed to our 'archaic heritage' (that is, to mental contents acquired through the experiences of ancestors and passed to subsequent generations through Lamarckian inheritance). Even more importantly, the mind's instinctual endowment, the course of psycho-sexual development, and 'the nucleus of the unconscious mind' itself were all to be explained in part by the long course of human history.

A look at the general index to the Standard Edition reveals that as these three doctrines were becoming more dubious, Freud's references to 'archaic heritage', 'phylogenetic inheritance', and 'primitive peoples' actually became more numerous. He did not try to recast the foundations of psychoanalysis, but continued to build higher. Freud's attitude was unfortunate in many respects, but I will consider just one significant error in interdisciplinary reasoning: he reversed the epistemic dependencies within his theory. If Lamarck was right and recapitulation true, then it was reasonable to construe childhood and neurotic behavior (which allegedly involved a regression to childhood forms) in terms of the practices and experiences of primitive humans; it was reasonable to hypothesize a primitive portion of the mind in which this material was stored. If the project of evolutionary anthropology could be carried out, then it would be reasonable to believe that hypotheses about the contents of that mental division (the 'Id') could be subject to independent confirmation.

The problem is that support could not run in the other direction. Psychoanalytic psychiatry and evolutionary anthropology, recapitulationism, and Lamarckianism, were not mutually supporting. The latter two theories gave credence to the former two. Psychiatry could provide no serious evidence for such specific biological hypotheses. Further, these hypotheses created the link between psychoanalysis and evolutionary anthropology. Without them, there was no reason to believe that evolutionary anthropology could confirm psychoanalytic hypotheses about the primitive or infantile Id. Hence, when Lamarckianism and recapitulationism were cast in doubt, Freud could not parry the threat by pointing to apparently fruitful applications of these doctrines in psychoanalysis.

Once a theory is launched and has some real or perceived successes, it tends to take on a life of its own. Further, having built the working assumptions of nineteenth-century biological and social sciences into the foundations of psychoanalysis, Freud became so accustomed to them that he no longer recognized how dependent he was on them. Hence he reversed the epistemic dependencies: psychoanalysis stood on its own, but could offer hints to prehistoric anthropology and, through its successes, help to vindicate two embattled theses of evolutionary biology. What he never fully appreciated was that without these important theoretical supports, his claims about the contents of the Id would appear fantastical and beyond the bounds of any possible confirmation – as they often do to contemporary critics.

Current interdisciplinary theorists are protected against most of the mistakes encountered in this episode. Whereas Freud isolated psychoanalysis in its own institutes, cognitive science is part of the academy, where lack of currency is strictly forbidden. However, the more subtle error of confusing epistemic dependencies within an interdisciplinary program still appears to be possible. As I read them, Jerry Fodor and Zenon Pylyshyn's well-known discussion of connectionism makes exactly this mistake.

'Classical' psychological theories, as they label the position they aim to defend, were made plausible by surprisingly consonant developments in two *prima facie* unrelated fields: Chomskian linguistics and 'classical' theories of computation. I repeat only the bare outlines of these familiar stories. Chomsky offered elegant arguments to show that speakers can enjoy linguistic competence only because they have internalized the complex grammatical rules of their language, which they apply to various levels of internal linguistic representations. At roughly the same time, workers in artificial intelligence and computer simulations showed that machines could carry out complex problem-solving tasks by applying rules specified in their programs to internal symbols. Since language use has long been regarded as a central case of intelligent thought and computer programs were designed to simulate thought at some level of abstraction, these developments made it plausible to model thinking and psychological processes generally in terms of the application of rules to internal symbolic representations.

In an influential series of books and papers, Fodor and, more recently, Pylyshyn have elaborated this picture of the mental and its implications for new and traditional issues in philosophy and psychology. The rise of parallel distributed processing (PDP) models of computation poses a significant threat to the classical program. This can be seen most easily by recalling a critical lemma in constructing the rules and representation model: no computation without representation. It is precisely this claim that is challenged by PDP models. Connectionist networks compute, but not by syntactic manipulations of internal representations.

Fodor and Pylyshyn propose to ward off the PDP threat with the following argument:

> Classical psychological theories appeal to the constituent structure of mental representations to explain three closely related feature of cognition: its productivity, its compositionality and its inferential coherence. The traditional argument has been that these features of cognition are, on the one had pervasive and, on the other hand, explicable only on the assumption that mental representations have internal structure. (1988, p. 33)

The argument proceeds by showing that connectionist networks cannot model these three features. My concern about this line of reasoning is that Fodor and Pylyshyn appear to be trying to argue from the soundness of their overall approach to the truth of one of its essential assumptions: no real computation or thought-like computation without representation. Again, however, the epistemic dependencies go in the wrong direction.

If language and computation require the presence of rules and representations, then it is plausible to regard psychological processes more generally in these terms. Without these assumptions, however, the regularities encountered in thinking are hardly strong enough to imply that any thought-like computation, including the processing or production of language, requires representations to be manipulated by strict syntactic rules or algorithms. So, for example, thinking could be compositional and productive – the thought that 'playing Bach is difficult' could be produced from simpler parts, such as the representation of 'difficult', and be related to thoughts such as 'psychology is difficult' – even though there is no algorithm that determines all and only those contexts in which 'difficult' may be appropriately used and no algorithm that characterizes the contribution of 'difficult' to any complex thought. Alternatively, as Fodor and Pylyshyn acknowledge, these three features are variations on the theme of systematicity, and thought is not so clearly systematic as to demand a strict rules and representation account.

Perhaps I have misunderstood the nature of their argument. The evidence for productivity, compositionality, and systematicity comes from Chomskian linguistics. So their point may be to defend one part of their program, a view about thought-like computation, by appealing to another, the truth of Chomskian linguistics: Chomskian linguistics implies that the computation underlying a central part of thought, language use, must involve the manipulation of representations by rules. This line of defense encounters problems of its own, however, since Chomskian linguistics is itself a hotly debated issue among linguists. Given this problem and their remarks about the coherence of the classical doctrine, I suspect that they are trying to argue from their general theory to one of its foundational supports. This will not work, however, because the rules and representations approach to psychology and classical Chomskian linguistics and classical computation are not mutually supporting. It is the latter doctrines that give plausibility to the former.

Error 3: Mistaking a common zeitgeist for the consilience of the evidence

Let me end with Freud's most pervasive interdisciplinary error, which is also, I believe, the error that poses the greatest threat to contemporary cognitive science. As Freud was coming to intellectual maturity, a number of diverse sciences agreed on what an ideal theory of the mind would look like. The mind was the brain and the human mind/brain, like those of other animals, came to have its current properties through a long process of evolution involving both physical and social environments. Through these interactions, the lowly human animal endowment was changed in two ways. The organs of thought themselves evolved and experiences of previous humans were passed on to their descendants, either by some unknown process of social evolution or by the inheritance of acquired characteristics, leading to the sophisticated and complex social creatures of today. Hence, it seemed both fruitful and necessary to approach the study of the mind/brain in two complementary ways. Anatomy and physiology would fathom the current neural wiring and evolutionary biology, sociology, anthropology, child psychology, and philology (or historical linguistics) would trace its lengthy history. Given this dramatic consilience of the sciences and their potential for mutual enlightenment, it was natural to hope that a unified, tolerably complete story of the origins of human mentality could be told and that it would be true.

The problem with this consilience was its source. To see the issue clearly, consider a more limited set of disciplines. The agreement in approach among evolutionary sociology, evolutionary anthropology, and evolutionary biology was no coincidence. The former disciplines began with the premise that the biological theory of evolution was correct and must be used as a benchmark for research in the social sciences. Historical linguistics predated Lamarck and Darwin, but – like the theory of evolution itself – was very much a product of nineteenth-century historicism. Biological evolution seemed attractive, in part, because it was a historical doctrine. When it emerged as a major scientific achievement, it reinforced the preexisting historical predilections of contemporary theorists and created a much tighter correspondence among the explanatory frameworks of the social and biological sciences. Towards the end of the nineteenth century, different sciences appeared to be converging on a unified approach to the problem of mentality, because they were all being guided by the same dominant intellectual force: basic historicism dramatically invigorated and made specific by the theory of evolution. The correspondences among the sciences were largely a reflection of this zeitgeist.

That different sciences operated under the sway of the powerful zeitgeist of evolutionary historicism did not diminish the validity of their results. But it undercut the probative value of their consilience. Under these circumstances, agreements among the sciences could not be credited to their correct, independent depictions of a common reality. Understandably, Freud did not appreciate this point. A devout evolutionist and system-builder, he looked for ways of integrating different branches of knowledge. When he found them, he did not question their source or recognize their common ancestry, but took them as prime indications that a unified theory of the mental was possible along evolutionary lines. Hence, although he always conceded the likelihood of errors of detail, he found it impossible to believe that the search for laws governing the development of human mental and social life from the beginning of civilization to the present might itself be completely barren.

As the predominance of evolutionary explanations led Freud to believe that the time was ripe for integrating the mental sciences, so the proliferation of computational or information-processing approaches has inspired the contemporary ideal of a unified, interdisciplinary cognitive science. Since the rise of computationalism is a fairly familiar story, I will note just four highlights. During the 1930s important results in logic demonstrated the power of formal methods. In particular, the results of Alan Turing and Alonzo Church showed that a universal Turing machine could, in principle, solve any problem that was decidable. When these and other results were supported by technological advances in the 1950s, it became possible to build computers and so to demonstrate their enormous practical utility in managing information. By the second half of the 1950s, the information-processing approach was beginning to take hold in the central discipline of psychology. Thirty years later, the proliferation of computational approaches across the mental sciences is evident in the listings of university catalogs. At my former university, the University of California at San Diego, for example, there are courses in computational psychology, computational anthropology, computational linguistics, and computational neuroscience.

The parallel with psychoanalysis is obvious. Freud was confident that a complete interdisciplinary theory of mind was within his grasp because he was fooled by the spurious consilience of evidence produced by evolutionary historicism. Contemporary cognitive science may be making the same mistake. So, for example, Howard Gardner notes two important 'convergences', the use of PDP models in theories of perception and in theories of cognition, and their use in both psychology and neurophysiology, Churchland and Sejnowski argue for the 'fecundity' of their particular brand of PDP model on the grounds that it may help with problems in perception, cognition, and motor control, as well as neurophysiology, and McClelland and Rumelhart conclude their two volume exploration of PDP models by surveying the possible fields that can be approached in this way: language, learning, neuropsychology, and neurophysiology. Notice that the argument is not simply that PDP models are an interesting new formalism that can be applied in a wide variety of areas, say neural modeling and astrophysics (although McClelland and Rumelhart sometimes voice that position). It is, rather, that different mental and brain operations that we antecedently believe to be related can be modeled in the same way, hence suggesting not just that this is a widely applicable modeling technique – but that these models are likely to be good approximations to reality.

The danger in misreading a common zeitgeist as a consilience of the evidence is not just an unseemly overconfidence. A dominant zeitgeist encourages an interdisciplinary approach, because when there is substantial agreement among the disciplines about the important questions to ask and the range of acceptable answers, then collaboration appears more fruitful. However, an interdisciplinary approach also leads to greater commonality of beliefs and attitudes. Thus, the adoption of an interdisciplinary research strategy increases the hegemony of a zeitgeist, which further encourages interdisciplinary integration, and so on.

An interdisciplinary research strategy also tends to preserve existing views, because it sacrifices an important mechanism for change. As work in related (but independent) fields can offer important confirmation, it can also cast doubts on accepted theories and offer hints about new approaches. The great danger in utilizing an interdisciplinary research strategy in the presence of a dominant zeitgeist is theoretical stagnation. Or, expressing the problem in computational terms: given a dominant zeitgeist, an interdisciplinary approach runs the risk of forcing research into a 'local minimum' by depriving it of any sources of energy that would enable it to climb out.

Let me just note that, with the rise of connectionist models, contemporary cognitive science is in danger of making a further interdisciplinary mistake that Freud was inured against. Late nineteenth-century theorists recognized the folly of *Hirnmythologie* (brain mythology), that is, of pretending to insight by restating psychological claims in neurophysiological terms. After Hebb's famous warning about confusing the central nervous system with the 'CNS', i.e., the conceptual nervous system, we should be equally attuned to this folly. Yet connectionist models are routinely described as neural networks. The problem is that when these models are offered for actual neural processes, the label presupposes the point at issue; when the label is used of models for mental processes, it implies that the models are neural models and so just the sort of models we want, regardless of their real degree of neural faithfulness. We might call this fault the error of mistaking hopeful labels for serious theoretical integration.

Conclusion

Given the negative tenor of this essay, I should say explicitly that my purpose has been neither to discourage interdisciplinary work in cognitive science nor to disparage Freud's pioneering efforts in interdisciplinary theory construction. I believe in the interdisciplinary approach for the same reasons that Freud and contemporary cognitive scientists do: since the mind is the brain, theories in psychology, linguistics, sociology, anthropology, computer science, and neurophysiology should all constrain and inform each other. My concern has been rather to show that, for all its many virtues, interdisciplinary theory construction can yield disastrous results. Freud's example should serve as a warning to contemporary theorists and thus provide some counter-weight to the many enthusiastic defenses of the interdisciplinary approach. But looking at Freudian psychoanalysis as an interdisciplinary theory also permits a more balanced assessment of its successes and failures.

Critics sometimes try to paint what they see as Freud's unwarranted influence as itself a scientific failing: it derived from his magnetic personality, the tight control he exercised over the institutions of psychoanalysis, or his strategy of going over the heads of the established scientific community to appeal to an uncritical lay audience. Upon closer inspection, however, none of these explanations is very plausible. Freud did not live in an age of mass communication, and he gave few public lectures. He could control only those who already wished to become members of the psychoanalytic community. He was a gifted writer – but he also had a very good story to tell. Freud himself understood well the secret of his success. In the *Introductory Lectures on Psychoanalysis*, he explained:

> [Psycho-analysis can] attract general interest in a way in which neither psychology nor psychiatry has succeeded in doing. In the work of psycho-analysis links are formed with numbers of other mental sciences, the investigation of which promises results of the greatest value: links with mythology and philology, with folklore, with social psychology and with the theory of religion. (Freud, S.E. 15, p. 167)

The self-diagnosis was exactly right. What attracted the educated public to psychoanalysis was its grand sweep, its seeming ability to bring so many aspects of mental life that people cared about – personality, social relations, religion, values, and, of course, sexuality – within the purview of a single unified theory that rested on an apparently solid foundation in biology and neurophysiology. Freud's theory was successful because it promised what educated people have wanted for over a hundred years and still want: a unified theory of mental life that does away with scientifically dubious distinctions between mind and body, humans and other animals.

Freud made serious mistakes in failing to appreciate how new scientific developments undercut the foundations of psychoanalysis – and, indeed, left it without any adequate basis in established science. What I have argued is some of his more costly mistakes should be attributed neither to scientific weakness nor to moral wickedness. Although wrong, they are the kind of mistakes that are much easier to see with the advantage of hindsight. Finally, I think that the interdisciplinary character of Freud's work offers some defense against a frequent criticism: he failed to probe the weaknesses of his theories, because he was so sure that he was right. Freud was sure that he was right. But, given the apparent consilience of biology, neurophysiology, and mental sciences about how complex mental processes should be explained, his attitude should be less surprising. It is just this sort of agreement among the disciplines that leads many to believe that the secrets of mentality are finally going to be unraveled in our own time.

References

Churchland, P., and Sejnowski, T.J. (1992). *The Computational Brain.* Cambridge, MA: MIT Press.

Fodor, J.A., and Pylyshyn, Z.W. (1988). Connectionism and cognitive architecture: A critical analysis. *Cognition,* 28, 3–71.

Freud, S. (1895/1950). *Project for a Scientific Psychology.* In: Standard Edition of the Complete Psychological Words of Sigmund Freud, *Vol. 1 (hereafter S.E., volume number),* J. Strachey (ed.). London: Hogarth Press, 1966–1974.

Freud, S. (1900). *The Interpretation of Dreams.* S.E. 4/5.

Freud, S. (1911). Formulations on the two principles of mental functioning. S.E. 12.

Freud, S. (1915). Instincts and their vicissitudes. S.E. 14.

Freud, S. (1916/1917). *Introductory Lectures on Psychoanalysis.* S.E. 15.

Freud, S. (1920). *Beyond the Pleasure Principle.* S.E. 18.

Gardner, H. (1985). *The Mind's New Science: A History of the Cognitive Revolution.* New York: Basic Books.

Hebb, D.O. (1982). Drives and the CNS (conceptual nervous system). Reprinted in Henry A. Buchtel (ed.), *The Conceptual Nervous System.* New York: Pergamon Press.

McClelland, J.L., and Rumelhart, D.E. (1986). *Parallel Distributed Processing. Vol. 2: Psychological and Biological Models.* Cambridge, MA: MIT Press.

Sherrington, C.S. (1906). *The Integrative Action of the Nervous System.* New Haven, CT: Yale University Press.

Smolensky, P. (1988). On the proper treatment of connectionism. *Behavioral and Brain Sciences,* 11, 1–74.

Index

Printed in the United States
100125LV00001B/123/A

9 780230 013391

DATE DUE

AP 0 4 0			
AP 0 2 08			
		SUBJECT TO	
		RECALL	